THE FRIARS

THE MEDIEVAL WORLD
Editor: David Bates

Already published

CHARLES THE BALD
Janet Nelson

CNUT
The Danes in England in the early eleventh century

M.K. Lawson

WILLIAM MARSHAL
Court, Career and Chivalry in the Angevin Empire 1147-1219

David Crouch

KING JOHN
Ralph V. Turner

INNOCENT III
Leader of Europe 1198-1216

Jane Sayers

THE FRIARS
The Impact of the Early Mendicant Movement on Western Society

C.H. Lawrence

ENGLISH NOBLEWOMEN IN THE LATER MIDDLE AGES
Jennifer C. Ward

JUSTINIAN
John Moorhead

BASTARD FEUDALISM
Michael Hicks

THE FRIARS

THE IMPACT OF THE EARLY MENDICANT MOVEMENT ON WESTERN SOCIETY

C.H. Lawrence

LONGMAN
London and New York

Longman Group Limited,
Longman House, Burnt Mill,
Harlow, Essex CM20 2JE, England
and Associated Companies throughout the world.

Published in the United States of America
by Longman Publishing, New York

First published 1994
Third impression 1996

ISBN 0 582 05633 0 CSD
ISBN 0 582 05632 2 PPR

British Library Cataloguing-in-Publication Data

A catalogue record for this book is
available from the British Library

Library of Congress Cataloguing in Publication Data

Lawrence, C. H. (Clifford Hugh), 1921-
The friars: the impact of the early mendicant movement on Western
society / C.H. Lawrence.
p. cm. - (The Medieval world)
Includes bibliographical references and index.
ISBN 0-582-05633-0 (cased). -ISBN 0-582-05632-2 (pbk.)
1. Friars-Europe-History. 2. Europe-Church history-Middle
Ages, 600-1500. I. Title. II. Series.
BX2820.L38 1994
271'.0604'0902-dc20   93-25750   CIP

Produced by Longman Singapore Publishers (Pte) Ltd.
Printed in Singapore

CONTENTS

Acknowledgements   vi
Abbreviations used in the footnotes   vii
Editor's Preface   ix

CHAPTER 1   The Medieval Church in Crisis   1

CHAPTER 2   St Francis of Assisi and the Origins of   26
             the Friars Minor

CHAPTER 3   The Growth of the Friars Minor,   43
             Crisis and Change

CHAPTER 4   St Dominic and the Order of   65
             Friars Preachers

CHAPTER 5   New Brethren   89

CHAPTER 6   The Mission to the Towns   102

CHAPTER 7   The Capture of the Schools   127

CHAPTER 8   The Complaint of the Clergy   152

CHAPTER 9   In the Houses of Kings   166

CHAPTER 10   In the Service of the Papacy   181

CHAPTER 11   Afar unto the Gentiles   202

             Epilogue: Loss and Gain   218

             General Bibliography   229
             Index   237

ACKNOWLEDGEMENTS

I am indebted to Dr Michael Sheehan OFM of Oxford Greyfriars for kindly reading chapters 2 and 3 in draft, and to Professor F.R.H. DuBoulay for reading the draft of chapter 8. Both offered valuable criticism. My thanks are due to Dr Jagger, the Warden of St Deiniol's Library at Hawarden for his kind and prompt help with an inquiry relating to the papers of the late Bishop Moorman. I should also like to record my gratitude to the students who attended my classes on the ecclesiastical institutions of the middle ages over the years and listened patiently to many of the views expounded in this book. Their friendship was a source of much encouragement in difficult times.

ABBREVIATIONS USED
IN THE FOOTNOTES

AFH	*Archivum Franciscanum Historicum*
AFP	*Archivum Fratrum Praedicatorum*
ALKG	*Archiv für Litteratur- und Kirchengeschichte des Mittelalters*, ed. H. Denifle and F. Ehrle 6 vols. (Berlin, Freiburg 1885–92)
AnA	*Analecta Augustiniana*
AOC	*Analecta Ordinis Carmelitarum*
1,2 Celano	The *Vita Prima* and *Vita Secunda S. Francisci Assisiensis*, edited by the Fathers of Quaracchi, 1926–7.
Chartularium	Chartularium Universitatis Parisiensis, ed. H. Denifle and A. Chatelain (Paris 1889–91)
Chron. Majora	The *Chronica Majora* of Matthew Paris, ed. H.R. Luard 6 vols. (RS 1872–84)
Eccleston	*Fratris Thomae de Eccleston de Adventu Fratrum Minorum in Angliam*, ed. A.G. Little 2nd edn (1951)
Esser *Opuscula*	Die Opuscula des hl. Franziskus von Assisi, ed. K. Esser 2nd edn (Grottaferrata 1976)
Habig	*St Francis of Assisi: Writings and Early Biographies*, ed. Marion Habig 3rd edn (Chicago 1972)
Hinnebusch *HDO*	W.A. Hinnebusch, *A History of the Dominican Order, Origins and Growth to 1550* 2 vols. (New York 1965–72)

JEH	*Journal of Ecclesiastical History*
Mansi	*Sacrorum Conciliorum Nova et Amplissima Collectio*, ed. J.D. Mansi (Florence 1759–98)
MEFR	*Mélanges de l'École Française de Rome*
MGH SS	*Monumenta Germaniae Historica Scriptores*
MOFPH	*Monumenta Ordinis Fratrum Praedicatorum Historica*
Moorman *HFO*	J.R.H. Moorman, *A History of the Franciscan Order from its Origins to 1517* (1968)
PL	Patrologia Latina, ed. J.P. Migne (Paris 1844–64)
Recueil	*Recueil des historiens des Gaules et de la France*
Reichert	*Acta Capitulorum Generalium Ordinis Praedicatorum*, ed. B.M. Reichert *MOFPH* III–IV (1898–9)
Répertoire	P. Glorieux, *Répertoire des maîtres en théologie de Paris au XIIIe siècle* 2 vols. (Paris 1933)
RS	*Chronicles and Memorials of Great Britain and Ireland* edited in the Rolls Series
Salimbene	*Cronica Fratris Salimbene de Adam*, ed. O. Holder-Egger *MGH SS* (1913)
TRHS	*Transactions of the Royal Historical Society*

EDITOR'S PREFACE

The thirteenth-century history of the Friars encapsulates the ideals, the paradoxes and the problems of the Christian Church during the Middle Ages. On the one hand, the Christian message has always possessed the capacity to inspire heroic acts of devotion and self-sacrifice. Its call to follow the teachings of Christ is superbly illustrated in the conversion and career of St Francis, who set out literally and absolutely to live in a state of poverty in imitation of Jesus' life. On the other hand, the medieval Church was a massive institution, unwieldy and often inward-looking, yet conscious of its responsibility to maintain the faith amongst a population, many of whom living in great poverty and ignorance, and extend it against the non-Christian peoples around the frontiers of a Christendom whose security they frequently threatened. In spite of their manifest radicalism and dynamism, both St Francis and St Dominic fully accepted a mission of service to the established Church, and, above all, the duties of preaching and education which meant that they and their followers had to involve themselves fully in lay society and accept the implications of a place within the ecclesiastical hierarchy. It is the great virtue of Professor Lawrence's contribution to the Medieval World series that he consistently and skilfully places the evolution of the Mendicant Orders of friars against the background of contemporary society. He charts with great sympathy and learning how the ideals of the early friars became a source of tension as their successors undertook a world-wide mission and how they had to be adjusted to meet the practical demands imposed by their role as educators, preachers and confessors.

Hugh Lawrence is one of the foremost specialists working on the thirteenth-century Church and on the history of the medieval religious orders. His book is as much a work of social as of religious history. It never loses sight of the complex interplay between religious idealism and worldly necessity. In his own words, the friars were 'a revolutionary answer to a potentially revolutionary situation'. The start of their history in the first years of the thirteenth century is placed in the context of a world where the religious monopoly of the medieval Church was being challenged by increasingly radical and entrenched heretical sects and was facing fresh demands under the impact of economic and intellectual change. The friars are shown combating heresy through preaching and the Inquisition, confronting in the universities the intellectual challenges posed by the rediscovery of Aristotle and the rivalry of masters from the secular clergy, and grappling with the demands of a more literate and critical laity and a burgeoning urban society. However, the paradoxes implicit in the poverty and spirituality of the earliest friars and the worldly mission they willingly accepted are never far from the surface in this history. Hugh Lawrence shows both how the successors of St Francis and St Dominic reached an intellectual justification for using property and how the Franciscan Order in particular was regularly wracked by controversies between a more fundamental and a more pragmatic wing. The book ends with the schism which split the Franciscans in 1322. Above all, however, it does full justice to the major contribution which the friars made to late medieval society and it explains with exemplary clarity the complexities at all levels of their history.

David Bates

Chapter 1

THE MEDIEVAL CHURCH
IN CRISIS

The orders of mendicant friars which appeared early in the thirteenth century represented a new and revolutionary version of the religious life. To the more perceptive leaders of the Church, like Pope Innocent III, they seemed to be a providential response to a spiritual crisis that was afflicting western Christendom. Reduced to its essentials, this crisis was a confrontation between traditional assumptions about the nature of the Christian life and the religious needs of a newly arisen urban and secular culture. Even the heresies which had taken root in parts of southern Europe were in some sense a by-product of this culture. It seemed that these needs could not be met by the established forms of religious organisation.

. . .

ECONOMIC AND SOCIAL CHANGE

The confrontation had been engendered by profound economic and social changes that had transformed Western Europe in the course of the twelfth century. The economic process underlying these changes is well known, if not easily explained. Beginning in the eleventh century, the West entered upon a phase of extraordinary economic and demographic expansion which was to continue with gathering momentum for the next two hundred years. Whatever the ultimate causes of this phenomenon – medieval Europe's economic miracle – its most conspicuous features were the rapid growth of international trade and commerce, the revival of urban life in the old lands of the Western Empire, and a sustained rise in population. Everywhere areas of unpopulated waste and primeval forest were cleared, brought under the plough and colonised. In the

1

wake of cultivation new villages sprang up, and new towns were founded by princes and enterprising landlords.

This development did not stop at the frontiers of Christendom. In the Mediterranean lands, expansion took an aggressive military form with the Norman conquest of Sicily from the Moslems and culminated in the planting of Frankish principalities in Syria and Palestine by Crusaders from northern Europe. Both these advances of the Latin frontier brought great wealth to the Italian maritime republics, whose fleets now dominated the eastern Mediterranean. East of the Elbe, which had marked the frontier of the kingdom of Germany in the early middle ages, in the wake of conquering princes a growing influx of German peasant settlers gave their names to innumerable villages in the sparsely populated Slav lands, and colonies of German merchants crept eastward along the shores of the Baltic.

It was in the life of cities that the greatest transformation occurred. Intensified commercial activity and booming industries enhanced the wealth of towns and attracted to them increasing numbers of entrepreneurs and artisans. Ancient towns outgrew their original boundaries and overflowed into new suburbs. The most spectacular growth was to be seen in the cities of north Italy, Flanders and the Rhineland – areas that were centres of a thriving textile industry and the terminals of trade with the east Mediterranean and the Baltic. Here several cities had by the end of the twelfth century attained the size and population of a modern town. A new world was emerging, one in which money, capital and credit played an ever increasing role. Its needs and aspirations found expression in such novel institutions as the city communes – self-governing city republics owning no lordship below that of king or emperor – and the nascent universities, and its religious sensibility was reflected in the naturalism of Gothic art.

Leadership of this urban society was in the hands of a bourgeoisie that derived its wealth from commercial profit. The rich merchant families which dominated the political life of the city-republics constituted a new civic aristocracy, which imitated, and in some areas superseded the old landed nobility in its patronage of the Church, learning and the arts. They formed the upper layer of a heterogeneous society which included professional men such as notaries and physicians, self-employed craftsmen and shop-keepers, and a large proletariat of artisans and wage-earners. It was a society more mobile and, at the upper levels, more affluent than before; one that was receptive to new ideas and ready to challenge the established authorities of church and state. Many of its values – especially the pursuit of commercial profit and the acceptance of market forces – were abhorrent to conservative churchmen; and communal autonomy had often to be won in the teeth of opposition from prince or bishop. To this day, the audacity of that challenge can be seen dramatically symbolised in the centre of the imperial city of Trent, where the campanile of the medieval commune still stands where it was erected, like a sore appendix, on the end of the episcopal palace.

It is a truism that city populations provided the most fertile seed-bed for religious dissent and anti-clerical agitation. Some recent studies have suggested that in the thirteenth century scepticism about some of the fundamental dogmas of faith was commoner among the rural peasantry than was once believed. Nevertheless, the closely regulated society of the rural manor and the inescapable intimacy of the rural parish exerted upon the individual an almost irresistible pressure to conform; whereas town living, with its relative freedom from customary bonds, its shifting population, its political self-consciousness and turbulence, and the constant stimulus of competition, fostered a more critical and individualistic mentality and provided readier opportunities for the dissemination of new ideas. The literate laity who formed the upper strata of the new urban society, dissatisfied with the passive role of a spiritual proletariat assigned them by traditional ecclesiology and aware of the educational and moral shortcomings of the secular clergy, were a natural forcing-ground both for ortho-dox criticism of the Church and for radical dissent.

This was the milieu out of which arose the most formidable challenge to its spiritual authority that the medieval Church had to face until the Reformation. It had been occasionally troubled in the eleventh century by groups of radical dissidents who expressed heretical opinions. By the middle of the twelfth century, it was confronted by dualist heresies which had won the spiritual allegiance of a significant part of the population over large areas of southern Europe. Heretical opinions travelled in the train of merchants and free-lance preachers along the arteries of commerce and found their audience in the inns and market-places. It was thus in Cologne, the

3

greatest of the Rhineland cities, that the heresy of the Cathars first broke historical cover in the year 1143, when some of the sectaries were put on trial; and it was in the towns of Lombardy, the Veneto, Tuscany and the Languedoc, the emporia of trade with the east Mediterranean, that it struck its deepest roots.

. . .

THE HERESY OF THE CATHARS

The doctrine of the Cathars in its fully developed form was nourished by missionaries and refugees from the Bulgarian sect of the Bogomils – latter day Manichees, who had found their way to the West in order to escape persecution by the Greek Orthodox Church and the government of Byzantium. The Cathars, known in France as Albigenses – a name derived from the town of Albi, one of their major centres – were dualists. They believed that the universe emanated from two conflicting principles, one good and one evil. God was a spirit, and the world he created was a world of spiritual beings. The visible and material world, on the other hand, was the work of an evil power or demiurge, and it was irredeemably evil. The flesh was an evil integument in which the human soul was imprisoned. It followed that most of the apparatus of Catholic Christianity, notably the sacraments, which used material things – water, bread and wine – as vehicles of supernatural grace, was to be rejected.

The sectaries, in fact, repudiated the Roman Church in its entirety. But they claimed to be Christians in the authentic apostolic tradition. Thus they appropriated to themselves much of the New Testament. But the Christ of their system was not the Christ of orthodox theology. He was a pure spirit. His bodily incarnation was illusory and so, necessarily, was his bodily resurrection Not all the Catharist groups were of one mind on such questions. The evidence suggests that the elaborate cosmography of the dualist universe was imported into the system from the East at a later stage. But hatred of the body expressed through a cult of negative asceticism seems to have been common to all the Cathar sects. For the individual soul, trapped in a physical body, salvation had to be sought through deliverance from the flesh, signified by a form of spiritual baptism called the consolamentum. This rite, which involved the laying-on of hands by the élite of the sect, the *perfecti*, promised the remission of sins and initiated the believer into complete membership of the Cathar church.

Those who received the consolamentum were required to live a penitential life of rigorous asceticism. They renounced personal property, marriage and sexual relationships, and followed a strict dietary regime which, besides fasting, involved permanent abstinence from all animal foods, including eggs, milk and cheese – from anything in fact that was the product of coition. The outward sign of their commitment to a life of penance and prayer was a black robe they wore.

The consolamentum initiated the recipient into the ranks of the elect, the *perfecti*. Women who received it normally retired to live a monastic life in one of the houses maintained by the sectaries. The men either lived in small communities or embarked upon a ministry of itinerant preaching and teaching. Having embraced voluntary poverty, they depended for their support upon the alms and hospitality offered by the faithful of the sect, in this respect anticipating the life-style of the mendicant friars. Obviously the obligations associated with the rite of solemn initiation were not to be undertaken lightly. The majority of believers understandably preferred to subscribe to vicarious holiness rather than embracing a life of such chilling asceticism, and it was common practice to postpone reception of the consolamentum until death was imminent.

The Cathars won adherents in many parts of Europe, but their most conspicuous success was in the cities of northern and central Italy and in the Languedoc. Here they were numerous enough to establish a hierarchy of their own, parallel to that of the Catholic Church. They had bishops in charge of territorial dioceses, assemblies, and deacons responsible for subordinate areas. But the Cathar churches displayed the fissiparous tendencies that are a feature of most dissident bodies. A visit from a Greek heresiarch, the bishop Nicetas, in the year 1166, seems to have led to theological dissensions which thereafter continued to divide the sectaries. Before the end of the century, the believers of Lombardy, Tuscany and the March of Treviso were the spiritual subjects of six Cathar dioceses which were in conflict with one another, each of which in effect excommunicated its rivals.[1]

1. A. Dondaine, 'La hiérarchie cathare en Italie': *AFP* 19 (1949), pp. 280–312; 20 (1950), pp. 234–324.

The Cathar faith was not confined to the towns; it had adherents among the rural peasantry. In the relatively tolerant society of the Languedoc, where the sectaries enjoyed the open approval and protection of the aristocracy, Catholics and Cathars lived side by side, even under the same family roof. 'It has penetrated everywhere,' wrote Count Raymond V of Toulouse, 'it has thrown discord into every home, dividing husband and wife, father and son, daughter-in-law and mother-in-law. Even the priests have succumbed to the disease'[2] Raymond's impassioned plea for help was written in 1178. Such few statistics as are available suggest that he had overstated the scale of the problem if not the social penetration achieved by the sect.[3] But his lament is a symptom of the panic evoked in the rulers of church and state by the increasingly public face of the Cathar religion.

Heresy is not a symptom of apathy but of religious fervour. In the twelfth century it was one aspect of the spiritual and intellectual awakening that gave birth to new religious orders, new forms of pious association and new scholastic institutions. Recent students of the phenomenon have stressed the contribution of indigenous orthodox piety, as opposed to eastern influence, in preparing the soil for the seeds of dualist teaching. The doctrine of the sectaries succeeded because it met an eager response from growing numbers of lay people whose religious aspirations the orthodox clergy seemed unable to satisfy.

The appeal of the Cathar system for people in search of a personal spiritual life is easy to understand. A cosmology that derived the material world of the senses from a demonic source offered a plausible explanation for the miseries of the human condition and the waywardness of the flesh that everybody experiences. It solved the eternal conundrum posed by the existence of evil in a world created by a good and omnipotent God. Moreover, it touched a responsive chord in orthodox Christianity, which contained a strong ascetical tradition that was all too easily tilted into dualism by preachers and writers of ascetical theology. Had not the author of the

---

2. J. Madaule, *The Albigensian Crusade*, transl. Barbara Wall (1967), p. 52.
3. In 1209, when the bishop of Béziers compiled a list of those defamed of heresy in his city, he named only 220 people out of a population of circa 10,000: W. L. Wakefield, *Heresy, Crusade and Inquisition in Southern France 1100–1250* (1974), p. 71 and n.

Epistle to the Galatians said 'the flesh lusteth against the spirit and the spirit against the flesh, and these are contrary the one to the other'? (Gal.v.17). The sinful proclivities of the flesh, the virtue of sexual abstinence, the heroic acts of asceticism practised by the saints in order to subdue the body, and the omnipresence of demons – evil spirits roving the world to lure souls to their destruction – were the commonplaces of sermons and didactic literature. Unsubtle minds must have found it hard to distinguish the message of the dualists from the moral teaching of the orthodox Church. It is significant that in some towns of the Midi Catholics and Cathars shared the use of the same church.

The negative factor that helped the spread of heresy was the failure of many of the orthodox clergy to meet the spiritual needs of the laity. Paradoxically, the Gregorian Reform had aggravated this problem. In their efforts to eradicate the abuses of lay patronage, to exalt the sacerdotal office and raise the standards of pastoral care, the reformers had drawn the attention of the laity to the shortcomings of the clergy. Gregory VII had, in fact, invoked the assistance of lay people in opposing unworthy candidates for bishoprics and in bringing public opinion to bear upon priests who flouted the rule of celibacy. The Gregorian papacy thus helped to create a climate of opinion that stimulated spiritual aspiration and was critical of the failings of the secular clergy.

In the south of France, the reform movement had not made much headway before the end of the twelfth century. The spiritual head of the ecclesiastical province covering the Languedoc, archbishop Berengar of Narbonne, whose worldliness and negligence were the subject of an angry denunciation by Pope Innocent III, was one of those mitred aristocrats whose chief preoccupation was with enlarging the wealth and power of his see. His suffragans were hardly more impressive. By 1213 several of them had been deposed or suspended on account of incapacity, scandalous conduct or their failure to take action against the heretics. The lower clergy – the vicars and chaplains who served the parishes in place of their absentee rectors or monastic proprietors – were no different from their colleagues elsewhere. The differences were not in themselves but in their environment – the fact that they were surrounded by devotees of a rival religious system, including some members of the higher aristocracy. Recruited largely from the peasantry, given to regular or occasional concubinage, and short on formal education, most of them compared unfavourably with the élite of the Albigenses. They lacked the intellectual equipment even to instruct their own flock, much less to meet the sectaries in argument. By contrast, the austere life of the perfect provided an inspiring example, which commended their teaching to people disillusioned with the performance of their own clergy.

Faced with the manifest inability of the local clergy to check the spread of Catharism in the Languedoc, Innocent III called upon the Cistercians to conduct a mission to the territory, and appointed the bellicose Arnald-Amaury, abbot of Cîteaux, to oversee the effort. The Cistercians failed, however, to make any impression on the problem. This, and the evident unwillingness of the Count of Toulouse, Raymond VI, to move against the heretics, finally persuaded the papacy to invoke the aid of the secular power in a policy of violent repression. At the end of 1207 Innocent appealed to the king and baronage of France to undertake a crusade to the Midi and confiscate the lands of the heretics. His call led in 1209 to the descent of the northern feudality upon the Languedoc under the command of Simon de Montfort and a war of expropriation, made hideous by the atrocities committed against the townspeople of the area, which lasted with intervals until 1229. In the years that followed hostilities, the work of extirpating the sectaries was pursued by the papal Inquisition.

.   .   .

LAY LITERACY

Grave though it was, the challenge the dualist heresy posed for the Church was less pervasive and easier to meet than the problems thrown up by the emergence of a new society. One of the most significant signs of this was the spread of lay literacy. Until the eleventh century literacy in Western Europe had been largely confined to the clergy. The classical dichotomy between the clerk, who was said to be *literatus*, and the layman, who was *idiota* – meaning illiterate – corresponded roughly with the facts. Literacy meant, of course, the ability to read and write Latin, the language of the Church, of administrative and legal record – the only language in which men wrote serious books. To be a scholar, or to be merely literate in a formal sense, meant to be a clerk. The point was underlined by Philip of Harvengt, abbot of Bonne-Espérance, who wrote a treatise on the studies appropriate for the clergy: 'the custom of speech has it that when we see a man who is lettered, we immediately call him a clerk'.[4] 'To be sure', he goes on, casting an uneasy glance over his shoulder at the literate laymen of his own time, 'one sometimes meets an educated knight and an illiterate clerk, but this is an anomaly'.

By the middle of the twelfth century, when Philip was writing, his simple classification looked out of date. Literacy had ceased to be a clerical monopoly. Commercial activity on any scale demanded of its practitioners at least a degree of formal literacy; and by this period the ability to read and write the vernacular, and even Latin, was quite common in the larger Italian towns. Well-to-do merchants sent their sons to the city schools, while their daughters and wives attended classes and learned to read the Latin Psalter.[5] A more complex society, in which commercial transactions were commonplace, also created a demand for an increasing number of educated laymen instructed in law and notarial skills. This is evident from the surprisingly large number of public notaries who were able to find employment in the cities of north Italy. A notary's function was to draw up contracts, recognizances and other documents in correct legal form and witness them; he performed, in fact, the functions discharged by a solicitor in modern times. In the early thirteenth century, a big city like Milan and even smaller towns like Verona and Pistoia could find work for several hundred notaries.

It was not only the merchant community that provided a forcing-ground for new professions. Economic expansion had its counterpart in the enlargement of government activity. The sacral kingship of an earlier age was superseded by royal administration working through written communication and

---

4. *PL* 203 col. 159.
5. Thomas of Cantimpré has an anecdote about a poor girl (apparently in a city of Brabant where he preached and heard confessions) who was sent to learn to read the Psalter under the tuition of a *magistra* who taught the daughters and matrons of well-to-do citizens: *Bonum Universale de Apibus*, ed. G. Colverinus (Douai 1627), pp. 93–4. Christina of Markyate, the daughter of a rich family of Huntingdon, was able to recite the Psalter when she fled the family home in *c.* 1115: *The Life of Christina of Markyate*, ed. C.H. Talbot (1959), pp. 92, 98.

record-keeping. Both church and state were served by bureau-cracies; and as the techniques of government became more sophisticated, there was an increasing demand for the services of educated and articulate men. In the course of the twelfth century we see a growing intake of men from the schools into the service of kings, city-republics and bishops, and not all of these men were clerks, even in the technical sense of having been tonsured. Many of the doctors of civil law and the canonists who taught the jurist universities of Bologna were laymen; and it was common practice for the Italian communes to appoint such men to the office of *podestà* – the supreme magistrate and executive officer of the city-republic.

For clerk and layman alike the road to blossoming career prospects lay through the schools. Here was a vital link between economic growth and that other parallel movement that changed the face of western society – the intellectual renaissance of the twelfth century. The rising flood of intellectual and literary activity associated with the scholastic movement of the twelfth century gained its momentum from the secular ambitions of innumerable young men. Widening prospects of advancement open to merit led to an escalating demand for higher education and a growing student population. Economic factors alone cannot account for the originality and creative energy displayed at this period in philosophy, letters and the plastic arts, as well as in the vocational studies of law and medicine. The wind bloweth where it listeth. The enthusiasm for learning that induced so many young men to set out for the schools in distant lands was kindled by the fame of great teachers and by a sense of living in an expanding mental universe. But it was the possibility of employment at the end of the road that made families and patrons willing to pay for it all.

. . .

NEW LEARNING AND NEW TEACHERS

The scholastic movement, which culminated in the creation of the first universities, presented the Church with a huge intellectual and social challenge. The expansion of the schools that had begun before the end of the eleventh century was associated with the recovery by western scholars of the lost intellectual capital of the ancient world in the form of Greek and Arabic philosophy and science, made available through the medium of Latin translation, and with the revived study of classical Roman law. In the course of the twelfth century these discoveries revolutionised both the content and the methods of learning.

Aristotle's works on logic, metaphysics and natural science, and Arabic medicine and mathematics, confronted scholars with a whole new universe of scientific knowledge and speculation, which could not be readily fitted into the traditional academic programme of grammar and Biblical studies appropriate to the clergy, and which called in question its hierarchy of values. Moreover, as the new learning was gradually assimilated, it became obvious that there were elements of the Aristotelian system and in the work of its Arab interpreters which were irreconcilable with the Biblical account of creation and the Christian belief in personal immortality. This conflict between Greco-Arabic science and the data of Christian revelation was to erupt in the thirteenth century into a major intellectual crisis, which had its epicentre in the Arts Faculty of the University of Paris.

Besides extending the range of the medieval curriculum, the new learning brought about a change in the method of study. With the application of dialectic or analytic logic to the study of the texts, the *questio*, or disputation, took its place alongside the lecture as the favoured instrument of instruction. In the universities men graduated to the status of Bachelor and Master by attending lectures on the prescribed books and taking part in disputations. In response to the demands of the scholastic method and the growing number of pupils, a new class of teachers arose – the *magistri* or secular masters, who were expert purveyors of the new learning. 'I became an emulator of the Peripatetics,' wrote Abelard, 'travelling and holding disputations wherever I heard there was interest in the art of dialectic.'[6] He was the prototype of the new class of professional scholars who made a career in the schools and gained a livelihood by teaching for fees. By the end of the twelfth century such men were legion.

Moved by a desire to improve the education of the clergy, the Third Lateran Council of 1179 decreed that every cathedral church should allocate a prebend to support a master, so

6. *Historia Calamitatum*, ed. J.T. Muckle in *Mediaeval Studies* XII (Toronto 1950).

that he could teach poor students free of charge. But the decree reflected the assumptions of a vanishing society in which services were supported by landed endowment or gifts. The schoolmen belonged to the new world of commerce and free movement in which services were proffered and bought with money. Abelard confessed that fame and money were the spur that goaded him; and in the towns of twelfth-century France both were available to an inspired teacher.

. . .

THE RISE OF THE UNIVERSITIES

Before the end of the century, a concentration of teachers offering the new learning and the confluence of students into a number of cities had generated the first universities at Bologna, Paris and Oxford. These were spontaneous associations or syndicates of scholars – in the case of Bologna, two universities of law students governed by their own student rectors, but at Paris and Oxford associations formed by masters. Urban growth meant that in many places, for the first time, conditions existed in which a large floating population of students could be accommodated; and the growth of international credit and currency arrangements made it possible for students to change money freely, to travel on credit notes and arrange loans, and thus to reside for long periods abroad.

The rise of these autonomous and turbulent academic societies was viewed with misgiving by many conservative prelates. The licence to teach had long been a monopoly of the Church, jealously controlled by bishops and cathedral bodies within the territory of their jurisdiction. The claim of the masters to be the sole arbiters of scholastic competence, and thus to control conferment of the magistral licence and admission to the teaching corporation, challenged these entrenched prerogatives. Early in the thirteenth century it was to be the subject of a prolonged tussle between the University of Paris and the capitular chancellor, who endeavoured to strangle the nascent academic association at birth.

It was more than a dispute about privileges. The dialectical method of the schoolmen, especially when applied to elucidating the sacred texts, aroused the mistrust of churchmen who had been schooled in the older traditions of monastic theology. The free speculation in the schools and the authoritative status accorded the opinions of the leading masters were seen as a challenge to hierocratic authority and a threat to the dogmas of faith. From the eminence of Ste Geneviève on the Mount, Stephen of Tournai looked down at the schools of Paris pullulating on the south bank and the island, and he did not like what he saw. 'As if the works of the holy Fathers are not enough,' he complained, 'they dispute publicly against the sacred canons concerning the incomprehensible Deity; they divide and rend the indivisible Trinity, and there are as many errors as there are masters.'[7]

For some time, in fact, the role of the masters as interpreters of the Sacred Page was difficult to define, and the place of the academic societies in the structure of the Church was unclear. In northern Europe, bishops tended to regard the universities in the same light as other clerical corporations within their diocesan territory, and only slowly and reluctantly abandoned the attempt to choose their officials and oversee their teaching. In Italy, the rulers of the city communes endeavoured to control the communities of alien scholars in their midst by providing a salaried professoriate. It was the papacy that, thanks to the far-sighted intelligence of Innocent III in the first place, perceived the possibilities of the scholastic revolution for the service of orthodox faith and the renewal of the Church. Innocent had been through the schools himself, and as pope proved himself a formidable champion of the Paris scholars. He and his immediate successors believed that the universities could be harnessed to serve the cause of reform by educating a new kind of clerical leadership.

The popes also recognised that in the immense task of building up the common law of the Church and establishing the judicial sovereignty of the papacy the masters and scholars had a vital part to play. The new law of the Church, the *ius novum* of the new age, was decretal law, compounded of innumerable legal and moral judgements made by the popes mostly at the request of individual petitioners. If it was to be universally known and have legal force, some agency was needed to disseminate it. This was to be the work of the law schools. Beginning with a compilation authorised by Innocent III in 1210, official collections of decretals were published by the expedient of sending them to the jurist universities of Bologna, wrapped up, as it were, in papal bulls commending

7. *PL* 211 col. 517.

them to the scholars. There they were expounded and glossed by the doctors, and copied for the benefit of students, who were required to possess the official texts; and from the schools men went out to staff the episcopal chanceries and ecclesiastical courts of Christendom. Thus through the university classrooms the new law was fed into the bloodstream of the Western Church.

It was the prospect of these services to the Christian community that caused the popes to cherish the universities, to flatter them, and generally to protect them from the pressure of local ecclesiastical authorities and from occasional attacks by city magistrates. In this they displayed a breadth of vision that was sometimes lacking from their other administrative expedients. Recognising this special relationship, the canonists gradually devised a place for the scholastic community in the ecclesiastical structure: along with the *sacerdotium* and the *imperium* – priestly and imperial authority – the *studium* was part of a threefold dispensation by which the Christian world was ordered and governed. This theory was precipitated in the term *studium generale*, which acquired clearer definition in the course of the thirteenth century. It meant a recognised school of the universal Church with a privileged status which only the pope could confer, and it became the hallmark of a university.

The rise of the universities and the creation of an international community of learning, in which men argued and wrote in a common scholastic idiom, signified the passing of intellectual leadership from the enclosed world of the monasteries. In the same way, the rise of an articulate town-dwelling laity in search of an inner spiritual life, and critical of the intellectual and moral shortcomings of the clergy, called in question the assumptions of monastic spirituality. Traditional piety had long taken it for granted that a serious commitment to the Christian life involved becoming a monk – that the Gospel call to personal holiness could only be realised in the cloister. For the great mass of mankind, enslaved to concupiscence and distracted by the material demands and anxieties of everyday life, there seemed to be only a tenuous hope of salvation. Safety was to be found only by repentance and conversion, which at this period of time meant flight from the world and entry to the monastic life. The term *conversus* that was used in monastic circles was the expression for an adult lay person who had taken the religious habit. As St Hugh of

Cluny explained to Philip I of France, Cluny was the chosen refuge of the penitent; let the king therefore resign his earthly kingdom while there was still time and lay hold upon the eternal kingdom by ending his days as a monk.[8] For those unable to commit themselves in this way, the best hope lay in sharing in the merits of a monastic community through association. This could be achieved by the gift of property or of children or, best of all, by formal admission to the privilege of confraternity with the monks.

. . .

THE APOSTOLIC LIFE

Understandably the notion of vicarious merit dependent upon the prayers of professional ascetics failed to satisfy the spiritual aspirations of an educated laity in search of personal religion. In any case, the credibility of this exclusive and world-negating ideal was weakened by the image the monastic Church presented to the outside world. The Benedictine abbeys were deeply implicated in the economic and political fabric of society as landlords, territorial rulers, holders of military fiefs and patrons of churches. It is not easy to view one's landlord as a paradigm of sanctity, especially when he raises the rent. It was, in fact, discontent with this image and the desire to discard worldly entanglements that inspired the eremitical movements of the eleventh and twelfth centuries, which assumed institutional form in Camaldoli and the Chartreuse, and provided the motive force for the reformed monasticism of the Cistercians.

In the twelfth century, besides these efforts to revive the monastic call to the desert, the spirituality of withdrawal itself was challenged by a growing awareness that the Christian vocation involved engagement with the secular world. Like the reformed monasticism, this reappraisal of the Christian life drew its inspiration from the model of the primitive Church presented by the New Testament. It was epitomised by the expression *vita apostolica* – 'the apostolic life' – an old term which acquired a fresh and dynamic meaning at this period.

The idea of the primitive Church is an historical one. It presupposes an awareness of the process of change and development. In the eleventh century it sprang from the heightened

8. *PL* 159 col. 9302.

historical consciousness of an age that was in the process of rediscovering the lost philosophy and science of the ancient world. The remote past had come alive again, and it seemed to offer an inexhaustible fund of lessons for those who knew how to interpret it. Thus an appeal from the present to Christian antiquity was central to the strategy of the Gregorian Reform movement. It was the avowed aim of the Gregorian party to restore what they believed to be the order and discipline of the primitive Church. To this end the papal Curia encouraged scholars to search libraries and archives for early sources of canon law, and in due course new collections were produced containing the 'ancient law' – the law that governed the Church of the early centuries.

The model of the primitive Church that attracted attention was the life of the apostolic community at Jerusalem as it is briefly described in the Acts of the Apostles: 'they continued steadfastly in the apostles' doctrine and fellowship, and in the breaking of bread and in prayer. And all who believed were together and had all things in common; and sold their possessions and goods and parted them to all men as every man had need' (Acts ii.41–5). This text had long been invoked by apologists for the cenobitical life of monks. To them the essence of the apostolic life was life in an ascetical community, based upon renunciation of marriage and personal property and organised for corporate prayer. In the ninth century, the abbot Smaragdus spoke for a well-worn tradition when he claimed that the Apostles were monks and the originators of the monastic life.[9] It was this conviction that helped to fuel the Gregorian drive for a celibate clergy living, where feasible, in religious communities, and thus provided a theoretical basis for the new orders of canons regular or clerical monks.

Under the impact of the reform movement, this controversial appeal to the apostolic Church opened vistas that extended far beyond the traditional confines of the cloister. For the idea of the apostolic life was a fertile one that meant different things to different people. It found a new and congenial soil in the urban society of the twelfth century. There was a growing recognition that a mode of life modelled upon that of the Apostles should involve not only renunciation of worldly goods but also a commitment to evangelism. The primary role of the

9. *Commentarium in Regulam S. Benedicti: PL* 102 col. 724.

Apostles, after all, had been to bear witness to their risen Lord – to preach the Gospel – and this meant an active engagement with the secular world as a preacher. The seventy disciples sent by Christ to announce the kingdom of God were the model; when he dispatched them, he instructed them to take neither purse nor bag for the journey but to depend upon the hospitality of the towns they entered.

It was this perception of the apostolic life that had moved individual ascetics like Robert of Abrissel and St Norbert of Xanten to adopt the role of an itinerant preacher while depending upon begging for their food and shelter. But neither of them succeeded in translating their personal vision of the apostolic life into the institutions they founded. Both the Order of Fontevrault and the Premonstratensian canons conformed to the accepted norms of monastic organisation. It was among the town-dwelling laity and the educated secular clergy – especially the university students and their teachers – that the idea of the *vita apostolica* won its most enthusiastic promoters.

In the later decades of the twelfth century, new and radical forms of lay piety began to appear, which drew their inspiration from first-hand study of the New Testament. Literate lay people, whose minds were unencumbered by the tradition of allegorical exegesis, drew from the Bible fresh and more radical interpretations of the apostolic life. The authentic apostolic life was seen to be one modelled upon the earthly life of Jesus, as it was revealed in the Gospels – the imitation of Christ. For those who would be perfect, this involved voluntary poverty, the renunciation of wealth and a mission to the unconverted; for all would-be disciples it meant a life devoted to prayer, penance and service to their neighbours. One of the ways by which this ideal could be realised was by membership of one of the penitential confraternities which sprang up in many parts of southern Europe at this period.

This model of the apostolic life was not the exclusive property of a cloistered élite; it did not involve flight from the world, but engagement with it; and it was accessible to every Christian, clerk and layman alike. It offered an ideal of sanctity and a programme that could be realised without abandoning marriage and secular responsibilities, and as such it commended itself to lay people in search of a religious vocation appropriate to their circumstances. It provided them

17

with an active role and a spiritual status that were denied them by monastic theology and classical canon law.

Realisation that a fully committed Christian life could be lived by lay people and without withdrawal from the world was slow to penetrate the mind of leaders of the Church schooled in traditional ecclesiology. One of the signs of a gradual reorientation was the recognition accorded, either by popular acclaim or by official canonization, to lay saints. Apart from martyrs, almost all the saints whose names had hitherto filled the calendars of the Western Church had been prelates, monks or crowned heads. The official models of sanctity were drawn exclusively from the ruling hierarchy of church and state or from an enclosed spiritual élite. But at the end of the twelfth century this socially exclusive tradition was broken, significantly in Italy, the land where urban political institutions had produced a mature lay culture. The canonization of St Homobuonus by Innocent III in 1199 proposed for the veneration of the faithful a new model of sanctity recruited from the ranks of the urban laity. Homobuonus was a merchant of Cremona and a married man, who had distinguished himself in the city by charitable work for the poor and his activities as a peace-maker. He was the first of many lay people, some of humble status like the wine-porter Albert of Villa d'Ogna, whose lives of penance and devotion to the needy made them the object of popular cults in the cities of northern Italy.[10]

The rise of an articulate town-dwelling laity in search of personal religion and critical of the assumptions of monastic spirituality presented the medieval Church with a pastoral challenge it was ill-equipped to meet. The diocesan and parochial structures of the Church had developed to serve the needs of a rurally based population. Its clergy, apart from an educated élite which was absorbed by the schools and the ecclesiastical bureaucracy, were largely recruited locally from the ranks of the free peasantry. Educationally most of them were barely above the level of their rustic parishioners. The medieval Church never devised institutions for training the clergy; the diocesan seminary was an invention of the sixteenth century. Few of the parish clergy possessed the educational or

10. André Vauchez, *La sainteté en occident aux derniers siècles du moyen-âge* (Ecole française, Rome 1981), pp. 224–9, 275–6.

theological equipment necessary to preach or instruct their people. The numerous churches to be found in some medieval towns were generally appropriated to monasteries or collegiate bodies, and the residue of the endowments left by the appropriator was too poor to attract the services of educated clerks. Lay people hungry for spiritual direction were sometimes driven to self-help, like the people of Metz, who were delated to the pope in 1199 for holding conventicles and preaching to one another.[11]

.   .   .

NEW EVANGELISTS

Initiative in forming penitential fraternities and groups of active evangelists professing the apostolic life came in many cases from the more affluent and articulate sections of the urban laity. One such group, which in its early stages anticipated many features of the Franciscan movement, was the fraternity of Poor Men of Lyons or Waldenses. Its founder, Waldes, was a cloth merchant and banker of Lyons, who had grown rich on the profits of money-lending.

We know nothing of Waldes's family or background before his dramatic conversion from the fleshpots. This occurred in or about the year 1176.[12] According to the chronicler of Laon, his spiritual crisis was brought on by hearing a minstrel in the street reciting the story of St Alexius – the rich young nobleman who was said to have renounced bride and patrimony on his wedding night and embraced poverty for the love of God; he ended by living incognito below the stairs of his father's house. The Alexius legend – a reverse version of the Cinderella theme – had a strange fascination for people of the twelfth century. In the case of Waldes, the impact of the tale suggests a mind already troubled by the fulminations of the Church

---

11. *Die Register Innocenz III*, II ed. O. Hageneder, W. Maleczek and A. Strand (Rome 1979), pp. 271–5.
12. The primary source for the conversion of Waldes is the chronicler of Laon in *MGH SS* XXVI (1882), pp. 447–9, who is, however, confused about the date of the event, which apparently coincided with a famine in the year 1176. For modern discussion of the Waldenses see J. Gounet and A. Molnar, *Les Vaudois au moyen-âge* (Turin 1974); R. Manselli, 'Il Valdismo originario' in *Studi sulle Eresie del secolo XII* (Rome 1953), pp. 69–87 – at once the most balanced and penetrating study; and Christine Thouzellier, *Vaudois languedociens et Pauvres Catholiques* (Cahiers de Fanjeaux 2, Toulouse 1967).

against usury. Smitten with compunction, he sought the advice of a schoolman about changing his way of life. The master referred him to the Gospel injunction: 'If you would be perfect, go, sell what you possess and give to the poor, and you will have treasure in heaven; and come, follow me' (Matt.xix.21). Moved by this advice, Waldes embarked upon a spectacular act of renunciation.

House and lands were settled on his aggrieved wife – her consent to her husband's religious odyssey seems not to have been sought. His two daughters were provided with a dowry and placed in a convent of Fontevrault. Those from whom he had extorted money were repaid; and the rest of his fortune was given away, some of it in the form of cash, which he distributed to the poor in the streets of the town. This done, he set off on a career of itinerant preaching, supporting himself solely by begging. In a short time he began to acquire disciples, who adopted his way of life. As he later explained, they all vowed themselves to absolute poverty, refusing to hold reserves of money, food or clothing: 'we have decreed to be poor, so as to take no care for the morrow; nor will we accept gold or silver, nor anything from anyone, except only food and clothing for the day'.[13]

In order to preach, the fraternity needed to have access to the Scriptures. Alain of Lille, one of the fiercest contemporary critics of the movement, says that Waldes was unlettered (*sine litteratura*), but in the language of the schoolmen this could mean no more than an inability to read Latin. As a successful merchant and banker, Waldes belonged to a class of men for whom basic literacy, at least in the vernacular, was an essential tool of their trade. That he was able to read is suggested by the fact that he commissioned two clerks to provide him with a Provençal translation of the Gospels and the Psalter.

It is not now possible to identify these early Waldensian versions of the New Testament. They were one of a growing number of unauthorised vernacular versions of parts of the Bible that were becoming available in the last decades of the twelfth century. To the ecclesiastical mind, direct study of the Bible by uninstructed lay people was fraught with peril – it was almost bound to engender anti-clericalism and heresy.

13. A. Dondaine, 'Aux origines du Valdéisme: une profession de foi de Valdès' in *AFP* 16 (1946), pp. 191–235. This study is of fundamental importance for the study of the early Waldensian movement.

Lambert le Bègue, a zealous parish priest of Liège, who translated the Acts of the Apostles for the use of his people, was accused of heresy for his pains and imprisoned by the bishop. The people of Metz, whom we have already encountered in the complaint laid before Innocent III, were denounced for having caused the Gospels, St Paul's Epistles, the Psalter, the *Moralia in Job* and many other books, to be translated into French, and making free use of these translations. Innocent's response was cautious: a desire to understand the Scriptures and to use them for exhortation was commendable; let the bishop send him more information about the character of the translators and the orthodoxy of those using the translations.[14]

In the eyes of his critics, the cardinal sin of Waldes, like that of the people of Metz, was that he was a layman who persisted in preaching without authorisation. When challenged, he and his followers claimed that by preaching and begging for their livelihood they were responding to a divine call to embrace the apostolic life, which they had received through studying the New Testament: were not the Apostles also laymen and illiterate like them? Bernard, the abbot of Fontecaude, who wrote a tract against them, briskly disposed of that argument: it was true that the Apostles were unlettered, but that was before they were called; afterwards, the Lord opened their minds so that they understood the Scriptures, and infused them with the Holy Spirit before sending them out to preach. Men cannot preach unless they have been sent. The etymology of the word *ecclesia*, he adds, unconsciously offering a hostage to his adversaries, is 'house of clergy'.[15] Worse even than preaching without authority, the Waldenses pilloried the moral shortcomings of the clergy and ridiculed their lack of education.

Rebellion, as Grosseteste declared, was as the sin of witchcraft. In official eyes Waldes was guilty of rebellion, but there is no evidence to show when, if at all, he adopted heterodox religious opinions. He had gone to Rome to seek papal approval of the vow of poverty taken by members of his fraternity a step he would not have contemplated if he questioned the authority of the ecclesiastical hierarchy. When, in 1181, he

14. *Die Register Innocenz III*, II, pp. 275–6.
15. *Contra Waldenses PL* 204, cols. 809, 838.

was summoned to answer for his conduct before a synod at Lyons presided over by the cardinal legate, Henry of Albano, he made an elaborate profession of faith in the form of assent to a series of doctrinal propositions. He swore on the Gospels that he believed in the validity of the sacraments irrespective of the merits or demerits of the priest who administered them, the efficacy of infant baptism, the remission of sins through sacramental confession and penance, and the value to the dead of almsgiving and masses celebrated on their behalf.[16]

These articles of faith presented to Waldes at the synod were precisely those that the Waldenses were accused by Alain of Lille of having denied.[17] Of course, Alain was writing his jeremiad many years later; but the selection of these specific items by the synod suggests that already by 1181 a number of Waldes's nomadic evangelists had moved into a radically unorthodox position, and that he was losing control of the movement he had initiated; the future parting of the ways between the orthodox Waldenses and the more radical brethren had already begun. But this may be to read too much into the acts of an assembly whose primary concern was with identifying adherents of the Cathar sects.

Despite his profession of orthodoxy, Waldes himself continued to insist on his right and duty to preach. In the face of his accusers he quoted St Peter's answer to the sanhedrin: 'We ought to obey God rather than men.' To conservative churchmen, lay preaching usurped the function of the official ministry. It was synonymous with subversion and heresy, especially when it drew attention to the failings of the clergy. The initial reaction of authority was to stamp on it. Thus Waldes's doctrinal orthodoxy was not enough to protect him and his followers from the ire of the new archbishop of Lyons, Jean Bellesmains, who had them expelled from the town. Worse still, in 1184 the Poor Men of Lyons were included, along with the Humiliati, in a general condemnation of heretical sects published in a council at Verona by Pope Lucius III – the decree *Ad abolendam*.

The anathemas of Verona in effect drove the Waldensian movement into schism. They hardened the radicals, who adopted an increasingly anti-sacerdotal position, and precipi-

16. Dondaine, *Aux origines du Valdéisme*, pp. 231–2.
17. *Contra Haereticos PL* 210, cols. 383–9.

tated a division within the movement itself. Some groups remained irreconcilable; others – the so-called Poor Catholics – stayed with Catholic orthodoxy despite their repudiation by the official Church, and after the death of Waldes found new leaders in the Spanish priest Durandus of Huesca and Bernard Prim. They asked nothing more than to be allowed to continue with mendicancy and preaching, which was directed primarily against the Cathar sectaries in Lombardy and the Languedoc. It was left to the shrewd intelligence and inspired pragmatism of Innocent III to reconcile these orthodox groups and to authorise their pursuit of the apostolic life. He also gave his approval to the Humiliati.

The Humiliati, like the Waldenses, anticipated some of the most conspicuous features of the mendicant friars. They were a lay pietistic movement of the late twelfth century, which had striking success in the cities of Lombardy and the Veneto. The source of their inspiration was the same: the Humiliati sought to realise in their lives what they conceived to be the life-style of the primitive apostolic Church, represented by voluntary poverty, simplicity in food and dress, penitential discipline, regular prayer and preaching. The movement re-cruited largely among the aristocracy and urban patriciate, who established houses for their communities in Milan, Pavia, Brescia, Bergamo, Cremona and Verona and other cities of northern Italy. Jacques de Vitry, a tireless observer of the religious scene, encountered them on his way to Rome in 1216, and credited them with possessing a hundred and fifty houses in Milan alone.

From an early stage they seem to have formed two echelons: one – the original group – consisting of married people, living in their own homes and pursuing their secular trade or occupa-tion, but following a penitential rule of life as members of a lay confraternity; the other group comprising quasi-monastic communities of celibates pursuing a cenobitical life, though without any recognised rule, and preaching in the streets and market-places. It was, of course, their unauthorised preaching activities that provoked the hostility of the clergy and got them included among the heretical sects in the condemnations of 1184.

Endowed with a keener intelligence than Pope Lucius, Innocent III perceived the potential value of the movement in the struggle against the élite of the Cathar sects. He therefore accepted a delegation from the Humiliati in 1201, and after examining their doctrine and practice, announced their rehabilitation. The papal privilege approving their form of life outlined their constitution. They were divided into three orders: the first order, which included houses of women as well as those of men, was a regular canonical order whose male members were ordained; the second order was also recognised as a monastic order, but its members were lay people, both men and women, who were celibate and lived in cenobitical communities; and the third order consisted of married people, who observed a penitential way of life in their own homes. Their obligations included the recitation of the Divine Office, a requirement which assumed that the lay members were literate and Latinate.

The most remarkable thing about the orders of the Humiliati, which particularly struck Jacques de Vitry, was the fact that their lay members had been authorised to preach: 'their brethren, both clerks and literate laymen, have authority from the supreme pontiff, who has confirmed their rule, to preach not only in their own congregation, but in the city squares and secular churches'.[18] Innocent's decision to authorise lay preaching legitimated an extraordinary breach in the sacerdotal professionalism of the medieval Church. It is true that he hedged it about with the proviso that the preaching of the lay brethren should be confined to spiritual exhortation and should avoid questions of dogmatic and sacramental theology;[19] but even with this limitation, a significant frontier had been crossed.

In their spirit the Humiliati bore some resemblance to the orders of friars. Where the friars were to differ from them was in pursuing a more radical ideal of poverty. In Milan and the other cities of northern Italy the communities of Humiliati enjoyed the security of well-endowed conventual houses. St Francis would have none of this. The scheme of evangelical perfection he proposed to his followers involved organised destitution. They were to throw themselves naked upon divine providence. They were to join the ranks of the holy beggars and threadbare evangelists who were becoming a scourge of

18. *The Historia Occidentalis of Jacques de Vitry*, ed. J.F. Hinnebusch (Spicilegium Friburgense 17, Fribourg 1972), p. 145.
19. 'ita quod de articulis fidei et sacramentis ecclesie non loquentur': G. Tiraboschi, *Vetera Humiliatorum Monumenta* II (Milan 1776), p. 133.

the ecclesiastical establishment. The two first and greatest of the Mendicant Orders of friars originated in the early years of the thirteenth century, and they grew side by side in a kind of symbiosis. Both had discernible roots in the twelfth-century ideology of the apostolic life, but their antecedents were rather different. The Dominicans were founded by an Augustinian canon, and from the outset they were a clerical order, which retained many of the features of the canons regular. The Franciscans, on the other hand, owed their origin to the liternal and uncomplicated vision of a layman. Like the evangelical movements that had preceded them, they represented the impact of the Gospel message upon the articulate laity of the new urban society.

Chapter 2

ST FRANCIS OF ASSISI AND THE ORIGINS OF THE FRIARS MINOR

The external life of St Francis is well chronicled and it is easy to trace the main events of his career. But it is less easy to penetrate his mind or to be sure that we have grasped his intentions. To his followers, he was a figure of momentous significance in world history. St Bonaventure (1221–74) and others identified him with the sixth angel named in the Apocalypse and credited his order with a messianic role, inaugurating a new phase in the Christian dispensation. This belief in the cosmic significance of Francis inspired a large body of hagiographical writing and anecdote about the origins of the friars in the decades following his death. The complex inter-relationships of these sources, the difficulty of distinguishing the original from the derivative, of disentangling genuine eye-witness report from pious fiction, have always posed serious critical problems. The search for the earliest testimony, which will offer us an image of the historical St Francis, is the essence of the 'Franciscan Question', which has exercised generations of scholars ever since Paul Sabatier published his classical *Vie de Saint François* in 1894.

The critical problem is aggravated by the fact that, as time went on, Francis became a sign of contradiction to his followers. As his small flock of devoted disciples expanded into a world-wide order, changes became unavoidable. Within four years of his death the leaders of the order were obliged to seek a papal interpretation of the Rule which declared his death-bed Testament to the brethren to be without binding force, and provincial ministers were ordering copies of it to be burned. There were some friars of the first generation who regarded the developments within the order as a betrayal of his ideals,

26

and their sense of malaise has infiltrated the written sources. Later in the thirteenth century, the order was rent by controversy over the meaning of his life and teaching; and eventually the conflict between the Spiritual party – the rigorists for absolute poverty who claimed to be the authentic custodians of the founder's message – and the 'Conventuals' ended in the Spirituals being driven into schism.

These dissensions, which became a lasting and tragic feature of Franciscan history, infected the hagiographical tradition: many of the later sources reflect the viewpoint of the Spirituals. For instance, the *Fioretti* or Little Flowers of St Francis – a classic of early Italian literature which in translation has enchanted generations of English readers – is a collection of anecdotes and legends which assumed its existing form in the Marches of Ancona during the fourteenth century. Ancona was a province that harboured many of the hermitages where the Spirituals had found retreat, and the idyllic picture of the Franciscan morning in the Umbrian countryside presented by the *Fioretti* depicts the beginning of the movement as it was seen though the eyes of the Spirituals, and it is deeply tinged with their preconceptions and disappointments.

The earliest Life of St Francis was by Thomas of Celano, who was commissioned to write it by Pope Gregory IX. Although it is couched in the rhetoric of official hagiography, as a historical source it has two important merits: it was begun in 1228, within two years of Francis's death, and it was the work of a friar of the first generation, who had met him – it contains, in fact, a vivid pen-portrait of the *poverello*; and it was written before the outbreak of troubles in the order had tainted the wells.

Sixteen years later, Celano was commissioned by the general chapter of the Franciscans to write a second and fuller Life; and to assist him with the task the Minister-General, Crescentius of Iesi, sent out a circular letter asking all who had personal memories of Francis to commit them to writing and dispatch them to him. Celano incorporated much of this new material into his second Life. But although he provides a lot of fresh detail, his selection has clearly been influenced by the pressure of later events. There are significant omissions and changes of contour which apparently reflect a desire to gloss over the deposition of Brother Elias – the successor Francis had chosen to govern the order – and also perhaps the need to

27

placate lay opinion in the town of Assisi. For the first Life begins with an attack upon the worldly values of the parents of the town who are accused of encouraging their children in dissolute and debauched living, a jeremiad that Celano thought it prudent to omit from his second work.

Continued heart-searching in the order and the proliferation of apocryphal anecdotes prompted the general chapter of Narbonne in 1260 to commission a third and definitive Life of the founder. This was the work of St Bonaventure. The foremost theologian of the Franciscan school at Paris, and Minister-General of the friars at the time of writing, Bonaventure was deeply concerned with the need to reconcile conflicting views in the order; and this preoccupation marked his Life of St Francis, which was based on Celano's work. Its diplomatic omissions and sandpaperings display the unmistakable marks of the official hagiographer. Following its adoption as the authorised version by the chapter of 1266, order was given to destroy the two earlier Lives by Celano.

In the search for primitive and authentic testimony, special interest has focused upon a letter addressed to Crescentius of Iesi by three of the earliest companions of Francis – 'we who were with him, though unworthy' – Brother Leo and Brothers Rufino and Angelo. The letter is dated 11 August 1246. They write in their old age from the hermitage of Greccio in response to Crescentius's request for reminiscences of the *poverello*. Unfortunately it is not entirely clear which if any, of the surviving collections of anecdotes represents the dossier that was attached to this letter. Some scholars have identified it with the Legend of Perugia, of which the earliest copy dates from the fourteenth century; others identify it with the Legend of the Three Companions, which is also known only from late copies.[1] Both these compilations contain many anecdotes about the life of Francis and his disciples, not all of them

---

1. The accompanying text is identified as the Legend of Perugia by Rosalind Brooke, see her edition with translation: *Scripta Leonis, Rufini et Angeli, Sociorum S. Francisci* (1970), and by L. di Fonzo, 'L'Anonimo Perugino tra le fonti Francescane del secolo XIII' in *Miscellanea Francescana* 72 (1972), pp. 117–483. For discussion and translation of the Legend of the Three Companions see Marion A. Habig (ed.) *St Francis of Assisi: Writings and Early Biographies* 3rd edn (Chicago 1972), pp. 855–956. A new approach to the problem based upon form criticism was made by Raoul Manselli, *Nos qui cum eo fuimus: Contributo alla Questione Francescana* (Istituto Storico dei Cappuccini, Rome 1980).

complimentary or uncritical, which have the flavour of authenticity; but it is no easy critical task to separate genuine oral testimony from subsequent 'improvement'. Some of the stories and reported dialogues clearly reflect later anxieties within the order over a slippage from the observance of poverty.

Some of this chronic controversy over Franciscan poverty has rubbed off on modern historians as well as on the medieval biographers. Sabatier, who was a Protestant pastor, saw the early history of the Friars Minor in terms of an inevitable conflict between the pure religion of the spirit, represented by St Francis, and the religion of authority, represented by Ugolino, the cardinal protector of the infant order, who became Pope Gregory IX and sought to translate the charismatic movement into traditional legal structures. Thus the original ideal of Francis was progressively diluted and smothered by the institutional Church. This viewpoint, which some modern scholars have adopted, derived some support from those sources that transmitted the tradition of the Spirituals.

In the search for the historical Francis through the thicket of the literary sources, the surest compass is provided by the handful of his own writings. Those that survive are the first and second Rules, a brief Rule he composed for brothers who elected to live in hermitages, the Testament dictated in his last illness, which contains his reflections on the beginnings of the movement, and a few letters. There are also the short Italian lyrics, of which the most famous is the Canticle of Brother Sun, for Francis was a mystic and a poet. Guided by these, we can endeavour to reconstruct a brief biography based primarily upon the Lives by Celano. In what follows it will be argued that the critique of the Spiritual party was not so much historically false to St Francis as misplaced, that the subsequent dilution of his ideal was not a betrayal but a necessary condition for the development of a permanent organisation.

. . .

THE EARLY LIFE AND CONVERSION OF ST FRANCIS

Francis was born in 1181, a child of one of the turbulent urban societies of twelfth-century Italy. His father, Pietro Bernadone, was a prosperous cloth merchant; and as a member of a well-to-do bourgeois family, the son took his place among the children of the chivalric class and the urban patriciate of the little hill town of Assisi. In their company he rode to war against the neighbouring commune of Perugia, was captured, imprisoned along with others and later released. Besides sharing in these military escapades, he had begun to take his place as a partner in the family business. In his eagerness to compete in chivalric society, he planned to join the crusade of Walter de Brienne against the agents of Hohenstaufen imperialism in southern Italy. He was in his twenty-fourth year when, probably in the spring of 1205, he set out for the campaign in Apulia. But on reaching Spoleto he heard the call of Christ in a dream, which made him abandon his quest for military glory and return home: 'as a dream when one awaketh; so when thou awakest, thou shalt despise their image'. In a dramatic gesture he renounced his patrimony and the family home. Old friends and frivolities were put from him, and in their place he adopted a solitary life of penance and prayer, sheltering in caves and ruinous chapels and begging his food from door to door. He was now embarked upon a spiritual quest the end of which he could not yet see.

It was only by degrees that he identified his vocation after his dramatic act of renunciation. We cannot be sure how or when he encountered the various ideals of the ascetical life that were abroad at the beginning of the thirteenth century. The level of his formal education, gained at the local school of San Giorgio, was that possessed by many of the town-dwelling Italian laity of his class at that period. His surviving letters, including the autograph of his blessing for Brother Leo, now preserved in the sacro convento at Assisi, show that he could understand Latin and could write it, if in a crude form. He also spoke French – the lingua franca of the merchant community. He was not a bookish man, either in his youth or in later life; but at any period, ideas that are widely current can be absorbed without recourse to books.

It is probable that in the course of his travels on business he had encountered exponents of the apostolic life such as the Humiliati and the Waldenses who devoted themselves to preaching and lived by begging. He may equally have been influenced by meeting some of the hermits who populated the forested hills of Umbria and Tuscany. In the first phase of his spiritual saga, when he haunted solitary places, it was evidently the eremitical ideal that took possession of his mind. The experience of these years left a permanent mark not only upon him but also upon the religious institution he founded. Even after he had acquired a group of disciples from the young men of Assisi, it was far from clear to him that the eremitical life was not his proper vocation. When he took them to Rome to seek authorisation, a perceptive cardinal suggested he could best fulfil his spiritual aspirations as a hermit. Possibly it was this hint that inspired a significant discussion among members of the party on the return journey from the Curia, which is reported by Celano. They had stopped over night in a deserted spot among the tombs outside the town of Orte – a scenario that recalls the Life of St Antony the Hermit – and they discussed 'whether they ought to live among men, or betake themselves to solitary places'.[2]

In fact, Francis opted for the cenobitic life of the religious fraternity and the active role of the evangelist. But the solitary life continued to exercise a compulsive attraction for him. It was his practice throughout his career to retreat at intervals, especially during Lent, to a remote spot in the mountains where he could meditate in solitude, with the support of two or three of his closest companions. It was in one of these retreats at Fonte Colombo, where he occupied a cave in the ilex forest above the valley of Rieti, that he pondered the text of the third and final version of the Rule. Although missionary activity was to be the *raison d'être* of his order, he recognised the need of those of the brothers who were drawn like him to the contemplative life to withdraw at intervals from the community, and for their benefit he composed a brief and simple Rule for those who lived in hermitages. In his last years he himself increasingly withdrew from the affairs of the order and the pressure of his worldly admirers to a remote hermitage in the fastnesses of Mount La Verna.

· · ·

ST FRANCIS AND THE APOSTOLIC LIFE

It was some time after he had left the family home and adopted the life-style of an impoverished hermit that another form of religious life was planted in his mind. This was the apostolic life – the life of the disciples of Jesus as it was

2. *1 Celano* c. 195.

revealed in the Gospels: a life of poverty devoted to evangelis-
ing the unconverted in which the missionaries were supported
by alms. The idea came to him, as he wrote in the Testament,
as a personal and immediate revelation: 'When God gave me
some brethren, there was no one to tell me what I should do;
but the Most High revealed to me that I ought to live
according to the model of the holy Gospel.'[3] Celano pinpoints
the moment when the idea took possession of his mind with
sudden and overwhelming force. He was attending mass at
the little church of St Mary of the Angels – the Portiuncula –
in the valley below Assisi. It was the feast of St Matthias in
the year 1208, and the Gospel lesson of the day (Matt.x.7,9)
described the sending out of the disciples: 'Preach as you go
saying "The kingdom of heaven is at hand" . . . Take no gold
or silver, nor copper in your belts, no bag for the journey, nor
two tunics, nor sandals, nor a staff for the labourer is worthy
of his food.' Celano reports that when the priest expounded
this passage to him, Francis cried, 'This is what I want; this is
what I am seeking.' And he immediately removed his shoes,
made a tunic of roughest material, and began to preach to all
the need for repentance.

The sole model for his fraternity was to be the life of Christ
and the disciples as depicted in the Gospel accounts. According
to Celano, the first draft of a Rule he submitted to the pope –
the so-called *Regula Primitiva*, now lost – contained little else
than a collection of texts from the four Gospels. This simple
and literal understanding of the Bible was characteristic of
Francis. His vision was always direct, literal and concrete,
uncomplicated by the conceptual analysis of the clerk who
had been through the schools. His imagination was not encum-
bered by the traditional gloss which elaborated the allegorical
senses of the Bible text. His apprehension of God took the
form not of analytical language but of concrete symbols – the
painted crucifix in the church of San Damiano which spoke
and commanded him to go and restore the church, the living
crib at Greccio, and the seraph which left on his body the
physical stigmata of crucifixion. Symbols like these were signs
of a new orientation of Western religious sentiment, marked
by a personal devotion to the humanity of Jesus, a concern

3. *Die Opuscula des hl. Franziskus von Assisi*, ed. K. Esser (Grottaferrata
   1976), p. 439.

with the circumstances of his earthly life, and a compassionate identification with his sufferings. They expressed a form of direct religious experience which was no longer confined to an enclosed spiritual élite and which the teaching of the friars was to make available to the ordinary Christian living in the secular world. Its inspiration came from a rediscovery of the literal sense of the Gospel.[4]

Other lay pietistic movements, like the Humiliati and the Poor Men of Lyons, had embraced a life of voluntary poverty in order to preach. But Francis went further than any of them in his radical understanding of evangelical poverty. Anyone who sought admission to his fraternity was required, as a precondition of acceptance, to sell all his possessions and distribute the proceeds to the poor. His small flock of disciples were to wander through the world without property or income, sleeping in borrowed barns and shacks, like the hut that was their first home at Rivo Torto, and performing casual labour or begging for their daily food. The significance for him of this way of life is directly stated in the words of the First Rule:

> The brothers shall appropriate nothing to themselves, neither a place nor anything; but as pilgrims and strangers in this world, serving God in poverty and humility, they shall with confidence go seeking alms. Nor need they be ashamed, for the Lord made himself poor for us in this world. This is that summit of most lofty poverty which has made you, my most beloved brothers, heirs and kings of the kingdom of heaven.

For Francis, this mystical destitution, the refusal to own houses, accept money or accumulate reserves, was not just a missionary expedient or an ascetical discipline; it was a literal imitation of the earthly life of Christ.

A belief in the absolute poverty of Christ and a desire to make it, and itinerant preaching, the model of their observance was a common feature of the evangelical movements of the twelfth century. It distinguished them from the accepted traditions of monasticism. The renunciation of personal property had always, of course, been required of monks. It was

---

4. On the evangelical revival of the twelfth century see M.-D. Chenu, *Nature, Man and Society in the Twelfth Century* transl. J. Taylor and L.K. Little (Chicago and London 1968), pp. 239–69.

enjoined by the Rule of St Benedict. But the individual who surrendered his possessions did so in the knowledge that he would be supported by the corporate property of his monastery. He was not making himself destitute. This was how monastic writers understood the 'apostolic life': it was a life modelled on the primitive Christian society described in the Acts of the Apostles, 'which possessed all things in common'. For Francis, as for Waldes, this traditional model of the apostolic life was not enough. He insisted that his fraternity should not only discard personal property; they were to forgo corporate property as well. The ideal he offered them was a total dependence upon divine providence, in Jerome's phrase, 'naked to follow the naked Christ'.

In the early years, Francis and his followers were an intimate fraternity of nomadic preachers, some like Brother Sylvester clerics, but most of them laymen, who moved from town to town in central Italy, preaching in market-places and attending mass in the churches. The outward sign of their poverty was the crude material of their habits secured round the waist by cord, and the fact that they went barefooted. For their daily keep they relied upon food given in return for doing manual jobs or upon begging for scraps. Francis did not call them monks, but Friars Minor or 'little brothers' (*fratres minores*), a name intended to signify their humble status. In 1209 he took his ragged party to Rome and persuaded Pope Innocent III, not without some misgiving, to authorise their activities.

Voluntary poverty is not an ideal that has much meaning for those who are poor by birth or force of circumstances. The poor of this world dream of getting rich. Understandably, therefore, although the early Franciscans recruited their members from all social groups except the unfree, their chief attraction was for the young of the more affluent classes and the clerical intelligentsia, young people who had never experienced real want. Francis himself and those of his companions whose antecedents can be traced were all children of well-to-do merchant or knightly families of the town of Assisi.[5]

---

5 Jacques Paul, 'La signification sociale du Franciscanisme' in *Mouvements franciscains et société française XIIe-XXe siècles*, ed. A. Vauchez (Paris 1984), pp. 9–25.

Salimbene, himself a friar of the second generation, a garrulous and snobbish man, boasted in his invective against the secular clergy that

> there are many in both orders of friars who, if they had been in the world, would have possessed the prebends they hold, and perhaps much better, for they are just as nobly born, as rich, powerful and learned as they, and would have been priests, canons, archdeacons, bishops and archbishops, perhaps even cardinals and popes, like them. They should recognise that we have given up all these things to go begging.[6]

The Friars Minor had some success in recruiting among artisans and peasants, but broadly speaking, Salimbene's boast was justified. Their ideal of the evangelical life attracted to their ranks some of the aristocracy and large numbers of the gentry or knightly class and of the urban patriciate. Their most spectacular trawl was among the masters, bachelors and students of the northern universities, a triumph fraught with momentous consequences for the future development of the order.

A conspicuous novelty of their fraternity was its social egalitarianism: it included men of widely differing social origins and different levels of education on equal terms. It was a fraternalism based upon a pragmatic but deep-seated conviction, perhaps peculiarly Italian, that in the sight of God all human beings are equally worthy of respect. Clerk and layman, patrician and peasant, lived together, shared their crusts, and slept side by side in their often cramped and insalubrious quarters. This challenge to the conventions of a sharply stratified society earned them abuse and mistrust as well as admiration. Aristocratic and bourgeois families were filled with dread when contemplating the possibility of their sons being captured by the friars and reduced, as it seemed to them, to the miserable status and impoverished life-style they associated with the lower class, the *popolo minuto*.

Their voluntary destitution identified them with the most deprived sections of society. Compassion for lepers – the pariahs of the medieval world – played a part in the conversion of Francis: 'When I was in sin, the sight of lepers nauseated

---

6. *Cronica Fratris Salimbene de Adam*, ed. O. Holder-Egger *MGH SS* (1913), p. 418.

me beyond measure, but then God led me into their company, and I had pity on them.'[7] And in its early days the fraternity spent much time on ministering to the needs of those in the local leper-house. In the towns, too, it was the poor – the carders of wool and the water-carriers, the occupants of hovels and basements – who were the first to be evangelized.

Modern film directors, fastening upon the poetry of Francis, have tended to represent him and his companions as proto-nature worshippers. In reality, although their compassion for the poor and oppressed attunes with modern sentiment, the spirit of their life-style and the themes of their preaching had little in common with the mentalities of the modern secular world. Their sense of kinship with the natural world sprang from the vision of Francis, for whom the cosmos was a vast picture-book filled with signs of its creator's love. The major theme of their preaching was the need for repentance and penance – the perpetual theme of the evangelist. Their renunciation of worldly comforts and their ragged tunics belted with cord identified them as exponents of the penitential movement that was gaining many adherents in the towns of northern and central Italy. When preaching in the March of Ancona, they were asked who they were by the local people, and they answered, 'we are the penitential men of Assisi'.[8] Thomas of Spalato, who heard Francis preach at Bologna in the *piazza communale*, records that he talked about the need to repent old hatreds and feuds and make peace. His style of oratory was simple, direct and emotive in its appeal. Mime had an irresistible attraction for him. Celano recalled that when he preached to the people on the hillside at Greccio during the midnight mass of Christmas day, he constantly pronounced the name 'Bethlehem' as if it were the bleating of a sheep.

In his Testament, recalling the early days of the brotherhood, Francis observed that the clerical members – among whom he included himself – recited the Divine Office at the canonical hours, while the lay brothers recited the Psalter or said *Pater Nosters*. According to Bonaventure, he and his companions were tonsured by Innocent III during their visit to the Curia, thus formally incorporating them into the clerical

---

7. The Testament in Esser, *Opuscula* p. 438.
8. The Legend of the Three Companions, cited by G.G. Meerseman, *Dossier de l'ordre de la pénitence au XIIIe siècle* (Fribourg 1961), p. 3.

order of the Church. Nevertheless, it was out of the question for them to imitate the elaborate choral liturgy of the monastic orders, if only because their poverty precluded possession of the battery of service books that would be needed. They either recited the Psalter, as was common practice among devout and educated lay people of the thirteenth century, or adopted the shorter order of service in use at the Roman Curia, for which in time they managed to obtain breviaries.[9] It was the need for a place where the brothers could chant the Office in common that persuaded Francis to seek a church for their own use. The bishop of Assisi had nothing to offer him, but the Benedictines of Monte Subasio made over to him the tiny dilapidated church of the Portiuncula, and beside it the brothers built themselves a humble residence of mud and wattle.

Because of its associations with the genesis of the order, the tiny ill-lit chapel of the Portiuncula in the valley of Spoleto always had a special place in Francis's affections. It, and the adjacent dwelling, conformed to his desired model of poverty and simplicity. The brethren were taught to regard it as their mother-house, and as numbers grew, it became the place of assembly where they congregated to hold their chapters. It was at the Whitsun chapter of 1217 that the decision was taken to launch the brethren on a universal mission. In this and the following years parties of friars were dispatched to the countries beyond the Alps, provinces were defined, and provincial ministers were appointed to lead them.

. . .

THE ORGANISATION OF THE ORDER

As the order expanded and its organisation began to take shape, Francis himself increasingly withdrew from its active direction. He had long cherished an ambition to evangelise the Moslems in the East, and in 1219 he sailed to join the Crusader army outside Damietta and secured an interview with the Sultan of Egypt, Al-Kamil. But before embarking upon this heroic mission, he had taken steps to provide for the oversight of his order during his absence. Some time before, during a visit to Florence, he had won a new admirer and an

9. S.J.P. Van Dijk and J.H. Walker, *The Origins of the Modern Roman Liturgy* (1960), pp. 179–201.

important patron in Ugolino, the cardinal-bishop of Ostia, who was at the time papal legate in Tuscany. Francis secured his agreement to act as protector of the order at the Curia, an arrangement that was later ratified by Pope Honorius III. Ugolino in fact proved himself to be a devoted friend and counsellor, and afterwards, as Pope Gregory IX, a powerful promoter of the Friars Minor. At some point, either before or after his expedition to the East, Francis formally resigned command of the order to one of his earliest disciples, Peter Catanii. He returned from Syria in 1220, but he never resumed the government of the friars. After the death of Catanii in March 1221, he designated Brother Elias to take his place.

In the six years between his return from the East and his death in October 1226, Francis adhered to his decision of self-imposed abdication. Yet, despite his solemn profession of obedience to the successors he had appointed, he remained for his followers the patriarch and model, and as such, the ultimate authority. It was during this period that he composed the Second Rule – the so-called *Regula Bullata* – which was approved by Pope Honorius III in 1223. Some scholars have seen in its careful provisions the guiding hand of Cardinal Ugolino, for Francis was no legislator. The task of translating his intense vision into the structures of a religious institution was left largely to other hands. The compulsion of his mystical experience, and a desire to escape the excited throng of devotees who pressed round him on his preaching tours, caused him increasingly to take refuge in the mountain hermitages like Greccio and Fonte Colombo, where he could devote himself to prayer. The toll taken by an internal complaint that was to kill him, the unhealing wounds of the stigmata and growing blindness, forced him to travel on a donkey instead of walking barefoot. At the end, after he had been nursed for a time in the palace of the bishop of Assisi, he had the brethren carry him down to the Portiuncula and lay him on the floor of beaten earth for his encounter with death.

Was his retirement from a directive role prompted by more than a desire to escape the distractions of worldly business? Possibly it was in part an anti-hierarchical demonstration: in his fraternity all should be equal, and he wanted to be on the same level as the brethren. But there may also have been an element of disappointment or disillusionment in his wish to relinquish office. There are some indications that in the last years he found himself out of sympathy with the direction the order was taking, that he sensed a new generation had diluted, if not betrayed, his ideals of poverty and simplicity. 'They were content with one habit, patched inside and out,' he recalled wistfully in the Testament, 'and we refused to have anything more. We made no claim to learning and we were submissive to everyone.' During his last illness, he was visited in the bishop's palace by Brother Richard of Ancona, who asked for reassurance that the scholar-friars like himself, who possessed books, were not infringing the rule of poverty. Francis's reply was unequivocal: 'This was my first and this my final intention – if the brothers had but believed me – that no brother should have had anything except a habit, as the Rule allows, with belt and breeches.'[10]

. . .

THE PARADOX OF POVERTY

To the end, he had not wavered in his belief that the imitation of Christ involved an absolute poverty that excluded all possessions – even the possession of books. In the Rule he had expressly forbidden the brethren to own buildings or to touch money in any form whatsoever. But this ideal of sanctified destitution, which was realisable by the small flock of disciples at Rivo Torto, posed insuperable problems when the fraternity expanded into a world-wide missionary order. How could preachers and priests be educated for their task if they had no books or writing materials or rooms in which to study? How could the friars preach and administer the sacraments if they had no churches? And how could any of these essentials be acquired without funds? Churches might be built for them by rich laymen and houses were lent them by city communes, but the largesse of the laity was too irregular to form the basis of a stable organisation.

After the death of Francis, efforts to reconcile his ideal of poverty with the practical needs of a pastoral mission were to involve heroic gymnastics of conscience. The practical problems posed by the prohibition of money forced the provincial

10. Rosalind Brooke, *Scripta Leonis* (ed.) pp. 202–3.

ministers in 1230 to seek an authoritative interpretation of the Rule from Gregory IX which in effect mitigated its force. The pope declared that they were permitted to appoint a *nuntius* or 'spiritual friend' as a trustee with power to receive and hold money on behalf of the brethren, to whom they could apply to pay for necessities. They were thus enabled to accept gifts of money, notably the legacies that were showered upon them by grateful penitents. 'What are necessities?' inquired the Four Masters who were commissioned by the chapter of 1241 to expound the Rule.[11] They conclude that ministers must resort to the 'spiritual friends' in order to clothe the brethren and provide for the needs of the sick; also for the provision of houses and books; they may accept any gifts, apart from money, on the understanding that they have the use of everything, but own nothing. Gregory's privilege *Quo elongati* that had authorised these concessions represents the beginning of the inevitable retreat from Francis's uncompromising ideal of absolute poverty.

Any residual misgivings about the possession of buildings were allayed by a legal device sponsored by Pope Innocent IV in 1245: by the privilege *Ordinem vestrum* he vested ownership of all the goods of the Friars Minor in the Apostolic See, except where donors had reserved their own rights. This pious fiction allowed them the undisturbed use of their houses and churches without infringing the letter of the Rule that denied them any right to property. Such compromises were the inescapable consequences of growth. The homelessness of the pauper Christ that Francis desired for his fraternity could not provide the necessary conditions for a universal missionary enterprise. As parties of mendicant friars arrived in the towns of Germany, France and England, enthusiastic individuals and city corporations offered them houses, which became places of fixed residence; and in the 1240s they began, with the help of patrons, to build their own churches. At Assisi itself, the unresolved paradox at the heart of Francis's ideal was given visual expression by the exquisite and costly basilica begun by Brother Elias on a spur at the foot of Monte Subasio to house the tomb of rough-hewn rock. A source of continuing delight to aesthetic as well as pious pilgrims, it was a cause of offence

11. *Expositio Quatuor Magistrorum super Regulam Fratrum Minorum, 1241–42*, ed. P.L. Oliger (*Storia e Letteratura* 30 Rome 1950), p. 134.

to some of the surviving elders who could remember the adventure of the early days at Rivo Torto.

Among the survivors who continued to bear witness to the spirit of the primitive Franciscan fraternity one of the most significant was Clare of Assisi. She was one of Francis's earliest and most illustrious converts. A girl of aristocratic family, she quietly slipped away from the family home one night in the spring of 1211 and made her way to the Portiuncula, where she took vows to follow Francis in poverty and the imitation of Christ. The ideal of voluntary poverty was not a male monopoly and Clare, like Francis, attracted disciples. Jacques de Vitry, who was in Italy in 1216, noticed groups of Minoresses – sisters who worked alongside the Friars Minor ministering to the sick and destitute in the towns, but living apart in their own residences. Francis assigned to Clare and her sisterhood the restored church and house of San Damiano just below the walls of Assisi. The extreme poverty and simplicity of the living conditions she maintained there continued to provide an instructive example to a generation of friars who had never known St Francis.

If Francis and Clare contemplated an active collaboration in the pastoral ministry of the friars by his female disciples, they must have been disabused by the pressure of social convention as well as by ecclesiastical disapproval. There existed a general assumption that the chastity of women without male escorts needed to be protected by the high walls of a convent. The Rule that Cardinal Ugolino gave to Clare's sisterhood in 1219 provided for a regime of strict enclosure based upon the Rule of St Benedict.[12] Female mendicancy seemed unthinkable, so while reiterating the monastic call to personal poverty, Ugolino's Rule authorised the sisters to hold property in common.

This was not how Clare understood her discipleship of St Francis. She, who described herself as the *plantula*, 'the little plant of our blessed father Francis', had promised him to live in poverty 'according to the perfection of the Holy Gospel'. She was happy with the enclosed life of the contemplative, but she was not willing to bow to any authority that would force her to compromise her vow of absolute poverty. In the end,

12. Ugolino's original rule for the Clares is lost, but as Pope Gregory IX he reissued it in revised form in 1239, see Moorman *HFO*, pp. 38–9.

she herself composed a new Rule for the nuns at San Damiano, applying to them the words of the Second Rule of St Francis – 'the sisters are to appropriate nothing to themselves, neither house nor place nor anything': they were to hold no property either directly or through an intermediary.[13] In other words, they were to depend for their food and other necessities upon the uncertain almsgiving of the faithful. With the help of the Cardinal Protector, confirmation of this was obtained from Innocent IV two days before her death on 12 August 1253. But it was a personal privilege that was not to be applicable to other convents of the order. Thus although the Second Franciscan Order – the order of the Clares – cultivated a relatively poor and simple life-style, in other respects it became an enclosed monastic order of the traditional type. Here too the compromises that Clare had fiercely rejected in her lifetime were symbolised by the magnificent gothic church of Santa Chiara that was built at Assisi to house her body in the decade after her death.

---

13. Text of her Rule with French translations in *Claire d'Assise: Écrits*, ed. M.F. Becker, J.F. Godet and T. Matura (Sources Chrétiennes, Paris 1983), pp. 142, 146; and English transl. in *Francis and Clare, the Complete Works*, ed. R.A. Armstrong and I.C. Brady (1982).

Chapter 3

THE GROWTH OF THE FRIARS MINOR, CRISIS AND CHANGE

. . .

MISSION AND SETTLEMENT

Most of the early recruits to the Friars Minor were Italians. This fact, and the existence of popular penitential movements, assured them recognition and ready acceptance in the Italian towns. By 1217 their numbers had grown dramatically, and they had established settlements in many of the cities of northern and central Italy. Of the twelve provinces into which the order was divided by the time Francis died, six were in Italy, including the southern provinces of the Terra di Lavoro, Apulia and Calabria. Expansion beyond the frontiers of Italy, on the other hand, suffered an initial setback. In the years 1217 to 1219, groups of friars sent to Germany, France, Spain and Hungary met with an unfriendly reception and returned to report to the general chapter that nothing had been accomplished. Five of a party sent to Morocco failed to return at all, having been slaughtered by the local Moslem ruler.

'The time to send them had not yet come,' observed Brother Jordan of Giano.[1] But the fact was, these early failures were caused by lack of information or elementary planning. Francis had not seen the necessity of identifying contacts in the proposed areas of mission or of ensuring that the parties sent were properly accredited. Nor apparently had he taken account of the linguistic problems of communication. The

1. *Chronica Fratris Jordani*, ed. H. Boehmer (*Collection d'études et de documents* VI Paris 1908), p. 7.

party sent to Germany under Brother John de Penna contained no one who spoke any German. Having discovered that the word 'ja' proved to be an open-sesame when begging for food, they used it rather too freely in response to suspicious questioning by their hosts, and were consequently taken to be heretics. So they were imprisoned, stripped and beaten, and then sent home.

Thanks either to the more practical, if worldlier, intelligence of Brother Elias, or to the prudent guidance of Cardinal Ugolino, these omissions were remedied in the light of experience. The new expeditions that were dispatched by the chapter from 1220 onwards carried letters of recommendation from Pope Honorius III, and included at least one of the brethren who could speak the language of the territory they were going to evangelize. Direction of the new German mission was entrusted to Caesarius of Speyer, and his party of twelve clerical friars and fifteen lay brothers included three others of German mother-tongue. To our advantage it also included Brother Jordan of Giano – an unwilling recruit and fearful of martyrdom, he had not volunteered like the others but had been ordered to go by Elias. Forty years later he wrote a narrative of the adventure with all the vivid recall of an old man remembering the encounters of his youth.

The advantages of better planning now became apparent. Crossing the Alps by the Brenner, the party was welcomed by the bishop of Trent, who invited them to stay and preach in his diocese. After forty years Jordan could still recall the physical trials of the journey that followed as they made their way into Bavaria. For some days no one offered them any bread, 'and the brothers knew not how to beg'. Famished and weak at the knees from fasting, they tried to assuage their pangs by drinking from mountain streams. Eventually they reached Augsburg where bishop Siegfried received them warmly and assigned them his nephew's mansion. It was their first residence in Germany and the headquarters from which Caesarius dispatched brethren to make settlements in Mainz, Worms and the cities of the Rhineland. The year 1222 brought a flood of recruits, both clerks and laymen, and Caesarius was able to hold the first chapter of the new province at Worms. As the friary was too small for the numbers, he was invited by the bishop and canons to hold the chapter in the choir of the cathedral. In the following year Caesarius was replaced by

Albert of Pisa, who brought new reinforcements from Italy, and the organisation of the province was consolidated by its sub-division into the four custodies of Bavaria, Swabia, Franconia and Saxony.

Some of the secular clergy were hostile to the new arrivals, but in the light of later troubles, these early years, when the new apostles were carried forward by their sense of mission and were welcomed by more zealous prelates, seemed to Jordan a halcyon age of growth and confidence. A party sent to France under the leadership of Brother Pacifico had established itself at Saint-Denis in 1219, and in the 1220s, with the active favour of King Louis VIII and Queen Blanche and the appreciative help of some of the bishops, the friars made settlements at Rouen and many towns of north-eastern France. At the same period another group succeeded in planting communities in Arles, Montpellier, Perigueux and other towns of the Midi. And Franciscan missions also penetrated Portugal and Spain.

The composition and procedure of the party that founded the English province was much like that of the others. On 10 September 1224 a group of nine, consisting of four clerics and five lay brothers, all of them bare-footed and penniless, landed at Dover, having been ferried across the Channel by the monks of Fécamp. Four of the party were Italians, including their leader, Agnellus of Pisa, and three were Englishmen, including the only priest in the group, Richard of Ingworth. Two were youngsters – recent recruits who were still in the noviciate. At Canterbury they were kindly received by the monks of the cathedral priory, and they made their first settlement in the town, consisting of a room lent to them below the school-house. Four of the party proceeded to London, where a house was provided for them on Cornhill by the sheriff, John Travers; and quite soon, Ingworth and Richard of Devon moved on to Oxford. There, as had happened at London, they were given hospitality by the Friars Preachers, who were already installed in the town, until they were able to rent a house of their own in the parish of St Ebbes. 'There,' wrote Brother Thomas of Eccleston with exultant hindsight, 'sweet Jesu sowed a grain of mustard-seed that has since been made greater than all the plants of the field.'[2] And in support

2. *De Adventu Fratrum Minorum in Angliam*, ed. A. G. Little (1951), p. 9.

of his observation he pointed to the fact that at the time of writing, thirty-two years after their first arrival, the brethren numbered twelve hundred and forty-two and were settled in forty-nine different places in England.

Everywhere they made for the cities. The urban populations were their chosen mission field. And it was in the towns of northern Europe that the apostolate of the Franciscans began to take clearer shape. As it did so, the paradox inherent in the idea of St Francis came to the surface and disturbed the order with a prolonged crisis of identity. The need for fixed residences and for churches of their own, where they could preach freely and hear confessions, obliged provincial ministers to seek a mitigation of the Rule. Rulers, city communes and individual lay people were eager to give them land and money to build. And the scale and design of the buildings were dictated by lay patrons anxious to display their generosity and uninhibited by Francis's austere devotion to his Lady Poverty. Although the Franciscans did not become rentiers like the old monastic orders, the accommodation built for them in the town-centres increasingly resembled that of the Benedictine monasteries – a complex of stone buildings constructed round a quadrilateral cloister, one side of which was formed by the conventual church.

All this was a far cry from the humble circumstances of the Portiuncula. Even there, respect for lay patrons had stopped Francis stripping unwanted tiles from the roof. Some provincial ministers, like William of Nottingham, fought a losing battle to perpetuate the early spirit of poverty by insisting upon the use of crude building materials: he had the stone walls of the friars' dormitory at Shrewsbury pulled down and replaced with walls of mud. But the tide of lay benefaction proved irresistible.

It was not only the observance of poverty that posed problems. The simplicity and humble egalitarianism that Francis demanded of his followers seemed to preclude prelacy or the cultivation of learning. 'We were unlettered and the servants of all',[3] he wrote, and Celano reports him as saying 'My brethren who are led by curiosity for learning shall find their hands empty on the day of retribution', and begging

3. Esser, *Die Opuscula des hl. Franziskus von Assisi*, ed. K. Esser (Grottaferrata 19, p. 439).

Ugolino to debar them from accepting bishoprics.[4] Himself a man of mystical but simple piety, he wanted the brethren to convert others to discipleship of Christ by the example of their lives rather than by logic or learned discourse. His primitive fraternity had been largely lay in its inspiration and membership. Although it included some clerics, there was no distinction of status between them and the lay members. According to Bonaventure, Francis and his companions were tonsured by the pope when they went to the Curia in 1209. *The Legend of the Three Companions*, on the other hand, tells us it was Cardinal John of Santa Sabina who wanted them tonsured and made the necessary arrangements. The tonsure, of course, signified the conferment of clerical status. Celano is silent on the subject, and it is possible that we have here an apocryphal tradition generated by subsequent developments in the order. Innocent III had shown himself willing to authorise lay preachers. But to Bonaventure, a priest and schoolman writing half a century later, a lay ministry would have seemed an inversion of the proper order of things.

At some point in his career – we do not really know when – Francis was ordained to the diaconate; but to the end of his life he never became a priest. Apparently he regarded priestly ordination as incompatible with his ideal of self-abasement and humble service. Those who were closest to him followed him in this. Brother Elias, the chosen disciple to whom he entrusted the direction of the order, remained a layman throughout his life. Agnellus of Pisa, the first provincial minister of England, was a deacon on his arrival, and refused to be ordained to the priesthood until the general chapter ordered him to do so following a petition from the brethren of his own province.

Here too, as the order expanded, the idea of Francis became difficult to maintain. A preaching mission to the relatively sophisticated and critical people of the towns required education, especially theological education, and intellectual agility, as well as some degree of rhetorical skill. The mystical genius and charisma of Francis and his immediate disciples like Giles and Leo were personal gifts that could not be transmitted to their successors. His later followers would require training. In any case, the whole concept of a lay ministry conflicted with

4. *2 Celano*, p. 195.

the sacerdotal professionalism of the medieval Church. Moral exhortation was lamed unless the preacher could follow up his message by shriving his converts. As Salimbene, himself an ordained friar, observed, the hordes of idle lay brothers he met in the Italian friaries were useless for the vital pastoral tasks of hearing confessions and administering the other sacraments. The shortage of priests in the friaries created serious difficulties in the early stages of the German mission. Jordan of Giano recalled that for a whole long summer he was the only priest available to celebrate mass and hear confessions at the friaries of Worms, Mainz and Speyer.

This shortage of the necessary personal equipment for a pastoral mission was high-lighted by encounters with the Dominican friars. As the Franciscans made settlements in the towns of northern Europe, they came under the direct influence of, and into competition with the Order of Preachers. In Paris, Cologne, London and Oxford, they found the Dominicans already established and ready to welcome them. They thus found themselves working alongside an order which, like them, was dedicated to poverty and preaching, but which was largely clerical, theologically educated, and had a clearly defined missionary purpose. It also had a well articulated system of representative government of a kind that St Francis had never envisaged. The problem was accentuated for the Friars Minor by their success among the masters and students of the northern universities, which brought them an influx of highly educated clerics. Men of this kind, although they had been moved by the Franciscan ideal of poverty to abandon the race for preferment, were disinclined to accept direction by laymen less educated than themselves.

. . .

FIRST CRISIS AND CONSTRUCTION

These tensions culminated in a conflict with the Minister-General, Brother Elias, and led to his deposition. In the tradition of the Spirituals, Elias was cast for the role of the Judas who betrayed the ideal of St Francis. Certainly his life-style during his second generalate from 1232 to 1239 laid him open to criticism. Accustomed by virtue of his position to socializing with the great, he seems to have acquired a taste for grandeur, and latterly abandoned any personal effort to observe the spirit of Franciscan poverty. Salimbene refers indignantly to his plump palfreys, his retinue of page-boys, and the private cook who accompanied him on his travels. But other and more significant charges were laid against him.

The attack upon his regime came from the northern provinces. It was mobilised by a group of friars who were clerks and university graduates, among whom the most prominent were Alexander of Hales and Jean de la Rochelle, both Paris theologians, and the English scholar Haymo of Faversham. The indictment which was presented to the pope, contained a number of grievances. It was alleged that he had governed the order autocratically and had failed to convene a general chapter for many years; also that he had disturbed the brethren by sending visitors to the provinces to invite delations of mismanagement or wrong-doing, which were to be reported to him personally. More significantly, he was accused of having persistently appointed lay brothers to positions of authority as guardians of houses and provincial ministers.

Elias was not ordained himself, and there is no doubt that in promoting lay friars and refusing to accord ordained friars a privileged status he was faithful to the mind of St Francis. His paternalistic regime was also in accord with the founder's notions of authority, which included a belief in the virtue of corpse-like obedience to religious superiors. In many directions the order had expanded and prospered under the direction of Elias. Nevertheless, the disapproval of the provincial ministers prevailed, and in 1239, after a stormy meeting of the general chapter presided over by Gregory IX in person, the pope deposed him. His overthrow was followed by a reappraisal of the constitution and objectives of the order. Leadership passed to the graduate clerical members, and lay brothers were debarred from holding the offices of warden, custodian or provincial minister. In fact, the Friars Minor had been subjected to a clerical take-over from within. Later, the *zelanti* – the zealots who deplored the path taken by the order – looked for a scapegoat, and found one in Brother Elias. But in reality change had been dictated by growth and the need to give permanent effect to the vision of Francis. For the charismatic cannot survive unless it is institutionalised. The conversion of the Minorites from a penitential movement inspired by lay piety into a recognisable clerical order within the ecclesiastical hierarchy was the inescapable outcome of a pastoral strategy that involved the cure of souls.

The two decades following the crisis of 1239 were a period of heart-searching re-examination and constitutional construction. The practical difficulties raised by the Rule and anxiety about compromises over poverty prompted a general chapter of delegates held at Montpellier in 1241 to order an inquiry. The chapter commanded each province to set up a panel of *magistri* to investigate and report on doubtful points in the Rule. The exposition of the Rule by four Paris masters – the only one to survive – illustrates the problems that preoccupied the leaders of the order in these years. The masters address themselves at length to questions raised by the observance of poverty in a world that seemed eager to shower them with gifts. What constitutes ownership of movable goods? they ask; can the brethren buy, sell, exchange or contract loans? Clearly not if such transactions involve them in using money. Does the poverty enjoined by the Rule forbid them any fixed means of support, such as the perpetual rents some people wish to give them, or cultivable land? On this the masters are adamant: 'the poverty of the friars is perfect poverty, which retains nothing, but depends on God to provide, which is called mendicancy'.[5] This obviously excludes acceptance of rents or any other fixed source of income. But ministers may, in accordance with *Quo elongati*, apply to 'spiritual friends' to help procure houses and books.

Alongside this painful exercise in reappraisal, a process of legislation and constitutional construction went forward under the generalship of Haymo of Faversham (1240–4), Crescentius of Jesi (1244–7) and John of Parma (1247–57). All these men were representative of the new type of leadership: all were clerics and schoolmen from the universities, and all had reached middle age before joining the friars, thus bringing to their office a certain independence of judgement. The general chapter of 1239 that had deposed Elias took some immediate steps to prevent a repetition of the despotic regime which had caused so much ill feeling. It approved statutes making the Minister-General responsible to the general chapter for his acts and requiring chapters to be convened at regular intervals. Various additions to these enactments, the text of which is now lost, were made in the years that followed. Finally, at

5. *Expositio Quatuor Magistrorum super Regulam Fratrum Minorum, 1241–42*, ed. P.L. Oliger (*Storia e Letteratura* 30 Rome 1950), pp. 156–8.

the end of this formative period, the previous legislation was codified and amended by Bonaventure, the then General, and his code was ratified by the general chapter of Narbonne in 1260. These statutes gave the order its permanent constitution.

The character of an institution is determined by the way in which its officials are chosen. The statutes of Narbonne provided for offices at the higher levels to be filled by a process of election. The General of the order was to be elected by a vote of the general chapter. In the same way, provincial ministers were to be elected by the chapters of their provinces and confirmed in appointment by the General. Below this level the arrangements were more authoritarian. For the purpose of supervision each province was subdivided into groups of houses called custodies, and the statutes decreed that the custodian – the head of the group – should be designated by the provincial minister; but in making this appointment, the provincial was required to take advice from representatives of the custody concerned. Wardens or guardians, the heads of individual friaries, were designated by the provincial at a meeting of the provincial chapter, though here too advice was to be sought from some of the brethren of the friary.

A conspicuous feature of the statutes was a desire to establish the principle of governmental responsibility by means of regular assemblies. A general chapter of the order was to meet every three years, alternately north and south of the Alps at places to be fixed by the General. It was to be attended by the provincial ministers, each accompanied by one companion, one custodian elected from each province, and a 'discreet' brother chosen by each provincial chapter. And to this body the General was to be answerable for his acts. On the first day of the meeting, the statutes require him to accuse himself of his shortcomings while in office. He is examined by the provincials and custodians sitting in conclave, and if they decide he should for whatever reason be removed, they will immediately proceed to elect a successor. Similarly, every province was to hold a chapter annually, and an important part of its business was to elect a committee of four members called *diffinitors* – the device was derived from the Dominicans – whose task it was to examine and, if need be, correct the provincial minister.

These constitutional arrangements borrowed several details

from the practice of the Order of Preachers; but they fell short of the thorough-going system of representation that the Dominicans established, at least in principle. There is an obvious kinship in the essentials. Both orders created an organisation to ensure that those in office were made accountable; both decreed the sovereignty of the general chapter; but whereas the Dominican chapter met annually, that of the Franciscans met every three years, leaving the General with greater freedom of action. The composition of the provincial chapters of the Friars Minor was left undetermined by the statutes, and seems to have varied from one province to another. Below the level of provincial, appointment to office was by designation, not by election. The paternalistic spirit in which the primitive order had been ruled was not wholly eliminated by the new constitutions.

Some of the most significant provisions related to education. The statutes laid down that in future no postulant for admission to the order was to be accepted unless he was either a cleric properly instructed in grammar and logic or a prominent layman, whose entry was likely to provide widespread edification. In other words, the Friars Minor had elected to become a learned or student order like the Dominicans, and now imposed an educational qualification on postulants. A rigorous application of this ruling would, of course, have excluded St Francis himself. The Franciscan convent at Paris had boasted a master teaching in the university faculty of theology since the admission of Alexander of Hales to the order in *c.* 1235; and the increasing slant towards learning is indicated by the rules governing the education and conduct of lectors – the trained theologians appointed to the convents to instruct the brethren. They formed an élite within the friaries, set apart to pursue higher studies, permitted, unlike anyone else, to work and sleep in a separate room, and equipped with books by their provincial. Francis's reported misgivings over the pursuit of scholarship by the brethren proved to be prophetic. The existence within each community of a privileged élite, who did not share the common dormitory and were exonerated from many of the common tasks, was bound to erode the bond of fraternity which he considered all important.

What light do the Narbonne statutes throw on the faithfulness of the order to the ideal of poverty thirty-four years after the founder's death? It can be said that they display a genuine intention to maintain the standards set by the Second Rule. The third chapter of the code, which deals specifically with the observance of poverty, reiterates the admonition that the friars may not own anything; they may not receive or store money or valuables (with the important exception of books) in their houses, or anything for the purpose of sale; they are not to travel on horseback except in cases of approved necessity, and they are to go unshod (the Four Masters had argued that this last prohibition did not extend to wearing sandals, for a shoe – *calceamentum* – was something that covered the whole foot). All must wear the same simple habit: 'be always a shining light of austerity, lowliness and poverty' (*reluceat semper austeritas, vilitas et paupertas*).[6] The brethren are told they must not allow collections to be taken on their behalf when they preach nor, when they hear confessions, must they ask penitents to make any offering either for themselves or for anybody else.

The code goes into detail on the subject of building and church decoration: superfluity must be avoided, whether in length, width or height; churches are to be simple structures without arcades or towers; and there is to be no refinement in paintings, windows or columns; windows are to contain no stained or historiated glass, with the sole exception of the principal window behind the high altar – this may display images of the crucifixion, the Blessed Virgin, St John, St Francis or St Antony, but no others. The most eloquent commentary on these regulations is the lower basilica at Assisi, covered from floor to ceiling with superb frescoes by the leading Tuscan painters, or the huge arcaded temple of Santa Croce at Florence. As Francis himself found, the enthusiasm of patrons was not easy to resist.

. . .

THE EVERLASTING GOSPEL

By the time of Bonaventure's regime, the process of development represented by the constitutions of Narbonne had already caused internal strains which threatened the cohesion of the order. He had, in fact, been designated Minister-General by his predecessor in order to resolve a crisis potentially more damaging than the conflict that had unseated Elias. The aged

6. *Die ältesten Redactionen des Generalconstitutionen des Franziskaner-Ordens*, ed. F. Ehrle in *ALKG* VI p. 91.

companions of Francis, some of whom, like Brother Leo and Brother Giles, were still living in the hermitages above the valley of Rieti, nursed their memories of the early days. But while old men dream dreams, young men see visions. There were younger men whose fervour for poverty and whose sense of the messianic mission of Francis and his followers found confirmation in the arcane prophecies of Joachim of Fiore.

Joachim, a Calabrian abbot, mystic and hermit, discerned in the events of the Bible the hidden outlines of a cosmic drama which was to haunt Western minds for centuries. Even in his lifetime he had acquired the status of a prophet whose counsel was sought by popes and princes. After his death in 1202, his writings were widely disseminated and his eschatological speculations were absorbed into the mental bloodstream of the thirteenth century. In his Biblical commentaries he advanced a new and revolutionary scheme of history, which claimed to elucidate the working of God in the historical process. His exegesis divided human history since creation into three stages or states, each of which represented the providential operation of one person of the Trinity. The first state was that of the Father, the second – inaugurated by the Incarnation – was that of the Son, and the third that of the Holy Spirit. The third age was the culmination of history in which, like Augustine's sabbath of the blessed, mankind would enjoy the perfect fruition of the Godhead. But its advent would be preceded by a period of great tribulation when the Antichrist – the mysterious superhuman enemy of God and man named by St John – would be loosed upon the world. According to Joachim, this transitional period of tribulation would be marked by the appearance of new spiritual men in the form of two orders – one of angelic contemplatives, the other of preachers – who would be raised up by God to lead the faithful safely through the time of their troubling into the new age of the Spirit.

In the late twentieth century, having lived with the possibility of a nuclear armageddon, we are better equipped than our grandfathers to enter into the minds of medieval people and to understand their fears and dreams when they contemplated the end of the world. They had long been accustomed to millennial musings which derived their inspiration from the Book of Revelation. Even the illiterate were constantly reminded of the terrors of the Last Days by the scenes depicted upon the tympana of their cathedrals and the walls of their parish churches. Joachim's prediction of the coming of the Antichrist was in a well recognised literary tradition, and it was this feature of his prophetic scenario that first attracted attention in the years following his death. But by the 1240s men had begun to read other signs of his world-picture in their own times. In particular, it seemed to some that the two orders of mendicant friars answered the description of the new spiritual men destined, according to Joachim, to lead mankind into the coming age of the Spirit. It was a messianic role that many Franciscans, especially the *zelanti* – the zealots for the absolute poverty prescribed by the Rule and the Testament – were eager to appropriate for their order.

Salimbene recorded in his chronicle that he had first heard of Joachim's prophecies in the 1240s when, as a young friar, he was living at the convent of Pisa. His informant was a refugee abbot from the south, who brought with him a complete set of Joachim's books and deposited them in the friars' library.[7] In the next few years the Franciscans played a leading role in circulating the writings of Joachim. A selection was brought to the English friar Adam Marsh by brethren from Italy, and he promptly passed them on to his friend Robert Grosseteste, the bishop of Lincoln.[8]

Dispatched to France to attend the schools at Paris, Salimbene was diverted to Hyères in Provence to hear lectures on Joachim by Brother Hugh de Digne. He felt privileged to attend Hugh's seminars, which attracted notaries and members of the local intelligentsia besides the brethren. To Salimbene, Hugh seemed a new Elijah 'one of the greatest clerks of the world, a boundlessly spiritual man'.[9] He was also, according to Salimbene, 'a great Joachite'. Nevertheless, Hugh's commentary on the Rule betrays none of the wilder interpretations associated with the *zelanti*, for whom the Joachite writings were a second Bible. In fact, he expressly warned Salimbene against swallowing the whole of Joachim: 'and are you infatuated with him like the others?'[10]

7. *Cronica Fratris Salimbene de Adam*, ed. O. Holder-Egger *MGHSS* (1913), p. 236.
8. *Adae de Marisco Epistolae*, ed J.S. Brewer in *Monumenta Franciscana* I (RS 1858), pp. 146–7.
9. *Salimbene*, p. 226.
10. 'es tu infatuatus sicut alii?': *ibid.* p. 238.

It was a timely warning. The danger of Joachite speculations as they were interpreted by the *zelanti* and their subversive possibilities became apparent a few years afterwards when, in 1254, a young Franciscan Bachelor at Paris named Gerard of Borgo San Donnino issued a book containing Joachim's major works together with an introduction and commentary by himself, which he called an *Introduction to the Everlasting Gospel*. In this he announced the advent of the age of the Holy Spirit, in which the Old and New Testaments were superseded and the carnal Church with its institutions – including the papacy and the secular clergy – was to wither away. And he identified Joachim's spiritual men of the new age with the friars, the humble and bare-footed people, destined to replace the clergy of the previous dispensation. This curious work of millennial fantasy fell with explosive impact into the midst of the fierce controversy then raging between the friars and the secular masters of Paris, and it provided welcome ammunition for those of the secular clergy who were coming to regard the pastoral activity of the friars as a threat to their status and livelihood.

The Everlasting Gospel was delated to Rome by the University of Paris and was condemned by the pope as heretical. The unfortunate Gerard, who had made the error of committing to writing opinions that were not uncommon among his religious brethren, was silenced and disciplined by the General. But the matter did not end there. The order had been tainted with a highly subversive heresy. Its role as a partner in the pastoral mission of the clergy was jeopardised. Only a public disavowal and dissociation from Gerard's views could save its future. The Joachites had to be purged. The most distinguished victim of the scandal was the Minister-General, the saintly and scholarly John of Parma. Although he had not subscribed to the aberrations of the Everlasting Gospel and had disciplined its author, he was known to be a convinced Joachite and it was known that he sympathised with the ideals of the *zelanti*; he had, in fact, referred in an encyclical letter to the possibility that the friars were to be identified with Joachim's new spiritual men. He therefore felt obliged to comply with the suggestion of Pope Alexander IV that he should abdicate the generalship. The general chapter summoned to Rome in February 1257 to receive his resignation accepted it with regret, but expressed its confidence in his leadership by authorising him to nominate a successor.

.   .   .

BONAVENTURE'S APOLOGY

Bonaventure of Bagnoregio, the man chosen to succeed, was at Paris, where he was a regent master in the theology faculty, when he received the summons of the general chapter to assume the leadership of the order. One of his first tasks was to purge the remnants of the heterodox Joachites. Gerard of Borgo San Donnino was committed to perpetual imprisonment; John of Parma was accused of heresy, but after examination was permitted by Bonaventure to retire in peace to Greccio. It was a difficult task. Many of the Friars Minor, and indeed many of their secular opponents, were inclined to accept Joachim's predictions of the Last Days. Bonaventure himself shared the belief of many of his brethren in the messianic role of the friars. By identifying St Francis as the angel of the sixth seal named in the Apocalypse he showed that he too had been touched by Joachite speculation. Joachim's eschatology was, in fact, a prevalent illusion of the epoch, rather in the way that Marxist historicism was that of the twentieth century.

In his efforts to remove the reproach of heresy and subversion and to steady the order on its new course of development, Bonaventure had of necessity to face both ways at once. He had to reassure the secular hierarchy, already alerted to the challenge posed by the highly privileged status of the Mendicants and now questioning their orthodoxy; he had also to reconcile the radicals among his own brethren, the *zelanti*, to the course the order was now taking. He was eminently equipped for the task. He had been a pupil at Paris of the theologian Alexander of Hales, and he was now the leading schoolman of his order. His classical commentary on Lombard's *Sentences*, his exegetical writings and his apologia for the ideal of evangelical poverty were to gain him the posthumous accolade of a Doctor of the Church. He was held in high esteem at the Curia. He resisted an attempt by Pope Clement IV to provide him to the archbishopric of York, but Gregory X created him cardinal-bishop of Albano a year before his death. In that capacity he helped plan the agenda of the Council of Lyons, which assembled in May 1274. His manifest saintliness, personal humility and devotion to the ideal of poverty, commended him to the *zelanti* and enabled him to reassure potentially rebellious elements among the radicals.

With some justice Bonaventure is venerated in Franciscan tradition as the second founder. Himself a highly educated cleric, the son of a professional family, he fully approved and promoted the image of the Friars Minor as a learned and clerical order, and he accepted the practical consequences of that reorientation. But he was well aware that it represented a divergence from the model of the primitive Franciscan fraternity. He took the point boldly in an apologia he wrote, addressed to an anonymous master, who was troubled by the apparent discrepancy between the Rule of St Francis and the observance of his followers:

> Do not be disturbed by the fact that the brothers were at the beginning simple and unlettered men; indeed, this ought rather to strengthen our faith in the Order. Before God I confess that it is this that made me most love the life of the blessed Francis – that it resembles the beginning and perfection of the Church, which first began with simple fishermen and afterwards advanced to most illustrious and learned doctors. You will see the same thing in the religion of the blessed Francis, so that God shows it was not devised by the prudence of men, but by Christ . . . this is shown to be the work of God when even the wise and learned have not disdained to step down and associate with simple men. [11]

This was a daring apologia for the new model of the Friars Minor. No one should be scandalised by the contrast between the learned order of the present, now becoming a nursery of scholars and bishops, and the simplicity of the early days. It was a mark of organic growth which was like that of the Church itself, and which for that reason bore the authentic sign of divine approval. The scholars, libraries, prelates and churches that the order now possessed, were all evidence that God was with it.

Alongside this striking theory of development, Bonaventure remained a passionate apologist of the evangelical ideal of poverty. His *Apologia Pauperum*, written in his later years in

11. *S. Bonaventurae Opera Omnia* VIII (Quarrachi 1898), p. 336.

response to a renewed attack by the secular masters of Paris, remains the classical exposition of the Mendicant ideal. He was fully conscious of the need to arrest tendencies towards a more relaxed kind of observance, to impose discipline upon the more unruly elements, and to reinforce the authority of the ministers. Before setting out from Paris to take up the Generalship, he penned a letter to all the ministers and custodians identifying the failings that were bringing the order into disrepute, and which he proposed to remedy. Among them he listed idleness, uncontrolled vagrancy, involvement in monetary transactions, importunate begging which made people dread the appearance of friars in their neighbourhood, excessive expense and refinement in buildings, the appointment to office of men who were untried and spiritually immature, and – a major source of friction – the appropriation of burial and testamentary rights that belonged to the parish clergy.[12]

The seventeen years of Bonaventure's Generalate (1257–74) did much to consolidate the new structure of the order and to hold the radicals and fundamentalists in check. The extent and limits of his success can be gauged from the fact that it was only after his death that the quarrel between the radicals – the Spirituals – and the so-called 'Conventuals' began seriously to disrupt unity. He had borne the full brunt of the secular polemic against the Mendicants. It was thanks in no small measure to his efforts that the attack on the friars mounted by the secular prelates at the Council of Lyons was diverted away from the Friars Minor and the Order of Preachers.

In the decade following his death the order was shaken by the first rumbles of dissent that were to lead to open schism. The compromises over poverty that he had castigated in his encyclicals to the brethren, particularly the acceptance of money bequests to individual friars, did happen, as a number of wills testify, but it is impossible to assess the extent of this lapse from the primitive observance. It was not only these failings on the part of individuals, but the whole drift of Franciscan observance represented by the acquisition of great churches, opulent buildings, security of income and a position of power in the councils of church and state, that aroused the

12. *ibid.* pp. 468–9.

misgivings of radical groups in the order. It was as much to satisfy their demands as to defend the mendicant ideal against its secular critics that the General Bonagrazia sought a fresh papal declaration of the principles upon which the order was based. This was provided by the constitution *Exiit qui seminat*, issued by Pope Nicholas III in 1279. The bull, which was clearly influenced by Bonaventure's *Apologia*, reiterated the legal fiction that the pope was the sole proprietor of everything the friars possessed, and vindicated Franciscan poverty as a way of life modelled upon that of Christ. A belief in the absolute poverty of Christ was thus elevated to the status of an official doctrine.

THE *USUS PAUPER* CONTROVERSY

The issue that was to preoccupy the internal critics of current observance was not ownership but the use and quality of the order's possessions. Anyone who has known the advantages of living in a well-appointed institution such as a college or an officer's mess will be aware that the ownership of the property by somebody else is no hindrance to the enjoyment of the facilities by those who use them. Enjoyment may, in fact, be enhanced by the absence of financial responsibility. The radicals or zealots among the Friars Minor held that the vow of poverty was not fulfilled by the simple renunciation of ownership; the friar's vocation involved restricting his possessions to the barest necessities – to cultivating an impoverished lifestyle. This what was meant by the expression *usus pauper* – poor possession – which gained currency among the zealots at this period. It was given its classic exposition in the writings of the Provençal friar Pierre Olivi.[13]

It was as lector to the friars of Narbonne that Olivi established his reputation as the chief exponent of the *usus pauper*. In his 'Questions on Evangelical Poverty' delivered to the brethren – he later claimed they had never been intended for general publication – he argued that a restricted use of material goods was implicit in, and integral to the Franciscan vow, that without it the renunciation of ownership was ineffectual and meaningless: 'As form is related to matter, so is *usus pauper*

---

13. On Olivi see M. Lambert, *Franciscan Poverty* (1961), pp. 151–9, and especially David Burr, *Olivi and Franciscan Poverty. The Origins of the usus pauper Controversy* (University of Pennsylvania Press 1989).

related to the renunciation of all right of ownership.'[14] Thus the Minorite was committed by his profession to a life of indigence. Those who denied this were no true religious. Olivi went on to single out the practice of accepting money and grandiose buildings as manifest breaches of the vow of evangelical poverty. These assertions were not startlingly new. There was probably nothing in them that would not have commanded the assent of Hugh of Die or Bonaventure. The fact that their orthodoxy was questioned and that they were delated to the Minister-General was an indication of a growing tension between those satisfied with a more relaxed observance and the zealots or 'Spirituals', who were beginning to challenge the leadership and to question the direction the order was taking.

The General, Bonagrazia, referred Olivi's writings for examination to a commission of Franciscan theologians at Paris, and in 1283 this body censored his opinions as erroneous and dangerous. As a consequence his works were banned in the order and confiscated. So far from being crushed by this, he addressed an eloquent letter of apologetic to the commission, defending his orthodoxy in matters of faith; and, in fact, his defence was approved by the general chapter of 1287. A new General, Matthew of Aquasparta, appointed him lector to the Franciscan school of S. Croce at Florence. He died at peace in 1292; but afterwards his name was taken as a logotype for those who protested against the decadence of the order. His tomb at Narbonne became the focus of a cult by the Spirituals, and the zealots of Provence and Ancona circulated his writings on evangelical poverty and drew from them inferences of which he would scarcely have approved.

The continuing dispute over the meaning of poverty not only threatened the unity of the Franciscan Order; it spilled over into the relations between the Friars Minor and the Dominicans and brought them into a damaging collision with the papacy. Rivalry between the two orders of friars, which was sharpened by academic controversy, often drifted into mutual recrimination over their observance. The Dominican understanding of voluntary poverty represented a sensible compromise. The Friars Preachers had not been committed by their founder to a regime of organised destitution. They

14. F. Ehrle, 'Olivis Leben und Schriften' in *ALKG* III, p. 508.

begged for alms, but nobody questioned their right to own their churches and conventual buildings; nor were they troubled by the Franciscan abhorrence of money gifts. What did disturb them were the claims of the Friars Minor to be better exponents of the evangelical life than their rivals because they had embraced a more absolute poverty.

A sharp dispute was touched off at Oxford between the two communities in 1269 by a Dominican brother named Solomon, who taunted the Franciscans with accepting money like everybody else, contrary to their profession of poverty. The claim of the Minorites that they practised greater poverty because they did not accept money (it was accepted and held on their behalf by an intermediary) was a sham: 'I am not a great clerk or a man of great learning,' averred Solomon, 'but I firmly believe this and, if need be, I will maintain as much in the presence of the pope.'[15] The ensuing controversy, puerile though it was, continued to flare up and embitter relationships between the two orders for many years, despite efforts at pacification by the Chancellor of the university. Leading schoolmen were drawn into it on both sides – Kilwardby and Thomas Sutton for the Dominicans, Pecham for the Franciscans.

. . .

THE RUPTURE OF UNITY

Brother Solomon had touched a raw nerve. It was the contention of the moderate or 'Conventual' party, which formed the majority of the Friars Minor, that they were faithful to their founder's ideal of evangelical poverty as they had renounced all rights of ownership – their buildings and land were the property of the Apostolic See or remained the property of the donors, and any funds at their disposal belonged to the 'spiritual friends' or intermediaries of the order. While Dominican sceptics were suggesting that this was a legal fiction of no practical significance, the complacency of the 'Conventuals' was being vociferously challenged by the Franciscan exponents of the *usus pauper*. As time went on, the struggle within the order for a more rigorous observance became increasingly bitter and violent. In the March of Ancona and Provence, leaders of the zealots or Spirituals were harassed and impris-

15. A.G. Little, *The Greyfriars at Oxford* (1892), p. 321.

oned by superiors trying to defend the *status quo*. A further effort was made to suppress the writings of Olivi, which were condemned by a general chapter meeting at Lyons in 1299. In Tuscany, where the Spirituals found an eloquent advocate in Ubertino da Casale, they pleaded for papal recognition of two Franciscan orders each having its own superiors, following respectively the rigorist or the relaxed observance. A group of radicals, in fact, seceded from Florence and set up an independent house in Sicily.

In the end the papacy was drawn into the conflict. The Minister-General, Michael Cesena, himself an advocate of strict observance, appealed to Pope John XXII to proceed against the secessionists and restore peace in the order. John had no sympathy with the radicals. He ordered the dissolution of the groups of dissidents – the 'Fraticelli' – who had set up houses in defiance of their superiors. A number of them were summoned to the Curia at Avignon, charged with heresy and imprisoned. Those who remained obdurate were delivered to the Inquisitor of Provence, and in May 1318 four of them were burned in the market-place of Marseilles.

The belief in the absolute poverty of Christ and the Apostles, which lay close to the heart of the controversy, came to be regarded by John as a subversive error that needed to be rooted out if peace was to be restored. He was not to be deterred by the fact that the doctrine had been formally approved by his predecessor forty three years earlier. Whether from weariness with the endless debate or provoked by a letter from the Franciscan chapter reaffirming the doctrine, he resolved to settle the argument once for all. In the bull *Ad conditorem canonum* of 8 December 1322 he renounced the Church's ownership of the possessions of the friars; and in November 1323 he issued the bull *Cum inter nonnullos* which declared it heretical to hold that Christ and the Apostles had divested themselves of all proprietary rights, both severally and in common. Thus with two blows of the axe the pope severed the branch that support the claims of both the Conventuals and the Spirituals to be the authentic practitioners of the evangelical life.

John's heavy-handed demolition of a belief about the poverty of Christ that had been shared by all parties in the Franciscan movement drove some of the moderates, including Michael Cesena, as well as the Spirituals into schism. The rebellion became politicised when Cesena, William of Ocham, and two others fled the papal court at Avignon and placed themselves under the protection of the emperor Louis of Bavaria, whose claims to the imperial crown were not admitted by the pope. This tragic episode of Franciscan history had long roots in the past. The germ lay in the message of St Francis. The conflict was the outcome of a hundred years of effort to contain and institutionalise an ideal which, if literally understood, was simply impracticable.

Chapter 4

ST DOMINIC AND THE ORDER OF FRIARS PREACHERS

The Friars Preachers or Black Friars differed from the early Friars Minor both in their spirit and the circumstances of their origin. Their institution was the creation of two men of genius – the Spaniard, Dominic of Caleruega, and the German, Jordan of Saxony. From the start they were a clerical and learned order, a stepchild of the canons regular, to whom their founder belonged; and while they devoted themselves to an active apostolate in the street and market place, they retained many features of monastic observance. This mark of their monastic parentage was visibly indicated by the dress that gave them their popular name: a black cloak worn over the white habit and scapular of the Premonstratensian canons. Their fraternity sprang from the pastoral demands of the south of France, the Languedoc, where the ascendancy of the orthodox Church was threatened by the entrenched counter-church of the Catharist heretics. It was St Dominic's preaching mission to combat the Cathars that gave birth to the new order.

· · ·

THE EARLY CAREER OF ST DOMINIC

Dominic was a Castilian priest, probably of aristocratic birth – a late medieval tradition connects him with the noble family of Guzman, which owned property at Caleruega, his birthplace. He had been educated as a clerk in the schools of Palencia, and as a young man he had been given a canonry in the cathedral of Osma. At the time he joined it, the chapter of Osma had only recently been reconstituted as a community of canons regular living according to the Rule of St Augustine. The canons regular were a hybrid order of clerical monks. They had come into existence during the eleventh century in response to the propaganda of the reform party, which exhorted the secular clergy to live in communities on the model of the early apostolic Church. Their houses embraced a wide variety of observance, but all their customaries provided for a monastic regime based upon the renunciation of personal property and a community life of shared refectory and dormitory, organised round the demands of singing the Divine Office at the canonical hours. This experience of monastic life in the first flush of renewed fervour at Osma was to be transmitted by Dominic to his fraternity of preachers and gave his institution its distinctive shape.

As compared with that of St Francis, Dominic's personality remains a little elusive. He did not inspire the great outpouring of hagiographical literature and legend that transmitted the image of St Francis to posterity; nor did his life-story become a source of dissension among his followers. The history of his spiritual development largely eludes us. Yet the lineaments of a portrait are discernible between the conventional and repetitive phrases used by the hagiographers and still more through the statements of those who testified at his canonization process. These men, who had known him well, spoke, as was to be expected, of his heroic preaching journeys, his personal austerities and his prayerful vigils, but they also testified to his humanity. As with all great leaders, there was an inspirational quality about his strategic decisions: 'Do not contradict', he said to Montfort, the bishop and the brethren, when they objected to his sudden decision to disperse the Toulouse community and abandon the Albigensian mission, 'I know perfectly well what I am doing.'[1]

The charisma of his personality was sweetened by gentleness – 'he was a great consoler of the brethren' – and by a pleasing spontaneity: travelling in bad weather, he would encourage the company by breaking into song, and at times when he was overcome by weariness he would simply lie down at the roadside and go to sleep. Brother Ventura of Verona observed that he paid for the night hours spent in prayer by frequently falling asleep at meals.[2] The same spontaneity showed in his

1. *Acta Canonizationis S. Dominici*, ed. A. Walz *MOFPH* XVI (1935), p. 144.
2. *ibid.* p. 127.

quick sympathy for a woman who told him that her brother was being held prisoner by the Saracens; Dominic immediately offered to sell himself to redeem the captive, but, wrote Peter Ferrandus with evident relief, 'the Lord did not permit'.[3] A characteristic that most strongly impressed his intimate companions was his humility and determined self-effacement. He habitually travelled on foot and unshod, but to avoid publicity he put his shoes on before entering a town or village and removed them again afterwards. Several witnesses repeated the comment that 'he held himself in contempt'.'I am fit to be deposed,' he told the chapter at Bologna, 'for I am useless and negligent.'[4] Possibly his wish to abdicate was prompted by the example of St Francis, who had withdrawn from directing the Friars Minor the year before. At any rate, the chapter refused Dominic's request. Whether this diffidence was innate or the product of his piety, it was consumed by a burning sense of mission; he had, as the hagiographers put it, 'a mighty zeal for souls'. Perhaps some of the combative fervour of the Crusader that marked his missionary activities derived from his Spanish upbringing in a society preoccupied with the *reconquista*.

It was in the summer of 1203, when accompanying his bishop, Diego of Osma, on a diplomatic mission to the court of Denmark, that Dominic made his first direct acquaintance with the strength of the Catharist heresy in the society of the Languedoc. Staying over night at Toulouse, he was aghast to discover that the host of his inn was a member of the sect, and sat up all night arguing with him. The task of combatting heresy in the Midi had been assigned by the pope to the Cistercians under the direction of Arnaud Amaury, the abbot of Cîteaux; but the official mission had made little headway against the sectaries, who were well organised and enjoyed the patronage of the local aristocracy. In 1206, on their return journey from a second expedition to the Danish court, Diego and Dominic encountered the Cistercian legates at Montpellier, and after hearing the report of their failure, decided to join in the enterprise themselves.

At this point Jordan of Saxony – Dominic's successor as Master of the order and its first chronicler – reports a signifi-

3. *Legenda S. Dominici*, ed. M.H. Laurent *MOFPH* XVI (1935), p. 225.
4. *Acta Canonizationis* p. 151. One witness at the canonization process said 'se valde despiciebat et tanquam nullum se reputabat': *ibid.* p. 183.

cant conversation between the two parties of missionaries. Diego argued that the Cistercian abbots were hampered by their prelatical style and large retinues: 'You should not, I think, proceed thus. See how the heretics, by presenting an appearance of holiness, and feigning to be an example of evangelical poverty and austerity, persuade simple people to accept their ways.'[5] Only humble practitioners of the *vita apostolica* could hope to secure a hearing as authentic preachers of the Gospel. It was a question of competing with the *perfect*, the spiritual élite of the Catharist sect, who were famous for their personal austerity and their renunciation of worldly goods.

. . .

THE DOMINICANS AND THE *VITA APOSTOLICA*

The apostolic life, as it had been interpreted for the previous fifty years, meant the life of an itinerant preacher, who had renounced personal property and was dependent upon alms for food and clothing. This was the model that Diego was suggesting to his clerical colleagues. The two Spaniards persuaded the abbots to join them. The bishop set the standard by sending his servants and clerks home with the horses. The party then set out on foot on an itinerant preaching tour, holding public disputations with the Cathar leaders at Servian and Béziers and other towns of the Midi.

It has sometimes been said that the Dominicans borrowed the ideal of absolute poverty – the rejection, that is, of both personal and corporate ownership and dependence upon mendicancy – from the Franciscans; but this is an over-simplification. Francis and Dominic admired one another. According to Celano, they met in Rome in the household of Cardinal Ugolino.[6] But if such a meeting took place, it cannot have been earlier than 1217, when Francis secured Ugolino's protection and friendship. The fact is, the mendicant idea was adopted by Dominic and Diego independently at a time when they could scarcely have heard of Francis. To them it was

---

5. *Libellus Iordani de Saxonia*, ed. H.C. Scheeban *MOFPH* XVI (1935), p. 36.
6. *2 Celano* c.109. According to the *Vitae Fratrum*, *MOFPH* I (1896), pp. 10–11, the meeting took place in the Lateran, where Dominic had gone to seek papal approval for his order, i.e. in 1215. On the Dominican conception of voluntary poverty and the alleged Franciscan influence see Hinnebusch *HDO* I pp. 154–6.

simply the practical application of the twelfth-century notion of the *vita apostolica* – a life dedicated to evangelism and voluntary poverty. It would have been a perfectly familiar concept to a well-read Augustinian canon like Dominic, for whom St Norbert provided an inspiring precedent. At the beginning of the thirteenth century such ideas were in the air.

Where the Franciscan example may have influenced the policy of the Order of Preachers was over the question of corporate ownership. In 1215 Dominic had been given houses in Toulouse, where he founded an establishment for the fraternity of preachers, and Bishop Fulk of Toulouse assigned them a portion of the tithes of his diocese. In this way they acquired a regular income to support their activities. Unlike Francis, Dominic sought from the outset to create a fraternity of educated clerks, equipped with the skills needed for a special preaching mission. It was hard to see how such a plan could be realised without endowments. In any case the Church would not ordain a man unless he had a recognised 'title' – unless, that is, a particular church or a bishop or some religious body would guarantee his support. Dominic himself had begged for his keep on his preaching journeys. This was how he understood the evangelical life, and he had seen its power to captivate others. But the question was whether his personal ideal could be made the basis for a stable institution. Any such doubts were apparently dismissed by the first general chapter, which was held at Bologna in 1220. The chapter renounced all its properties in Toulouse and decreed against accepting any properties other than churches or any revenues for the future. Thus a year before his death, Dominic had persuaded his order to opt for corporate poverty and to commit itself to mendicancy. It is possible, though we cannot be sure, that the decision was influenced by the example of the Friars Minor.

Two years after the enterprise had begun, Diego returned home to die. But Dominic continued his preaching and pastoral ministrations in the Midi throughout the grim years of the northern crusade against the Albigenses and the social upheaval that followed it. He had made his first base at Prouille. It was here that, at the suggestion of Diego, he founded the earliest house of his order for women, to provide a refuge for female converts, mostly noblewomen, who had been won over from the Cathars. From there he moved to Fanjeaux. But it

69

was at Toulouse, where he established his headquarters in 1215 at the end of the Albigensian war, that he attracted and trained a community of helpers which formed the nucleus of a new preaching order. The foundation had been made possible by the steady patronage of Fulk of Toulouse, who donated the church of St Romain for the use of the fraternity.

. . .

THE FORMULATION AND GROWTH OF THE ORDER

Himself a Cistercian and sometime abbot of the Thoronet in Provence, Fulk had come to see Dominic's preachers as the best hope of salvaging what was left of the orthodox Church in his diocese. In the autumn of 1215 he had decided that the new institution should be given official status, and took Dominic with him to Rome to seek Innocent III's authorisation of an Order of Preachers and to get confirmation of its endowments. They were received kindly at the Curia. Letters confirming the properties of Prouille were obtained without difficulty. But over the proposal to create a new religious order for the express purpose of preaching, the pope temporised.[7] Preaching and the licensing of preachers were *ex professo* the function of bishops. To vest it in a monastic body looked like an anomaly; all the more so as canon law debarred monks from ministering in public churches.

At the time Dominic presented his petition, the prelates of Christendom were assembling for the Fourth Lateran Council – greatest and most famous of the medieval councils – and the regulation of religious orders was on its agenda. Apparently out of a desire to stem what now seemed to be an uncontrollable flood of religious experiment, the fathers of the council in due course decreed that, owing to the multiplicity and confusion of orders, nobody was to found a new one. Anyone who desired to found a new fraternity was instructed to adopt an existing rule that had already been approved.[8] Faced with this check to his plans, Dominic returned to discuss the situation with the brethren at Toulouse. The solution they adopted was the obvious one: they placed themselves under

---

7. In his brief chronicle Peter Ferrandus reports that 'the pope was difficult over this': *Cronica Ordinis*, ed. B.M. Reichert *MOFPH* I, p. 323.
8. Mansi XXII, cols. 1002–3; *De religiosis c. 9 X iii, 36.*

the Rule of St Augustine, to which Dominic was already vowed.

The Rule of St Augustine, in the attenuated form that was current at the end of the twelfth century, was derived from Augustine's letter No. 211, which had originally been addressed to a community of nuns. One of the curious things about it was its generality. It was little more than an exhortatory treatise on chastity, poverty, charity and concord, designed for those who wanted to embrace the life of a religious community. It offered little practical guidance on how to organise a monastery or construct a timetable. Thus by adopting it for his fraternity, Dominic left himself free to plan the organisation and observance of his preachers as he thought best. Papal confirmation, obtained from Honorius III in 1216, was a stereotype privilege which did no more than recognise the existence of the fraternity and confirm its possessions at Toulouse. The privilege *Religiosam vitam* did not ratify any specific Rule comparable to that of the Franciscans. The organisation subsequently enacted by the general chapters, which gave the order its remarkable constitution, was never confirmed by the papacy. Nor was confirmation sought. Officially, the Order of Preachers was simply a branch of the canons regular.[9]

Hitherto the fraternity at Toulouse had confined its preaching activities to the province of Narbonne. They had been called into existence by the need to reinforce the orthodox clergy of the area in their struggle with the Cathars. But in the summer of 1217, Dominic announced to the brethren his decision to scatter them. They were to embark upon a universal preaching mission. Possibly it was during his stay in Rome that the plan for this wider and more daring enterprise was formulated in his mind. It was not only the lawyers who thought of Rome as 'the common fatherland of all men'. It was the religious emporium of the Western world. Its antiquities, shrines and venerable relics, and its cosmopolitan throng of petitioners and pilgrims, all impressed upon the reflective visitor the universality of the Church in time and space. And the universality of the apostolic mission was most strikingly demonstrated by the great council, representing the whole of

9. On the scope of *Religiosam Vitam* see M.-H. Vicaire, *Saint Dominic and his Times*, transl. K. Pond (1964), pp. 219–23.

Western Christendom, that assembled in the Lateran basilica in November 1215, while Dominic was present at the Curia.

If his experience at Rome had enlarged Dominic's plans, his decision to put them into effect was precipitated by the situation at Toulouse. Innocent III had placed Count Raymond of Toulouse under the ban of the Church and, although he had been reconciled after public penance, the Lateran Council ratified the expropriation of his territory by the northern feudality. But in the summer of 1215 Count Raymond was preparing to invade the province to recover his lost county with the help of an army raised in Aragon. Toulouse was about to become the epicentre of the renewed war. In face of this threat to his work, Dominic decided to send all but a handful of the brethren elsewhere. There was a diaspora of the Toulouse community. In the summer of 1217 some were dispatched to Paris, some to Spain, and a few months later some to Bologna. The preachers were thus launched upon a wider mission. They were accredited to prelates everywhere by papal letters, obtained from Honorius III in 1218, instructing the clergy to render them all possible assistance with their ministry of preaching.

The selection of Paris and Bologna as early objectives highlighted an element in Dominic's strategy that was vigorously pursued by his successors. His friars not only sought to provide for the theological education of the preachers; they made it their aim to capture the leading intellectual centres of their time. At Paris, by August 1218 they had already taken occupation of the house of Saint Jacques on the left bank that was to be made famous by a succession of outstanding schoolmen. At Bologna, they were given the church of St Nicholas (later rebuilt as San Domenico) in the heart of the university quarter, and built a house and cloister alongside it. The same strategy was evident in the English mission dispatched by the general chapter of 1221. The party of thirteen led by Gilbert de Fresney was welcomed by archbishop Langton, who offered them a residence in Canterbury; but this was declined. They pressed on to London, and from there to Oxford, which was evidently the goal of their journey.

In pursuit of this programme the leadership of the order concentrated on recruiting from social groups that were educated – clerks, the sons of professional people like notaries, burgesses and the lesser nobility. Among those attracted by the mendicant ideal and the apostolic enthusiasm of the Preachers were several members of the older monastic orders. But recruits of this kind were liable to create legal as well as social problems for the friars. The canonists had established the principle that a monk could only be released by his own monastery and transfer to another provided that the reason for his move was a desire to join a stricter order (*ordo arctior*), which in practice usually meant the Cistercians or Carthusians. But nobody had defined the position of the Mendicants in the scale of austerity. To avoid recriminations, Honorius III decreed that the Preachers were to accept no recruits from the Cistercians except in cases specifically authorised by the pope; and this prohibition was reaffirmed by the Dominican general chapter. But in 1240 the chapter rescinded this restrictive decree.[10] Evidently in the eyes of the papacy, corporate poverty and mendicancy had raised the friars to a frosty peak of austerity even higher than that of the Cistercian monks. So a monk might leave his abbey to become a friar without being treated by the Church as a runaway and apostate.

The early statutes required postulants to have already learned their grammar before acceptance by the order. Not all those who were technically clerks could have met this requirement. It was above all among the masters and students of the newly fledged universities of Europe that the Preachers found their most outstanding recruits. Here some early catches baited the nets for a swarm of younger fish. Brother Gerard of Fracheto reported how the little fraternity at Bologna, intimidated by their surroundings and struggling with a loss of confidence, were hugely heartened by the sudden appearance of Roland of Cremona at their gate, requesting immediate admission to the order. Roland was one of the élite of the university community, a regent doctor in the schools. Rightly perceiving that his arrival would prove a turning-point in the fortunes of the Bologna friary, the brethren celebrated the occasion by ringing the bells and chanting the *Veni Creator*.[11]

---

10. *Acta Capitulorum Generalium Ordinis Praedicatorum*, ed. B.M. Reichert *MOFPH* III (1898), pp. 14, 19, 22. The prohibition of Honorius III is referred to in a letter of Gregory IX : dated 11 July 1235 *Bullarium Ordinis Fratrum Praedicatorum* ed. E.T. Ripoll and A. Bremond (Rome 1729–40), I p. 77. According to Gregory, the poaching was a two-way process – the Cistercians had also recruited from the Friars Preachers.
11. *Vitae Fratrum*, p. 26.

The policy of recruiting in the class-room was eagerly pursued by Jordan of Saxony, who succeeded Dominic as Master-General of the order in 1222. He had himself been a young Bachelor of Theology at Paris when he experienced the pull of the mendicant ideal. Promotion was quick in those early years. He had not been in the order for two months before he was sent to represent the Parisian house at the general chapter, and a year after his admission he was appointed prior provincial over the province of Lombardy. Once elected to the generalship he embarked upon a tireless itinerary of visitation and preaching, concentrating his best efforts on the universities. 'He gave all his might to attracting good people to the order,' recalled Brother Gerard, 'and therefore he always stayed in places where there were scholars, and especially at Paris.'[12] He has left a record of his successful trawl of the scholastic community in the letters of direction he wrote to Diana d'Andolo and the sisters of the newly founded Dominican nunnery at Bologna. 'Your prayers for the scholars of Padua have been heard,' he wrote triumphantly, 'twenty have entered our order.'[13] In 1226 he was at Paris and reported a fine crop: 'Within four weeks of our arrival, twenty-one brethren entered, among whom were six Masters of Arts, and the rest Bachelors.'[14] At Vercelli 'the Lord gave us many of the best and most learned men.'[15] 'At the university (*studium*) of Oxford,' he wrote, 'where I am at present, the Lord has given us great hopes of a good catch.'[16] And in the event his hopes were realised. His preaching to the university in November 1229 brought a flush of recruits from among both Masters and students.

The schoolmen formed, of course, only a proportion of the numbers recruited. They constituted an intellectual élite, a reservoir of learned men, from which the order could draw its generals, provincials and other officers; they also supplied the lectors whose role was to instruct their brethren. The general chapter made it a rule that no new priory should be inaugu-

12. *Vitae Fratrum*, p. 529.
13. *Beati Iordani de Saxonia Epistulae*, ed. A. Walz *MOFPH* XXII (1951), p. 4.
14. *ibid.* pp. 38–9.
15. *ibid.* p. 16.
16. *ibid.* pp. 19–20. The sermons he preached at Oxford were discovered and printed by A.G. Little and D. Douie, 'Three sermons of Friar Jordon of Saxony, the successor of St Dominic, preached in England, AD 1229': *EHR* 54 (1939), pp. 1–19.

rated without a minimum complement of twelve friars, one of whom must be a qualified theologian to act as lector. The rank and file of the Friars Preachers were recruited more widely. The basic educational qualification was required of all postulants who aspired to join the clerical ranks of the order; but it was relaxed for those – generally peasants and artisans – who sought admission as lay brothers.

The *conversus*, or lay brother, was a familiar figure in the economy of the monastic orders. He was a monk in the sense that he took the monastic vows, wore the habit and attended some at least of the liturgical offices; but he lived a separate existence from the choir monks. He was chiefly occupied with manual work, serving his community as ploughman, shepherd or carpenter. The Cistercians recruited *conversi* in large numbers, using them as a permanent work-force to cultivate their estates. Dominic's friars followed the monastic tradition in accepting men who were illiterate as lay brothers, but on a much more restricted scale. Since, as mendicant friars, they possessed no lands, they had no need of agricultural labour. Their lay brothers formed only a small proportion of their communities. They were used to perform the essential manual tasks in the house with the express purpose of releasing the clerical brethren for study. The early statutes debarred them from aspiring to clerical status, and they were forbidden to read books for the purpose of studying. All the same, in the mendicant houses there was no trace of the kind of social apartheid that was maintained between *conversi* and choir monks in the Cistercian abbeys. Like that of the Franciscans, the Dominican fraternity was a social leveller. The lay brothers joined the clerical brethren in choir during the Offices, served as sacristans, provided companions for preachers on their journeys, and played an active part in the daily quest for alms.

. . .

THE RELIGIOUS NEEDS OF WOMEN

Like Francis, Dominic attracted women followers as well as men. The first foundation at Prouille, which was largely the creation of Diego of Osma, had arisen out of the immediate need to provide a haven for female converts from the Cathars. As the preachers extended their mission beyond the French Midi, provision had to be made for new female disciples attracted by the call to embrace the apostolic life. A visit by Dominic to his Spanish homeland in 1218 set in train the process that led to the creation of a nunnery of 'Preacheresses' at Madrid. His apostolate among the women of Rome in 1219 brought to fruition a plan of Innocent III to create a convent of reformed observance at San Sisto. A community of women took up residence there under Dominic's direction in 1221, and he and his friars moved out to occupy the ancient basilica of Sta Sabina on the Aventine, which Pope Honorius III had given him.

For all his apostolic zeal, the cast of Dominic's mind was more clerical and traditionalist than that of Francis. Although he was sensitive to the religious needs of women, he accepted the assumptions of his time about their social role. The possibility that the sisters could collaborate in the active ministry of the friars or depend, like them, on begging for their subsistence, seems never to have entered his mind. The observance he prescribed for the nuns at Prouille was purely monastic, based upon the customs of Prémontré and involving strict enclosure. And he brought eight sisters from Prouille to instruct the nuns of San Sisto in this observance.

In the years that followed, many convents of women sought affiliation to the Order of Preachers. One of the most arresting social phenomena of thirteenth-century Europe was a widespread and growing demand for forms of religious life suited to the needs of women. It was primarily an urban phenomenon, and humanly speaking the explanation for it must lie in the demography of the towns. It points to a population imbalance: the number of marriageable women must have significantly exceeded the number of available men. Such an imbalance could be explained by female longevity and the inroads made upon the male population by clerical celibacy, warfare, and the hazards of travel. This situation had not been reflected in the pattern of monastic foundation. The new orders that had sprung from the spiritual revival of the twelfth century had been promoted by and for men. The foundation of nunneries had not at first kept pace with the foundations for monks. Moreover, the nunneries tended to be socially exclusive – they would only accept well-born ladies of the landed classes.

One of the most striking symptoms of frustrated female demand for the religious life was the rise and proliferation of the Beguinages in the towns of Northern France, Germany and the Low Countries, towards the end of the twelfth century. The Beguines were groups of pious women who formed quasi-monastic communities of a freer kind. They took no irrevocable vows, but a condition of membership was the renunciation of personal wealth and the cultivation of a humble and frugal life-style. Some of these groups supported themselves by organised begging, but many of their houses received endowments from recruits or patrons. Just as the established nunneries provided a home for the ladies of the armigerous classes, the Beguinages offered a religious haven for the daughters and widows of the bourgeoisie.

As the Friars Preachers made settlements in the towns of northern Europe, many of the Beguinages sought and obtained their services as confessors and spiritual directors. Many other convents, especially in Germany, placed themselves under the direction of the friars or petitioned to be incorporated into the Dominican Order, following the customary of San Sisto. The problem of the women's houses was aggravated by the tendency of the older men's orders to discard their female branches. In 1197 or 1198, the general chapter of Prémontré voted to admit no more women to the order, thus condemning the female branch of the order to a process of gradual extinction. Before long their example was followed by the Cistercians. After tardily and reluctantly admitting a number of nunneries to the order, the general chapter of Cîteaux decreed in 1220 that no more communities of women were to be incorporated. Although this prohibition was subsequently breached, it put a sharp brake on the affiliation of women's houses to the white monks. There were several reasons for this misogynistic policy. Fear of incurring financial liability for many communities without adequate endowments, the difficulties of overseeing and maintaining regular discipline in houses of women, who sometimes proved recalcitrant to male direction and, not least, anxiety about the spiritual safety of the small group of monks who had to be attached to these houses to provide sacramental and counselling services.[17] Having been turned adrift by their parent body or refused affiliation to the order whose Rule they had adopted, many nunneries sought adoption, or at least spiritual direction, from the friars.

17. For the problems involved in the pastoral care of the Cistercian nuns see C.H. Lawrence, *Medieval Monasticism* 2nd edn. (1989), pp. 228–30.

Dominic was conspicuously successful in his ministry to women, and his flair was inherited by Jordan of Saxony. It was he who brought to completion the plans for the nunnery of Sant'Agnese at Bologna, and he established a warm spiritual friendship with Diana d'Andolo, its patron and first prioress. Nevertheless, there were those among the leadership who regarded the pastoral care of women religious as an undesirable diversion from the order's primary task of preaching to the unconverted and securing the intellectual bases of faith. Fear and misogyny also played their part: the chapter acts harp upon the perils of hearing women's confessions and socialising with them.

Pressure for disengagement was already strong in Jordan's time: the general chapter of 1228 legislated to check the further extension of the ministry to nunneries. Twelve years later, under Jordan's successor, Raymond of Penaforte, the chapter took the more drastic step of forbidding friars to administer the sacraments to nuns, apart from penance – hearing their confessions. The chapter of 1242 decreed harsh penances – seven days on bread and water and seven scourgings – for those who had ministered to women's houses in defiance of this prohibition.[18] Only Dominic's own foundations of Prouille and San Sisto succeeded in getting exemption from this ruling through papal intervention. For a period, both the Dominican and Franciscan nuns came close to being cast off by their parent orders. It was only after several decades of struggle that the needs of the women's houses won recognition from the Dominican cardinal Hugh of St Cher, and the Master, Humbert of Romans (1254–63). Humbert acknowledged the obligation of the Friars Preachers to undertake the spiritual care of the nuns.

It is one of the arts of government to make a virtue out of changes that have become inevitable. In this instance, as in others, Humbert displayed political acumen as well as pastoral zeal. Yielding to aristocratic as well as to ecclesiastical pressure, he created arrangements allowing nunneries that petitioned entry to the order to be incorporated by acts of the general chapter. Also, using the customary of San Sisto as a basis, he drafted new constitutions for the women's houses so as to ensure uniformity of observance, and these were approved by the chapter of 1259. In this way he gave legal and

18. Reichert I p. 24.

permanent existence to the Dominican Second Order. By the year 1277, when a census was made, fifty-eight nunneries had been incorporated, forty of which were in the German province, including a number that had originated as Beguinages. It was a paradox, made inescapable by the assumptions of medieval society, that the mendicant orders, which had broken out of the monastic tradition in order to preach in the market-place, originated female contemplative orders observing a regime of seclusion and strict enclosure.

. . .

ORGANISATION AND OBSERVANCE

Despite the advantages of the residence at Sta Sabina, among which was proximity to the papal Curia, Dominic seems never to have contemplated locating the headquarters of the Preachers at Rome. Instead he made Bologna his preferred residence and the centre-point of his order. In fact, it was there that he died in August 1221. In his vision, Bologna, home of the jurists' universities, where men came from all parts of Europe to sit at the feet of the famous law doctors, and Paris – in whose theology schools 'the corn is ground,' as Pope Gregory declared, 'to feed the faithful of the whole world',[19] would be the poles of the intellectual axis about which the Friars Preachers would organise their mission to all parts of Christendom. Thus it was to Bologna that he summoned the first general chapter of the order in 1220, and he decreed that subsequent chapters should meet annually at Whitsun, alternating their venue between Bologna and Paris. After 1243, the meeting-places were more varied, being determined by the discretion of the then Master. But the original plan disclosed the thrust of Dominic's thinking.

The acts of the second general chapter held at Bologna in 1221, less than three months before his death, outlined the lineaments of an articulated religious order. Recognising the need to organise the settlements that had already been made, the chapter defined five territorial provinces of Provence, Spain, France, Lombardy and Tuscany, and designated provincial priors to govern them. Brother Jordan, to his surprise and consternation, found himself placed in charge of the huge and populous province of Lombardy – 'I who had completed

19. *Chartularium* I pp. 136–9.

but a year in the order'. The chapter also decreed arrangements for the foundation of new provinces in England, Germany, Denmark, Hungary, Poland, Greece and the Holy
Land. This provincial structure was to remain unchanged
until nearly the end of the thirteenth century. Like the Franciscans, the Dominican missionaries made for the major centres
of population. In Germany their first settlement was at Cologne, the greatest of the north-German cities, and plantations
in the other cities of the Rhineland quickly followed. By 1250
the order had established houses in thirty-eight of the greater
German towns, many of which were episcopal cities.

The strategy of Dominican settlement was clearly planned.
The cities were the chosen objective of the Preachers because
the urban populations were the most fertile seed-bed of heresy
and scepticism; it was there that the largest and most responsive audiences were to be found; and it was there that the
struggle for religious orthodoxy was to be won or lost. There
was also an economic factor, which enemies of the friars were
not slow to point out: only thriving commercial communities
possessed the surplus of property and disposable wealth that
made it possible to house and support groups of preachers
who depended on begging for their livelihood. As compared
with the Friars Minor, the Preachers showed a marked preference for larger settlements well above the statutory minimum
of twelve friars, big enough to sustain full community life of a
monastic type. In the early years concentrations were made
necessary by the scarcity of men qualified to act as lectors.[20]
This, and the policy of restricting recruitment to the educated,
explains the fact that the growth of the Order of Preachers
proceeded at a more restrained pace than that of the Franciscans. In Germany, thirty years after the arrival of the friars, the
Franciscans had upwards of a hundred houses as compared
with the thirty-eight priories of the Dominicans. By the year
1303 the whole Dominican Order possessed 590 houses, which
by 1358 had risen to a total of 635, as against the Franciscan
total of some 1400 houses.[21]

20. In 1251 the chapter observed that many priories lacked lectors; the
    visitors were instructed to seek out retired lectors or other suitable
    candidates: Reichert I, p. 100.
21. Lists of priories compiled in 1277, 1303 and 1358, were co-ordinated by
    A. Walz, *Compendium Historiae Ordinis Praedicatorum* (Rome 1930), p. 248;
    cited Hinnebusch *HDO*, pp. 262–3.

One of the gifts St Dominic had — one that St Francis conspicuously lacked — was a capacity for organisation. The earliest comprehensive body of statutes governing the life of the Friars Preachers was enacted by the general chapter of 1228, and it was codified by Raymond of Penaforte during his Mastership (1238–40), but the plan it embodied was largely the creation of Dominic himself. In their domestic observance the Preachers retained the marks of their monastic origin. Himself a canon regular, Dominic imposed upon his order a regime in which the framework of the day was determined by choral recitation of the Divine Office at the canonical hours; the community met in a daily chapter of faults; the monastic periods of fasting were observed; and the monastic rule of silence was kept everywhere in the house and at all times except in privileged places.

Obviously the plan to reconcile a strictly regulated monastic regime of liturgical prayer, silence and seclusion, with the multifarious activities of a pastoral mission presented problems. Mitigations were necessary to allow the preachers freedom to operate outside the cloister and to release lectors and their pupils for study and practice in the skills of disputation. Thus the monastic tradition of manual labour was discarded; the statutes decreed that the offices were to be sung 'shortly (*breviter*) and succinctly, so that the brethren be hindered as little as possible in their studies';[22] and any prior was authorised to dispense friars of his house from attendance at the offices for the sake of study or preaching. The chapter gave friars studying at Paris to equip themselves for lectorships a general dispensation to absent themselves from the non-festive offices on week-days, with the exception of Compline. That exception is itself indicative of a spirit of adaptation. Compline — the short concluding office of the monk's day which inaugurated the hours of the Great Silence — was converted by the Preachers into a public service. Sung at a time of day when most people's work was finished, it attracted townspeople to the churches of the friars. To increase its popular appeal, the Preachers gave it an added touch of solemnity: they concluded the service by chanting the *Salve Regina*, the anthem to the

---

22. *Constitutiones Antique Ordinis Fratrum Predicatorum*, ed. H. Denifle *ALKG* I, p. 197.

Blessed Virgin, processing as they did so out of the choir to kneel alongside the people in the nave.[23]

If the internal observance of the Dominican friaries was firmly anchored in the monastic tradition, the constitution of the order embodied a revolution in the theory and practice of government. It gave effect to the principles of representation and responsibility to an extent then unknown in either the ecclesiastical or the secular world. This was a conception of authority that found no place in monastic tradition. At every level, the superiors of the Order of Preachers were not only elected; they were made responsible for the conduct of their office to their constituents. The basic unit of the organisation was the individual convent or priory. Its head – the prior – was elected by his brethren in chapter. They also elected a companion, a *socius*, to accompany their prior to the annual meeting of the provincial chapter, and it was part of his role to carry a report on the state of his community and the conduct of their superior to the assembly.

The order was divided into territorial provinces, and the head of each province – the provincial prior – was elected by a special session of the provincial chapter, consisting of the heads of individual houses together with two representatives elected for the purpose by each priory. The provincial prior was answerable to the chapter. As the provincial chapter was usually a large body, the Dominicans quite early adopted the Cistercian practice of delegating business to a steering committee, in this case of four 'diffinitors', chosen by a poll of the chapter on the opening day; and this committee could receive complaints against the provincial and, if necessary, suspend him from office.

Dominic had determined from the outset that the sovereign body of the order should be general chapter. It met every year at Whitsun, alternating in the early years between the priories of Bologna and Paris. The general chapter was not in itself an innovation. It had been a feature of some monastic organisations for nearly a century. In fact, under the inspiration of Pope Innocent III, the Lateran Council of 1215 had pressed regional chapters upon those monastic congregations

23. On the origin of this practice, which was initiated at the Bologna priory, see W.R. Bonniwell, *A History of the Dominican Liturgy* (1945), pp. 148–66. For the exoneration of student lectors from attendance at the other ferial offices see Reichert I, p. 17.

that lacked such a general assembly. Where the Dominican chapter differed was in its representative character. It consisted of the Master-General, who presided, and one diffinitor elected by the chapter of each province. As the order had established only thirteen provinces before the year 1300, the general chapter must have been a relatively small and effective body. For two successive years, only these elected representatives of the provinces attended; but in the third year the provincial priors attended instead. This nice balance between the representative and official elements was reinforced by a proviso that any new statute must have secured the assent of three consecutive chapters before it acquired the force of law. This requirement not only insured against hasty and ill-considered legislation; it also allowed the official element to exercise a veto.

There was, of course, another severely practical reason for these arrangements which we, in the days of air and motorway travel, can easily overlook. Perpetuating the example set by St Dominic, the statutes insisted that friars should manifest the spirit of poverty and place themselves on the level of the most indigent classes of society by always travelling on foot. No exceptions were allowed for longer journeys; the general chapter of 1255 ordained that priors or other brethren who were unable to make their way to chapter on foot, should stay at home.[24] Travel to the general chapter from the more distant provinces had therefore to be reckoned in months rather than weeks. A journey from England to Bologna on foot would have taken anything between a hundred days and four months. If provincial priors had been required to attend every year, they would have spent most of their time on the roads and away from the provinces they were supposed to govern.

The head of the order, the Master, was himself elected by an enlarged session of the general chapter. And although he might hold office until resignation or death, the statutes made him answerable to the chapter for his stewardship: the diffinitors had the power to correct him or, in case of heresy or grave misconduct, to depose him. They were warned, however, to proceed with utmost caution in such an eventuality. In fact, although a Master sometimes resigned on account of ill health, as Humbert of Romans did in 1263, most incumbents of the office held it for life.

24. Reichert I, p. 77.

In order to ensure that the decrees of the sovereign body were observed and standards maintained, a system of regular visitation was devised. Four friars were chosen annually by each provincial chapter to inspect the houses within the province, and every third year visitors were appointed by the general chapter. The visitors were required to report their findings to the chapters that had appointed them. These arrangements for supervision were already incorporated in the earliest statutes;[25] later, in the years 1271–5, the general chapter ordered the subdivision of provinces into vicariates or visitations – groupings of houses into areas for the purpose of visitation.

Here then was a completely articulated system of representative government which in its essentials apparently sprang fully fledged from the minds of St Dominic and his successor, Jordan of Saxony, in the years 1220 to 1228. It succeeded, in a way that no other monastic rule had done, in giving institutional form to the ascetical principle of obedience to a superior without recourse to paternalism or prelacy. It proved to be a model that influenced many other organisations, not least that of the Friars Minor.

. . .

AN ORDER OF STUDENTS

A pastoral mission to the literate and relatively sophisticated people of the cities, as well as disputation with the élite of the heretical sects, demanded both mental agility and theological learning. Dominic and Jordan had perceived this from the outset. Behind the drive to recruit Bachelors and Masters from the universities was an awareness of the pressing need to provide instructors to educate the brethren and train them for their task. The Preachers had to be a student order if they were to be effective. 'Study,' observed Humbert, 'is not the end of the order, but is most necessary to secure its end, namely preaching and the salvation of souls, for without study neither can be accomplished.'[26] Every priory, therefore, had its classroom, where all clerical friars attended lectures and took part in practice disputations. The chapter constantly urged priors to chivy their young recruits into applying themselves to their studies. To provide systematic schooling, the

25. *Constitutiones*, p. 219.
26. *Humbert de Romanis Opera*, ed. J.J. Berthier (Marietti 1956) II, p. 41.

order as a whole was organised as a kind of disseminated university.

At the base of the structure was the priory school with its own lector. The lector's business was to lecture to the brethren on the Bible, the Biblical *Histories* of Peter Comestor, and the *Summa de casibus* – a treatise on penance and confession by the Spanish friar Raymond of Penaforte. As the testimonial letters of Pope Honorius had made clear, the mission of Dominic's friars was to hear confessions and counsel penitents as well as to preach. Those who were going to hear confessions had to be well instructed in the problems of moral theology; and for those of the brethren who were not going to proceed to a university or one of the higher schools, the instruction had to be given in their own priory. It was for their guidance that in the 1220s a number of lectors put together treatises on confessional practice, of which Raymond's *Summa* was the most famous.[27] Initially composed in 1225 for the use of the brethren in Spain, in its revised form it was adopted as the classical manual of instruction throughout the order. In the early years, it proved difficult to provide adequate staffing of schools at priory level, as the expansion of the order outran the supply of ready-made graduates who could act as lectors. In time the order produced its own teachers, but the education of a fully fledged theologian was a long process. The general chapter of 1259 remarked that in some provinces many priories were without lectors; the visitors were instructed to search out vacancies and commandeer the services of any friars who were qualified to teach.[28]

What was provided in the priory schools was Bible study and a basic grounding in their principles of dogmatic and moral theology. At a more advanced level, a study of the logical works of Aristotle – 'the books of the heathen', as the statutes refer to them distastefully – was an indispensable preparation for the study of scholastic theology. The Aristotelian logic formed a large part of the university Arts curriculum, but the friars refused to allow their men to attend the Arts course in the turbulent and randy society of the universities. Instead they provided the necessary philosophical grounding

27. L.E. Boyle, 'Notes on the education of the *fratres communes* in the Dominican Order in the thirteenth century': *Xenia Medii Aevi Historiam Illustrantia oblata Thomae Kaeppeli O.P.* (Rome 1978), pp. 249–67.
28. Reichert I, p. 100.

in their own schools. In the course of time, the Dominicans developed specialist centres to meet all their needs. Within each province a number of larger priories were given the status of major schools – *studia solemnia* – with a larger teaching staff to teach the subjects of the Arts curriculum. In the last decades of the thirteenth century, we find provincial chapters designating houses in each vicariate or visitation, some to be schools of logic, some to provide instruction in natural philosophy, and others to offer more advanced courses in theology.[29]

Those who were groomed for teaching were sent to one or another of the provincial schools to hear lectures and take part in disputations until they were ready to embark on the theology course at one of the order's 'general schools'. These *studia generalia* were in university centres, and they formed the apex of the order's scholastic structure. The earliest of them to be established and the most prestigious was the school of Paris, to which each province was entitled to send three of its picked men. In order to take the pressure off the Parisian priory and to meet the increasingly voracious demand for lectors, the general chapter of 1247 instructed the provincials of England, Germany, Lombardy and Provence, to set up a general school in their provinces in some suitable priory, to which other provinces might send a quota of two students each, and this led to the creation of general schools at Oxford, Cologne, Bologna and Montpellier. By the year 1300, additional centres of advanced study had been established at Florence and Barcelona.

The intellectually ablest, after completing courses in logic and philosophy were initiated into the study of theology in a provincial school through the medium of Peter Comestor's Biblical *Histories* and the *Sentences* of Peter Lombard, and were then dispatched to a *studium generale*. In due course, some – the men with an aptitude for pure scholarship – would be authorised to incept as Masters in the theology faculty of the university. Those selected for study at the provincial schools were wrapped in a cocoon of privilege. The Master of Students appointed to supervise them would assign each of them a separate cell. The friar who is assigned a cell is allowed by the constitutions to use it freely. In it he can read, write, pray, sleep or sit up during the night by lamp-light to pursue his

29. Reichert I, p. 38.

studies. He may be dispensed from attendance at the Divine Office on non-festal days, except the office of Compline. In other words, he is completely released from the horarium of the community. But the privileges were conditional upon effort. Here the statutes assume the tones of a disciplinarian housemaster: 'they should so apply themselves to study by day, by night, at home or travelling abroad, they should be reading something or meditating and memorizing ... if anyone, however, be found unfruitful in study, his cell shall be assigned to another.'[30]

This co-ordinated academic system was an extraordinary construction without parallel in the middle ages, except in those Mendicant Orders that copied it. It was far superior to the educational facilities available to most of the secular clergy or to the laity. It was all the more remarkable for being the creation of an order which had renounced endowments and most forms of permanent income in favour of begging. The purpose of it all was strictly functional – to prepare the preacher for his task. The earliest constitutions show a concern to ensure that only friars of tested competence should be allowed to preach in public. No one is to be authorised to preach outside the walls of his own community unless he is at least twenty-five years old and has heard lectures on theology for at least a year. If deemed suitable and adequately instructed by his prior, he may be licensed as an ordinary preacher (*predicator communis*), to preach within the territory of his priory.[31]

Besides the ordinary preacher, there was the more prestigious office of preacher-general *predicator generalis*, who was authorised to preach anywhere within the province of his order. To qualify for this appointment a friar was required to have studied theology for at least three years. He was appointed by the general chapter or, more commonly, by the provincial prior acting with the diffinitors of the provincial chapter. The preacher-general not only had a roving commission; he was involved in the government of his order and an *ex officio* member of the provincial chapter. He tended to be a man of affairs, a holder of other administrative offices, perhaps a prior or a lector. As the appointment was held for life and

---

30. *Constitutiones,* p. 223.
31. *ibid.* p. 223. On the training and grades of preachers see Hinnebusch, *The Early English Friars Preachers* (Rome 1951), pp. 282–96.

new candidates were constantly emerging from the schools of the order, the number of preachers-general rapidly increased in the 1240s, in some cases exceeding the number of priories in certain provinces. As a whole the system was admirably devised to achieve the objects of the order as they were defined by the earliest constitutions: 'it is known that our order was from the beginning instituted expressly for preaching and the salvation of souls; and our studies should be principally directed with fervour to the end of making us useful to the souls of our neighbours'.[32]

32. *Constitutiones* p. 194.

Chapter 5

NEW BRETHREN

The new version of the religious life created by the Friars
Minor and the Preachers deeply affected the way thirteenth-
century people thought about the Christian vocation. No
subsequent religious organisation could entirely escape their
influence. The ideas they represented – that it was possible for
the committed Christian to be in the world yet not of it, that
in this world the appropriate condition of those who aspired
to the Kingdom of God was one of simplicity and poverty,
and that the imitation of Christ involved an active mission of
evangelization and service to the poor – proved to be as
dynamic as they were dangerous. As these ideas were disseminated among the clergy and the devout laity, they fired
discontent with established ecclesiastical institutions and inspired new kinds of ascetical organisation. The numerous
confraternities of lay penitents that grew up around the
churches of the Mendicants were a paler reflection of the
friars' master-plan. But besides these, several new orders
sprang into existence which, whether or not they practised
organised begging, imitated the friars in making corporate
poverty and humble service the basis of their observance.
Most of them engaged in some form of active ministry, such as
preaching or serving hospitals for the care of the poor; a few,
while adhering to the principles of institutional poverty and
egalitarian fraternalism, opted at least initially for the contemplative life in complete or partial seclusion from the outside
world. One of this latter group was the small order of the
Servite Friars – the self-styled 'Servants of Mary'.

. . .

SERVITE FRIARS

The Servites originated as one of several communities of lay penitents at Florence. In the year 1246 seven of the fraternity – all of them members of the civic aristocracy – decided to retire to a collective hermitage on Monte Senario, which lay in the hills of the Mugello north of the city. Possibly their flight was prompted by the conflict between the Ghibelline and papal parties at Florence, for after a few years they returned to Cafaggio in the suburbs of the city under the patronage of the papal legate. Here they formed themselves into a regular cenobitical community professing the Rule of St Augustine. Although the hermitage of Monte Senario continued to be the spiritual focus of the nascent order, its centre of government now moved to Florence, where in 1254 work began on the new church and conventual buildings of the Annunziata.

Organisationally the Servites copied the constitutional arrangements of the Dominicans, and like the Mendicant Orders they pledged themselves to a regime of corporate poverty, refusing to own any form of real estate, either directly or through intermediaries.[1] They had begun as a society of recluses: the early constitutions of Buonagiunta, the first Prior-General, outline an observance that is purely monastic.[2] But in the course of the 1250s, the example of the other friars, pressure from their own recruits and the demand of their patrons, impelled them to issue out of their claustral solitude and engage in an active urban apostolate.

The confirmation of the Servite rule by Pope Alexander IV licensed the brethren to hear confessions and accept burials of lay people in their churches, and they opened their oratories to the public. Nevertheless, their association with mendicancy seems to have been brief. Within a few years they abandoned the attempt to subsist on alms in favour of accepting landed endowments, and they came to resemble Augustinian canons

1. F.-A. Dal Pino, *I Frati Servi di S. Maria dalle origini all'approvazione, 1233–1304* (Louvain 1972) II, pp. 848–50. The agreement to renounce all immovable property was reached at an assembly at Cafaggio in September 1251: 'una volontà di pauperismo radicale da parte del gruppo primitivo dei Servi'.
2. *Monumenta Ordinis Servorum Sanctae Mariae*, ed. A. Morini and P. Soulier (Brussel 1897) I, pp. 21–3.

more closely then friars – a quiet transformation that enabled them to survive the conciliar axe of 1274, which suppressed several small orders of friars.[3] In the middle ages the Servites remained a small order. They achieved their greatest success in the cities of central Italy; by the year 1300 the order had twenty-eight houses, of which twenty-two were in Italy and four in Germany.

THE CRUTCHED FRIARS AND THE MATHURIN FRIARS

Among other new orders that adopted some features of the Mendicants' organisation and abandoned claustral enclosure to engage in pastoral or social work were the Crutched Friars and the Trinitarians or, as they were known in France, the Mathurin Friars. Neither was strictly speaking a mendicant order, for both of them accepted the necessity of owning corporate property; but both emulated the friars in interpreting the *vita apostolica* as a form of religious life devoted to the active service of the world around them. The Crutched Friars – the *Fratres Cruciferi*, whose name derived from the white cross emblazoned on their black habit – devoted much of their effort, besides preaching, to staffing hospitals and hospices for pilgrims.

The Trinitarians were a product of the apostolic movement of the twelfth century. In fact, they predated both the Franciscans and Dominicans by some years Their founder, the Provençal John de Matha, was moved by the spectacle of Moslem prisoners he saw at Marseilles and by harrowing tales of the torments of Christians who had fallen into Moslem hands, to form a community for the purpose of recovering Christians from their Moslem owners either by exchange or purchase. In 1198 he and Felix de Valois secured the approval of Innocent III for a brotherhood devoted to this work. The Rule, which is set out in the papal privilege, had been composed at the pope's request by the bishop of Paris, Maurice de Sully, and the abbot of Saint-Victor.[4] It outlines a monastic observance similar to that of the Augustinian canons. In every house the community observes the traditional periods of the monastic

3. For this act of the Council of Lyons see below, pp. 158–9.
4. *Die Register Innocenz III*, I ed. O. Hageneder and A. Haidacher (Graz–Köln 1964), No. 481 pp. 703–8.

fast, and recites the Divine Office according to the customary of Saint-Victor. But in other respects the regime displays the impact of the new ideas about the religious life that were current at the end of the twelfth century and which were about to be realised in the Mendicant Orders. Thus, although the brothers owe obedience to their superior, there is an emphasis upon fraternity and a marked absence of prelacy. Each house is to have a complement of three clerks and three lay brothers and their head, who is to be called a 'minister'; and all seven – the limitation of numbers was later relaxed by a decree of Honorius III – live together, eat at a common table and sleep in a common dormitory. Corporate poverty is excluded by the need of the order to raise funds for its work; but a third of all income is to be allocated to the fund for the redemption of captives, and a further third to providing hospitality for pilgrims and the poor. The spirit of evangelical poverty is represented by the injunction to the brothers not to ride horses, but to travel on foot or, in case of necessity, to ride on mules.

Shortly after the pope had confirmed the Rule, the first mission set off for Morocco armed with papal letters to the Sultan proposing an exchange of prisoners. In an age of crusading, when preachers toured town and countryside appealing to able-bodied men to take part in the hazardous expeditions to the Holy Land and Egypt, the recovery of captives from the hands of the infidel was a cause that evoked an immediate and powerful response in popular feeling. So money and recruits multiplied, and the order received a flood of endowments in the form of land, advowsons and churches, the most famous of which was the church of St Mathurin in Paris, from which the brothers acquired their popular name of Mathurin Friars.[5] By the middle of the thirteenth century the Trinitarian brothers possessed more than a hundred houses scattered across Europe for the purpose of collecting resources. To govern this international organisation they evolved a representative system like that of the Mendicant Orders. Each house elected its own minister, and houses were grouped in territorial provinces. At the head stood the grand minister, elected by a general chapter, which met annually.

5. For an account of the early endowments see P. Deslandres, *L'Ordre des Trinitaires* (Toulouse–Paris 1903) II, pp. 2–18.

. . .

THE SUPPRESSED ORDERS OF FRIARS

The ideal of the evangelical life inspired several small orders of friars, such as the Pied Friars and the Williamites, which were suppressed by the conciliar decrees of 1274. The largest and most expansive of this group of Mendicants to fall under the ban was the order of Brothers of Penitence of Jesus Christ, otherwise known as the Friars of the Sack or *Saccati*. Their popular name referred to a mantle of sackcloth they wore over the habit, an outward and visible sign of their commitment to poverty and humility. They had come into existence in Provence, a land as fertile in mystics and religious revolutionaries as it was in poets, and Provence remained a major focus of their preaching activity. Their founder, a former Franciscan, succeeded in transmitting to the new organisation the ideals of the *poverello*, but as with the Friars Minor, the demands of an organised apostolate involved the order in a process of development and adaptation. In 1255 it received confirmation by Pope Alexander IV as an order subject to the Rule of St Augustine, and its constitution was modelled upon that of the Friars Preachers.

As preachers and confessors, the Friars of the Sack had much success with the town-dwelling laity. By the eve of their suppression they possessed upwards of a hundred communities scattered across the cities of Europe, and for the purpose of educating their preachers they had established houses of study in the university centres of Paris, Bologna, Oxford, Montpellier and Cologne. After the conciliar ban, most of these assets passed into the hands of the Dominicans or the Friars Minor, along with many of the brothers. Their popularity with the townspeople made their extinction a halting process – their house at Marseilles was still receiving bequests in the 1290s, two decades after the act of dissolution.[6] They were obviously a valuable addition to the pastoral resources of the thirteenth-century Church, a fact that makes their suppression difficult to understand. It seems they fell victim to the indiscriminate onslaught by the secular hierarchy at the Council of Lyons only because, unlike other major orders of friars, they failed to mobilise the political support necessary to defend themselves.

6. Micheline de Fontette, 'Les Mendiants supprimés au 2e Concile de Lyon (1274)': *Les Mendiants en pays d'oc au XIIIe siècle* (Cahiers de Fanjeaux 8, Toulouse 1973), pp. 193–215.

Besides these short-lived orders, whose pattern of religious life was inspired by the ideas of evangelical poverty and apostolic activity for which the early friars had provided the example, two other religious groups fell under the spell of the mendicant ideal and formed two orders of friars which came to rival the Franciscans and the Friars Preachers in scale and esteem. These were the Order of Our Lady of Mount Carmel and the Augustinian Friars Hermits. They had one peculiarity in common: both originated as groups of hermits, who subsequently adopted the ideals and organisation of the Mendicants. In doing this they more or less successfully reconciled the active apostolic vocation of the friars with the contemplative life of the desert. In both of them the original eremitical ideal – the compelling attraction the desert has for the mystic – persisted, as it did with the Franciscans, sometimes as a hampering or disruptive force. Neither order could point to any single founder comparable to Francis or Dominic, or give a satisfactory historical account of its origins.

. . .

THE CARMELITES

By contrast with the wealth of literary sources for the beginnings of the Franciscan movement, the sources for the early history of the Carmelites are extremely meagre. Later Carmelite writers endeavoured to fill the gap with pious legend: after the middle of the thirteenth century, younger brethren, when questioned about the antiquity of their order, were instructed to refer to the prophets Elijah and Elisha as the founders of their hermit predecessors who had come from Mount Carmel in Palestine. Modern scholarship has stripped the story of its fictional crust without being able to put much in its place. As John of Hildesheim, the Carmelite apologist, explained in 1374, the hermit founders had not generally been educated men;[7] and during the first troubled century of their migration to the West members of the order wrote little in the way of history.

7. A. Staring, *Medieval Carmelite Heritage: Early Reflections on the Nature of the Order* (Institutum Carmelitanum Rome 1989), p. 339. This scholarly work provides an edition of the earliest Carmelite writings relating to the history of the order, beginning with the so-called *rubrica prima*, a brief narrative which first appears as an appendage to the chapter constitutions of 1281.

The Carmelite Order begins to emerge from legend into the daylight of history towards the end of the twelfth century, when groups of hermits living on the slopes of Mount Carmel began to form an organisation that attracted the attention of the ecclesiastical authorities. They were apparently expatriates from the Latin West who had come to Palestine either as pilgrims or as Crusaders. At some point in the first decade of the thirteenth century, in response to their request the Latin patriarch of Jerusalem, Albert of Vercelli, provided them with a brief rule: they were to confine their settlements to deserted places, to occupy separate cells, and to assemble together only for a daily mass in their common oratory and to meet on Sundays for a weekly chapter. Possibly because it became a focus of contention in the order at a later date, the original text of this rule has been lost.[8]

With the collapse of the Latin Kingdom of Jerusalem the hermits lost the protection of their Frankish overlords, and in the 1230s a diaspora began. Impelled by the menacing attitude of the Muslim rulers of the area, the occupants of the mountain hermitages migrated in groups to the West, forming new settlements in Sicily, Italy, Spain, France and England. Most of what is known of this phase of Carmelite history comes from the occasional references of the Franciscan chroniclers. It is the Franciscan Eccleston who tells us that the first contingent to reach England from the East was brought by Lord Richard de Gray of Codnor in the year 1241–2, on his return from crusading in Syria. An earlier group of *émigrés* was brought to Valenciennes by Peter of Corbie in 1235, helped by the patronage of the Countess of Flanders.

Initially these immigrants from the waster places of Palestine sought out remote areas where they could pursue their contemplative way of life in solitude. The earliest English settlements were in such remote spots as Aylesford in the yet unpopulated Kentish Weald and Hulne in Northumberland. But in less than ten years strains became apparent. Younger recruits, untroubled by recollections of life on the holy mountain and sensitive to the apostolic ideals of their time, pressed for change. They wanted an order devoted to an active role of

8. The text was reconstituted from the papal register by G. Wessels, 'Excerptae historiae ordinis': *AOC* 2 (1910), pp. 556–61.

preaching and study, following the example of the Mendicants, which would engage in a pastoral mission to the towns.
In this identity crisis leadership fell to an English Carmelite,
the otherwise obscure Brother Simon, who was elected General
of the incipient order by a general chapter at Aylesford in
1247. Nothing is now known of Simon – the surname of
'Stock' attached to him in Carmelite tradition rests on no
contemporary evidence – beyond the fact that he was the
agent of the desired change. Although he had himself come
from the hermitage of Mount Carmel he bowed to the demands for an active apostolate, and petitioned the pope to
have Albert's rule modified.

Innocent IV set up a commission to investigate the case
consisting of the theologian, Cardinal Hugh of St Cher, and
William, bishop of Tartoûs, both men Dominicans, who might
be expected to sympathise with the desire of the Carmelites to
emulate the friars; and on the basis of their report he issued in
1247 the constitution *Quae honorem conditoris*, which made slight
but significant changes in the original rule.[9] It authorised the
order to make new settlements in any convenient place, including by implication the towns or centres of population, and
approved various cenobitical practices such as taking meals in
common; the regime of fasting was mitigated to bring it into
line with standard monastic practice. This opened a new road
to those who wished to take it. The order now adopted a fully
cenobitical pattern of life and an active pastoral role in
imitation of the Mendicants, and in the course of the following
decade began to establish houses in or on the fringe of cities.

The early stages of reorganisation are hard to trace owing
to the lack of documents. The earliest statutes that survive –
those enacted by a general chapter held at London in 1281[10]
– show the order modelling its structure on that of the Friars
Preachers, holding annual provincial chapters, and also imitating the scholastic organisation of the Dominicans. The logic of
its changing role made it a student order like the Dominicans
and Franciscans, and soon after the amendment of their rule
the Carmelites began sending their men to the schools at
Cambridge, Oxford, Paris and Bologna. The London ordi-

9. M.-H. Laurent (ed.) 'La lettre *Quae honorem conditoris*' in *Ephemerides
Carmeliticae* 2, fasc. i (Florence 1948), pp. 5–16.
10. L. Saggi, 'Constitutiones capituli Londinensis anni 1281': *AOC* n.s. 15
(1950), pp. 203–45.

nances of of 1281 provide, apparently for the first time, for the creation of a Carmelite *studium generale* at Paris – a house of studies for the whole order, to which each province was to send two men to study theology; those selected were to be the men suited by their intellectual capacity to become lectors.

Such a radical reorientation was bound to meet with internal resistance from more conservative members of the order. Some older men, who had renounced everything to embrace the eremitical life in Palestine, felt that the ideals of Mount Carmel had been betrayed. The struggles of the decades following the reappraisal of 1247 are largely hidden from us by the poverty of the sources. Some of the brethren who found the pace of change too slow quitted and sought admission to the Friars Minor or the Dominicans; some who were altogether opposed to it fled to the Cistercians. For a brief moment the heart-searchings and tensions that accompanied the change of direction are vividly illuminated by a curious tract called *Ignea Sagitta* – an Arrow of Fire – that appeared in the year 1270. This was an encyclical letter addressed to the brethren by the retiring General of the order, Nicholas the Frenchman. It is a last plea from an old man for the order to retrace its steps and return to the desert. He had, he explained, been roused from sleep by the cold wind of adversity – 'would it had blown through my garden twenty years before'. Now religion, which had flourished in the holy solitude, has been abandoned and perverted by her sons:

> Perhaps they will answer, 'It was never our intent to resist the divine will, but rather to follow it. For we desire to build up the people of God by preaching His word, hearing confessions and counselling, so that we can be useful to ourselves and our neighbours. For this reason, a most just one, we fled the solitude of the desert to settle among the people in the cities, so as to perform these tasks.' O foolish men! I will show you that in the city you accomplish none of this, but that in time past in the solitude you accomplished it all . . . What is this new religion discovered in the cities? . . . Tour the provinces, go to and fro among the superiors, and tell me, how many have been found in the order who are fit and adequate to preach, to hear confessions and counsel the people, as is proper for those who dwell in towns?[11]

11. *Nicolai Prioris Generalis Ordinis Carmelitarum Ignea Sagitta*, ed. A. Staring: *Carmelus* ix (Rome 1962), pp. 278–9, 281, 283.

This is a strange valediction from a man who had been entrusted with the direction of his order for many years. It suggests that a significant number of the brethren believed that the changes made since 1247 had been a mistake. Nicholas's tearful jeremiad is evidence of the internal stresses and conflicts engendered by the process of turning what had been an association of hermits into an order of mendicant friars. But those who felt as he did were increasingly isolated. The tide of change was now irreversible. Twenty-four years after his lament, the statutes of a chapter held at Bordeaux reveal that the White Friars (as they came to be known on account of their white habit) had become an articulated order divided into twelve provinces, governed by regular general and provincial chapters, organised for pastoral work, and provided with an elaborate scholastic structure to promote advanced studies.[12]

.   .   .

THE AUSTIN FRIARS

The origin of the Austin Friars was in some respects similar to that of the Carmelites, but is better documented. They grew from an amalgamation of groups of hermits living in Tuscany, Lombardy and the March of Ancona. The thirteenth-century popes displayed a constant concern to harness and control the anarchic tendencies of these self-generated religious movements; and in 1244 Innocent IV, himself a canonist of no mystical temper, instructed Cardinal Richard Annibaldi to accede to a request of the hermits of Tuscany for a collective organisation and a recognised rule. Annibaldi called representatives of the various bodies to Rome, formally accredited them to the Rule of St Augustine, gave them a constitution and appointed a Superior General. This union of the hermits of Tuscany, which was confirmed by Pope Innocent, was the first stage in the creation of the Augustinian Friars. A series of papal privileges exempted them from diocesan jurisdiction and authorised them to preach and hear confessions. Within a few years of Annibaldi's ordinance

12. L. Saggi, 'Constitutiones capituli Burdigalensis anni 1294': *AOC* n.s. 18 (1953), pp. 123–85.

they had begun to plant missionary settlements north of the Alps.

In north Italy the most conspicuous body of hermits was a congregation of penitents founded by St John Bono (1168– 1249), a layman of Mantua, and called after him the Bonites. Influenced by the example of the Franciscans, they seem to have spontaneously adopted a life of preaching and mendicancy, an initiative which drew a remonstrance from Pope Gregory IX that they were poaching the benefactors of the Friars Minor. The canonization process of Bono in the years 1251–4 attracted widespread notice and brought many new recruits, and the need to rationalize the various competing groups of Mendicants became pressing. So, acting under the instructions of Pope Alexander IV, Cardinal Annibaldi summoned delegates from the various houses to a meeting in the church of S. Maria del Popolo in Rome in the year 1256, and ordained an act of union, bringing together the Augustinian Hermits of Tuscany, the Bonites, the Williamites, the hermits of the March called the Brettini, and a number of small groups, into a single mendicant order. The bull *Licet ecclesiae catholicae* of April 1256, by which Pope Alexander ratified this grand union, formally constituted the Order of Friars Hermits of St Augustine, known in common parlance as the Austin Friars.[13] Annibaldi, who had master-minded the union, was appointed the first Cardinal Protector of the new order.

Like the Bonites and the Tuscan Hermits, the new friars professed the Rule of St Augustine, and they gradually modelled their constitution on that of the Dominicans. The prior of the Bonites, Lanfranc Septala of Milan, became their first Prior General. Thus the Austin Friars, like the Carmelites, moved from their hermitages into the towns, and followed the Friars Minor and the Friars Preachers into the scholastic world of the universities. Within three years of the grand union, Lanfranc Septala had purchased a house in Paris to serve as a school of theology for the intellectual élite of the order.[14] Among the earliest students to be sent there was Giles of Rome, the future Prior General, whose theological writings

13. Text of the bull in *Bullarium Ordinis Eremitarum S. Augustini*, ed. B. Van Luijk in *Augustiniana* 14 (Louvain 1964), pp. 239–41.
14. D. Gutiérrez, 'Los estudios en la Orden Augustiniana': *AnA* 33 (Rome 1970), pp. 75–149.

came to be approved by the general chapter as representing the official doctrine of the order.

In the last forty years of the thirteenth century the Austin Friars made foundations in, or on the outskirts of towns in Spain, France, Germany and England, and established houses of study in the universities of northern Europe; but their centre of gravity remained in Italy, from which they had sprung. Italy, including Sicily, contained eleven of the twenty-four provinces into which the order was divided by the fourteenth century. Of the eight men who held the office or acted as General before 1300, all but one were Italians; and it has been estimated that in the fourteenth century more than half the membership of the order was based in Italy.

Both the Carmelites and the Austin Friars, then, originated as groups of monks or lay penitents pursuing the eremitical life. Their conversion into orders of friars bears witness to the powerful impact of the mendicant idea upon the consciousness of religious people in the thirteenth century. Once the notion gained currency that the authentic imitation of Christ involved an active ministry of preaching and service, as well as voluntary poverty, it proved impossible to withstand. But the change in each case meant a radical reorientation which, however gradual, could not be accomplished without stress. Corporate poverty long remained a contentious issue. Many of the hermitages and penitential fraternities that had been merged in the Austin Friars owned modest properties donated by well-wishers or their own members, and more radical groups urged that these should be disposed of. One Prior-General, the saintly Clement of Sant'Elpidio, resigned over the question. The radicals had a brief triumph in 1290, when the general chapter of Regensburg decreed a regime of absolute poverty and ordered the hermitages to sell their properties; the proceeds of sale were to be used to acquire new houses in the same province, a quarter of the whole being reserved to buy a new site for the house of studies at Paris.[15] But common sense gradually prevailed over impracticable idealism. In the fourteenth century, the Austin Friars continued to rely upon mendicancy for part of their income, but they retained the possession of their residences and their modest endownments.

15. 'Antiquiores quae extant definitiones capitulorum generalium': *AnA* 2 (1907–8), p. 291; cf. F.A. Mathes, 'The poverty movement and the Augustinian hermits': *AnA* 31 (1968), pp. 9–154.

Another potential source of tension, which had troubled the Carmelites in the early stages, was the hankering felt by some friars, especially the older men, for the solitary life of the hermit, which had been abandoned in favour of a cenobitical regime and an active pastoral mission. To some extent the Austin Friars succeeded in accommodating this desire for the eremitical life within their organisation. In Italy, their spiritual homeland, they kept in touch with their hermitages, where communities continued to live. The greatest and most famous of these was the hermitage of Lecceto, situated in an ilex forest a few miles from Siena. From time to time it received recruits who felt a desire to disengage from the active life of the order. One of these was an English friar, William Flete, a Bachelor of Theology at Cambridge, who was later to become the friend and amanuensis of St Catherine of Siena. In 1359 he got the General's permission to retire to Lecceto as a recluse. At the same time two of his English fellow-friars were allocated to nearby hermitages.[16]

Twenty-one years later William wrote to his brethren of the English province. He had, he explains, been afraid to write earlier for fear of reawakening old affections long since dormant. Now the burden of his message was that they should not travel about to attend chapter meetings or university inceptions; nor should they frequent towns or villages, but stay in their cells: 'in the cell is peace; outside it nothing but strife'. [17] This advice, if literally understood, was obviously at odds with the mendicant way of religious life. But Flete's experience showed that the eremitical ideal could be contained within the framework of the order without posing a threat to its pastoral enterprise.

16. Aubrey Gwynn, *The English Austin Friars* (1940), p. 107.
17. *ibid.* pp. 195–6.

Chapter 6

THE MISSION TO THE TOWNS

. . .

PATTERNS OF URBAN SETTLEMENT

The friars set out to evangelize the new world of the cities. 'There', explained Humbert of Romans, 'preaching is more efficacious because there are more people and the need is greater, for in the city there are more sins.'[1] Themselves the product of the new urban society, they preached the Word to people whose language and mental habits they knew and understood. Because their mission was directed to the people of the towns, the distribution of their friaries and the local whereabouts of their settlements corresponded to the pattern of urban expansion in thirteenth-century Europe. The houses of the Mendicants were most numerous in those areas where urban density was the greatest. Initially they made for the larger and long-established cities, the major centres of commerce and exchange. It was there that the size of the population offered a ripe field for the evangelist and the existence of surplus wealth made it possible to support groups of missionaries who depended upon begging for their livelihood; there, also, could be found a reservoir of young people free from seignorial bondage, from which the mendicant apostles hoped to recruit new members.

They found these conditions in the rich and turbulent city-republics of central and northern Italy, the commercial and episcopal cities of the Rhineland, the Languedoc, the Paris basin and the Low Countries, and in some of the smaller but

---

1. *Humberti de Romanis de Eruditione Praedicatorum* II: *Maxima Biblioteca Veterum Patrum*, ed. M. de la Bigne XXV (Lyons 1677), p. 491.

prosperous towns of England. For the Dominicans, and to a lesser extent for the Friars Minor, a desire to recruit among the educated was one of the factors determining their choice of venue. For this reason the university towns of Bologna, Paris, and Montpellier were among their primary objectives. In England, while both orders made for London, their decision to settle in Oxford immediately afterwards was probably influenced less by the commercial importance of the town, which was a small one by continental standards, than by the attraction of the schools, which offered a promising hunting-ground for recruits. It was probably the same consideration that soon afterwards drew them to Northampton, which was an expansive scholastic centre in the early thirteenth century.

Although both the Franciscans and the Dominicans were quick to establish themselves in the major cities, there was a marked difference between them in the pace of their expansion. The Preachers were noticeably slower in making new foundations. In Germany by the year 1250, some thirty years after their arrival, the Dominicans had planted 38 communities, whereas the Friars Minor had established upwards of 100.[2] The same difference is to be seen elsewhere. In England, by 1250 the Dominicans had 26 houses, as against 43 founded by the Friars Minor. In France, by 1275 the Dominicans had 87 houses, compared with no less than 195 founded by the Franciscans. The differing pace of expansion is even more striking if we compare the English figures in the year 1234, just a decade after the arrival of the Friars Minor: in these ten years the Franciscans had planted 22 communities, as compared with 9 established by the Friars Preachers, who had been in the country three years longer.

External as well as internal factors may account for this difference in the rates of growth. Possibly it reflects a greater impact made upon lay people by the Franciscan ideal and by the cultus of St Francis. But the most cogent explanation for the more cautious expansion of the Friars Preachers is to be

2. Figures for Germany from J.B. Freed, *The Friars and German Society in the Thirteenth Century* (Cambridge Mass. 1977); for France from R.W. Emery, *The Friars in Medieval France. A Catalogue of French Mendicant Convents 1200–1550* (Columbia UP 1962); for England from M.D. Knowles and R.N. Hadcock, *Medieval Religious Houses: England and Wales* (1953). On general patterns of Mendicant settlement in France, see J. le Goff, 'Ordres Mendiants et urbanisation dans la France médiévale': *Annales* 25 (1970), pp. 924–65.

found in their own policy. Their earliest constitutions decreed that no new community should be founded except with the authorisation of the general chapter and without an initial complement of at least twelve brethren; and the party had to include a qualified lecturer in theology.[3] These requirements, which were designed to ensure that communities were big enough to sustain a full monastic regime and to provide for the theological education of the brethren, must obviously have put a brake upon over-carefree colonization. The Dominicans, in fact, showed a marked preference for larger communities, which in their major houses often numbered upwards of a hundred friars.

Arriving on the scene some thirty years later, the Carmelites and Austin Friars at first grew more slowly, but both orders began to establish houses in increasing numbers after 1270, more often than not in towns where the Preachers and the Friars Minor were already settled. By 1300 most of the major cities of Western Europe housed communities of four or five Mendicant Orders. For many newer towns, whose civic consciousness had been heightened by buoyant commercial prosperity and expanding population, the presence of the friars came to be seen as a desirable adjunct of civil society, a symbol of both divine protection and political importance. Thus at Bern and Zürich and several other new towns, the city council – the Rat – took the initiative and invited the friars to settle in their midst. The considerations that prompted overtures like this are explained in a letter of about the year 1240 addressed to the Order of Preachers by the city council of Saint-Julien in the Limousin:

> We have learned from sure testimony that cities and towns
> which you favour with your residence have quickly improved in
> both their spiritual and temporal affairs; for your brethren
> welcome people of peace, they give lustre to the native land, and
> free the people of God from the bondage of their sins. Therefore
> it has seemed good to us, being desirous of sharing in your
> prayers and good works, to beseech you, out of your prudence
> and charity, to be good enough to turn your footsteps towards
> the town of Saint-Julien.[4]

3. *Constitutiones Antique Ordinis Fratrum Predicatorum*, ed. H. Denifle. *ALKG* I p. 221.
4. M.H. Vicaire, 'Le développement de la province dominicaine de Provence' in *Les Mendiants en pays d'oc au XIIIe siècle* (Cahiers de Fanjeaux 8,

In the early phases of settlement the spots chosen by the friars followed a recognisable pattern which was reproduced in nearly all the cities they chose to evangelize. They were generally located in the suburbs – the *borgo* of the Italian cities – lying outside or in close proximity to the town walls. In Germany and England it was not unusual for their conventual buildings to be integrated with the mural fortifications. This recurring pattern can be seen in the settlements made by the Mendicants at Florence and London.

At Florence, the Friars Minor were the first to take up permanent residence. Coming apparently on their own initiative – Francis had already visited the town at the time of Cardinal Ugolino's legation – they at first had to be housed with the indigent in the hospital of San Gallo. In much the same way their first residence at Siena was in the hospital of St Mary Magdalen, and at Marseilles the Preachers were first put up in the hospice of St Michel for travellers. By 1221 the Franciscans had already acquired the site of Santa Croce in Florence close to the Arno, outside the city wall on the southeast, where they were to remain. The Dominicans arrived shortly afterwards. They were accommodated for a time in the hospital of S. Pancrazio, from which they made a bid to obtain possession of the church of St. Paul's, but this was frustrated by the opposition of the secular clergy, and they were given instead the church of S. Maria Novella in the extra-mural suburb of S. Paolo, on the west side of the city.

A fresh phase of Mendicant settlement began in 1250, when the Servites – the brotherhood of Florentine penitents returning from their hermitage on Monte Senario – reoccupied the plot at Caffagio in the northern suburbs from which they had fled, and there shortly afterwards they began building the church and convent of the Annunziata. They were joined in the same area by the Friars of the Sack. Some years later, the Austin Friars and the Carmelites established settlements across the river in the Oltrarno, a district which was still thinly inhabited in the middle years of the thirteenth century. The

Toulouse 1973), pp. 55–6. Cf. similar invitations by Zürich and other new towns of Germany in M. Wehri-Johns, 'Stellung und Wirksamkeit der Bettelorden in Zürich' in K. Elm (ed.) *Stellung und Wirksamkeit der Bettelorden in der städtischen Gesellschaft* (Berliner Historische Studien 3, 1981), pp. 77–84.

houses of the friars were thus distributed in an outer ring around the nucleus of the old city, which was just beginning to burst out of its confinement within the walls of the twelfth century.[5] Their churches were erected in a suburban periphery which was to undergo intensive development during the following hundred years. Away from the city centre dominated by the fortress of the *podestà* and the palaces of the aristocracy, they were well placed to serve the pastoral needs of new immigrants, tradesmen, artisans and the new bourgeoisie, whose villas were springing up along the outer highways radiating from the gates of the city.

The settlement of the friars in and around London displays a similar pattern. The Dominicans were the first to arrive. In 1224 they took up residence on a plot of land given them by Hubert de Burgh, the Justiciar, on the east side of Shoe Lane in the extra-mural suburb of Holborn. It was there that, after the site had been enlarged by further donations, they built their first church and cloister. The Holborn area, lying beyond the river Fleet, was still a rural suburb tenanted by market gardens and the palaces of noblemen and prelates in the early years of the thirteenth century.[6] During the following eighty years it was rapidly converted into a built-up district as it housed the over-spill of population from the area of intensive occupation within the city walls. Some twenty years after the Preachers, the Carmelites also acquired a site in the western suburbs further to the south, between Fleet Street and the Thames.

The Friars Minor, whose advance-party reached London towards the end of 1224, were to begin with given hospitality by the Preachers. They were then taken under the wing of John Travers, a sheriff of the city, who let them have a house in Cornhill; and finally they settled on a plot that had been offered them immediately within the city walls by Newgate, in the insalubrious area of the shambles. In the 1250s the Friars of the Sack established their first settlement outside Aldersgate. The Austin Friars, on the other hand, were found a site inside the northern ramparts.

5. Anna Papi, 'L'impianto mendicante in Firenze, un problema aperto' in *Les Ordres Mendiants et la ville en Italie centrale* (Mélanges de l'Ecole Française de Rome 89, 1977), pp. 40–68.
6. C.M. Barron, Penelope Hunting and Jane Roscoe, *The Parish of St Andrew Holborn* (1979), pp. 9–12.

The general propensity of the friars for settling in extra-mural suburbs, or close to the city gates, has led some historians to argue that their choice of location was the outcome of a deliberate missionary strategy – part of a plan to evangelize the newly arrived and socially deracinated populations round the periphery of the expanding cities, for whom the established parishes failed to make adequate pastoral provision. Because medieval parishes and collegiate bodies generally resisted any subdivision of their territories for the purpose of creating new parishes, many settlers in outlying areas were left without adequate pastoral care. Some cities had only a single church with parochial status.[7] But the prevailing pattern of Mendicant settlement admits of a simpler and more obvious explanation. The friars could only settle where their patrons offered them land or buildings. And in the densely populated area within the walls of the older cities vacant property was hard to find and expensive. Those of them who managed to acquire a location within the walls had to be content with less salubrious quarters in the shambles or in areas subject to flooding, which were shunned by all except the poorest residents.

It was not only high land-values that discouraged the friars from settling within the established boundaries of the cities; another factor was the hostility displayed towards the newcomers by many of the secular clergy. Even where a zealous and enlightened bishop welcomed the friars as pastoral assistants, his cathedral or parish clergy might resist what they regarded as an insupportable intrusion into the area of their spiritual jurisdiction. At Cologne, where Archbishop Engelbert had welcomed the Dominicans, a spokesman for the parish clergy protested to the legate, Conrad of Porto, that they had been admitted to the city 'to our damnation: they have put their sickle into another man's harvest'.[8] At Florence, despite the favour of Bishop Ardingo, a zealous reformer who had imposed regular observance on his chapter, attempts by the Dominicans to acquire the central church of S. Pietro Scheraggio

7. See the discussion of C.N.L. Brooke, 'The Church in the towns' in *The Mission of the Church* (7th Summer Conference of the Ecclesiastical History Society, 1970), pp. 59–83. For this problem in Germany see Freed, *Friars and German Society* p. 48.
8. Thomas of Cantimpré, *Bonum Universale de Apibus*, ed. Colverinus (Douai 1627), p. 39.

were frustrated by the opposition of the local clergy. At London, in 1275 Archbishop Kilwardby, himself a former head of the English Dominican Province, acquired for the Friars Preachers a new and more spacious area within the city walls south of Ludgate, formerly the site of Baynard's Castle. But the move of the Preachers into the city was opposed by the chapter of St Paul's cathedral, and the canons were only persuaded to relent by the intervention of the king.[9]

. . .

PATRONS AND BUILDINGS

Individual benefactors, guilds, and city communes or corporations, all collaborated in providing sites for the friars and in giving money or materials for building their churches and domestic quarters. In the early days their buildings generally conformed to the Rule of poverty enshrined in their constitutions. The Dominican statutes decreed that 'the brethren are to have modest and humble houses', and went on to prescribe a maximum height of twelve feet for their dwellings and thirty feet for their churches.[10] The Franciscans were warned by their statutes to avoid 'superfluity' in length, width and height, and to shun refinement (*curiositas*) in decoration.[11] They needed churches primarily for communal celebration of the Office, and to begin with, an oratory of modest size was enough for the purpose. It was this requirement that had impelled St Francis to ask the Benedictines of Monte Subasio for the tiny chapel of the Portiuncula. In the early years of their mission the friars preached alfresco in the squares and market-places or in parish pulpits lent them by well-disposed secular clergy.

The astonishing success of their ministry to the townspeople changed all this. A rapid growth in the number of postulants wanting to join the Mendicants made the early buildings inadequate. 'As the number of the brethren grew from day to day', explained Eccleston, 'the houses and sites that had

9. W.A. Hinnebusch, *The Early English Friars Preachers* (Rome 1951), pp. 55–6.
10. *Constitutiones Antique Ordinis Fratrum Predicatorum*, ed. H. Denifle *ALKG* I p. 225.
11. *Die ältesten Redactionen des Generalconstitutionen des Franziskaner-Ordens*, ed. F. Ehrle in *ALKG* VI, pp. 94–5.

sufficed them when they were few, could not suffice for a multitude. Moreover,' he adds without conscious irony, 'by the providence of God, persons of such degree frequently entered that it seemed right to make more honourable provision for them.'[12] Within a couple of years of the death of St Dominic, the community at Bologna found it necessary to extend the choir of the church of St Nicholas eastwards, nearly doubling the length of the building, in order to accomodate swelling numbers. But it was not only the growing size of the Mendicant communities that provided an incentive for rebuilding. In the 1240s a hardening of attitude on the part of the secular clergy increasingly debarred the friars from using parish churches for preaching. They were therefore forced to provide accommodation for the people in churches of their own. Encouraged by their lay benefactors, they embarked on a programme of enlargement and new building, constructing churches spacious enough to provide an auditorium for the large crowds attracted by their preaching.

The Dominicans at Florence had inherited an eleventh-century church at S. Maria Novella, but the crowds drawn by the sermons of Brother Peter of Verona – the Inquisitor St Peter Martyr of the Dominican martyrology – persuaded them first to petition the city to have the piazza west of the church enlarged, and then to start erecting a new and more commodious church alongside the old structure. The work was begun by 1245, and by 1279 it was far enough advanced for the old building to be pulled down. The new church, characterised by its lofty arcades, slender columns and long bays, producing a nave as light as it is spacious, inaugurated a new idiom in Italian Gothic architecture.[13]

A desire to outdo the Preachers, as well as the pressure of popular demand, inspired the Franciscans at Santa Croce to embark on a still more ambitious project. The new work, begun in the 1290s, was financed by leading merchant families such as the Bardi and Peruzzi, who were commemorated by family chapels, and by the Calimala guild – the association of foreign cloth merchants and most powerful of the major guilds

12. *De Adventu Fratrum Minorum in Angliam*, ed. A.G. Little (1951), p. 44.
13. On the architectural history of S. Maria Novella see W. and E. Paatz, *Die Kirchen von Florenz* III (Frankfurt 1940), pp. 664–8. On the phases of Dominican building in general see G. Meerseman, 'L'architecture dominicaine au XIIIe siècle': *AFP* 16 (1946), pp. 136–90.

which dominated the government of the city-republic. The Calimala, in fact, served as a repository and banker, receiving and dispensing funds contributed by individual citizens. The city itself entered into the spirit of the enterprise: from 1295 onwards the republic made an annual grant towards the cost of the building.[14] The great basilica, which was still unfinished in 1375, was intended to overtop all the other churches of the city, including the cathedral; according to an unverifiable tradition, it was designed by the cathedral's architect, Arnolfo di Cambio. At the same time as these grandiose churches were under construction, both the Dominicans and the Franciscans were aided by their benefactors to enlarge their cloisters and rebuild their conventual accommodation. A humble chapel, which the Preachers had inherited on the site of S. Maria Novella, was converted into a chapter-house, on the wall of which Andrea di Bonaiuto painted a huge composition symbolising the triumphs of the order.[15]

This process of extension and new building by the friars, which gained momentum after 1250, went on in many of the cities of Europe. Everywhere the generosity of princes, the bourgeoisie, and city governments enabled the Mendicants to erect huge preaching churches, which were often the largest buildings in the town. Where their existing sites were too constricted to allow building on the large scale now thought desirable, they sought an alternative location. This was what the London Dominicans did. In 1286 they moved to the new site south of Ludgate, which Archbishop Kilwardby had found for them and which the king donated, and sold the old premises at Holborn. And on the new site they began building a large and sumptuous aisled church with a broad nave a hundred and twenty feet long.

In London, as elsewhere, the cost of the friars' buildings was met by the leading merchant families who formed the aldermanic class. The first oratory of the Friars Minor was paid for by the mayor, William Joyner. In a phase of rebuilding they undertook between 1270 and 1290, a new dormitory was built for them by the mayor, Gregory de Rokesley, and a

14. Paatz, *Die Kirchen von Florenz* I, p. 499.
15. Converted at a later date to the use of the Spanish suite of the Duchess Eleonora of Toledo, since when it has been known as the Spanish Chapel.

new chapter-house and refectory were built through the largesse of two of the city's aldermen, Walter Potter and Bartholomew de Castell.[16] The latter was a large-scale contractor and supplier to the royal household. Gregory de Rokesley, himself a wealthy cloth and wine importer with a mansion in Cornhill belonged to a family that dominated the political class of London in the later decades of the thirteenth century. For men such as these, generosity to the friars was a mark of status which needed to be satisfied by building with some degree of ostentation. They were doubtless encouraged in this form of well-doing by the knowledge that they were imitating the practice of the royal almsgiving.

Kings and city governments led the way in contributing money and materials for the building operations of the Mendicants. Both Henry III and Edward I made frequent gifts, and the royal bounty was distributed to all the orders without distinction. The London Dominicans were granted ten pounds by the King in 1261 from the proceeds of the vacant bishopric of Winchester to construct a school in the cloister.[17] In 1269 the Crutched Friars received twenty marks to build their oratory;[18] and the following year the Carmelites were given a hundred shillings towards the cost of building their church.[19] Subventions in kind were much favoured by the Italian city-republics. At Siena, the earliest reference to the fact that the Servites had settled on the fringe of the city comes from an order of the commune granting them, a consignment of 20,000 bricks for their building.[20]

In all the cities where the friars settled, public and illustrious benefactors were imitated by a host of smaller people who bequeathed sums of money or modest properties. Of such were William of Colchester, who in his will which was proved in 1259, bequeathed the Crutched Friars of London a dovecote with pigeons, and Master Richard de Stratford, who instructed his executors to sell his tenements in London and

---

16. C.L. Kingsford, *The Grey Friars in London* (1915), pp. 146–65. For the importance of the Rokesleys in the government of London and for Bartholomew de Castell, see G.A. Williams, *Medieval London: from Commune to Capital* (1963), pp. 77, 247.
17. *Calendar of Liberate Rolls 1260–67*, p. 50.
18. *Calendar of Liberate Rolls 1267–72*, p. 81.
19. *ibid.* p. 113.
20. F. dal Pino, 'I Servi di S. Maria a Siena': *MEFR* 89 (1977), pp. 749–55.

use the proceeds to help the Blackfriars build their new chapter-house.[21]

How could this flood of funds for the erection of great churches and elaborate conventual buildings be reconciled with a rule of poverty which debarred the friars from owning any form of property and from holding or retaining money? Societies of merchants had no difficulty in creating devices by which this obstacle could be circumvented. The papal privilege *Quo elongati* which authorised the Friars Minor to make use of 'Spiritual friends', or trustees, to receive and hold funds on their behalf for building purposes and other necessities, sanctioned an arrangement which many would-be benefactors had adopted from the beginning. When the Dominicans settled in the suburbs of Florence, several rich merchant families were eager to provide them with funds to build a residence and cloister alongside the old church of S. Maria Novella. So as to do this without contravening the Mendicant rule against accepting money, the family of Berlinghieri – one of the benefactors in question – in 1224 founded the hospice of Fontemanzina for the poor. This charitable institution was administered by a confraternity of lay penitents, and it was able to receive bequests and other donations for the poor, among whom the friars were numbered by their profession. By this means money could be received, banked, and used to finance the building projects of the Dominicans.[22]

· · ·

LAY CONFRATERNITIES

The religious confraternity was one of the favoured channels through which the friars acted upon the laity and which in turn provided them with material and moral support. Voluntary associations of men and women for the purpose of mutual support in prayer and works of charity had long been a feature of urban parish life. The confraternity of voluntary penitents (*fratres et sorores de penitentia*) was a particular form of lay association that appeared in the cities of northern and central Italy towards the end of the twelfth century. The Humiliati were an association of this type, and the early

21. R.R. Sharpe, *Calendar of Wills enrolled in the Court of Husting* (1859) I, pp. 5, 52.
22. G.G. Meerseman, *Ordo Fraternitatis* (*Italia Sacra: Studi e Documenti* 24–6, Rome 1977), pp. 365–70.

disciples who attached themselves to St Francis were a similar form of brotherhood. The preaching of the friars did much to spread this penitential movement in the towns of Italy, France and Germany.

The men and women who formed themselves into these confraternities adopted an ascetical life-style, while living in their own homes and pursuing their secular vocations. Although most of the associations were city based, they transcended parish and even urban boundaries to form regional unions. In 1221 the fraternities in the Romagna region entered into a federation and drew up an ordinance which throws much light on the character and aims of these religious societies. The document sets out detailed prescriptions for the dress as well as the religious observances of members: their clothes are to be made of humble undyed material, not exceeding 6 sol. Ravenna in price. They observe the monastic periods of fasting and abstain from meat four days a week. Those who are sufficiently literate recite the Office or the psalms daily; those who are not, recite *Pater Nosters* in place of the Hours. They meet monthly for a mass, and on this occasion each member pays a subscription of a penny to the *massario* – the executive officer of the confraternity– for distribution to the poor.[23]

A major theme of early Franciscan preaching was reconciliation. And the Romagna ordinance makes it apparent that, alongside charitable works, peace-making between both individuals and groups was a central theme in the programme of personal sanctification which the confraternity proposed to its members. They engaged themselves to seek reconciliation with their neighbours and gave a solemn promise never to bear arms against anyone. This commitment to pacifism gave the confraternity a significant political role in the cities of Italy, many of which were torn by violent dynastic feuds. Possibly it provided an unavowed motive that led increasing numbers of the bourgeoisie to join the penitential movement. The associations had marked success in recruiting among the better-off citizens and married professional men, including those who held executive and administrative posts in the city commune.[24] But if organised pacifism helped to ameliorate

23. G.G. Meerseman, *Dossier de l'Ordre de la pénitence au XIIIe siècle* (*Spicilegium Friburgense* 7, Freiburg 1961), pp. 91–112.
24. G. Casagrande, 'Penitenti e Disciplinati a Perugia e loro rapporti con gli Ordini Mendicanti': *MEFR* (1977), pp. 711–21.

internecine strife, it also posed political problems. In the thirteenth century, warfare between the Italian city-republics was endemic; and their rulers were understandably reluctant to grant exemption from military service to an influential section of the citizenry. In 1221 the confraternity of Faenza found it necessary to invoke papal protection from harassment by the city authorities on account of the refusal of its members to serve in the militia.

Although the confraternities bore some resemblance to religious orders in their observances and in the demands they made upon their members, they were lay associations, formed and governed by lay people. In structure they were not unlike the urban commune which was their political environment. The Fraternity of St Mary of Mercy – the Misericordia – of Bergamo, the biggest of several in the city, had a constitution that was typical of many others. Its ruling body was a council of twelve elected by the whole membership; and annually on the first Sunday of Lent, the councillors elected a minister to head the fraternity. They also chose four treasurers, called 'massarii', to receive the regular alms required of members and bequests, and to dispense assistance to the poor. The Misericordia became, in fact, and remained for centuries the city's chief agency for the distribution of poor relief.[25]

Some confraternities pre-dated the advent of the friars, but many more sprang up in the wake of the revivalist preaching of the Friars Minor and the Preachers. In either case, they gravitated towards the churches of the Mendicants, which in many cases had been funded by their members. They looked to the friars to provide them with counsellors and confessors, and the friary church became the meeting place where they regularly met to hear sermons and where they stored their archives. In many cities separate fraternities were sponsored by both orders, as happened at Florence, where the brothers of penance who attached themselves to the Franciscan and Dominican churches became known in the city as the 'greys' and 'blacks' respectively. The fierceness of their rivalry was notorious until 1298, when the papal legate, Matthew of Acquasparta, intervened and forced them to unite in a single body.

25. Lester K. Little, *Liberty, Charity, Fraternity. Lay Religious Confraternities at Bergamo in the age of the Commune* (Smith College Studies in History 51, Northampton Mass. 1988), pp. 58–9, 114–17.

Many confraternities were directly sponsored by the friars. Some of these associations, like the Societies of the Faith, founded at Milan and Florence by Peter of Verona, were militant organisations created specially to combat heresy and pressurise the civic authorities into applying sanctions against heretics. Others, like the associations of the *Laudesi* – the singers of the divine praises – and the fraternities of the Blessed Virgin, which were to be found attached to churches of the friars in many parts of Europe,[26] were organised solely for the purpose of religious observances and works of charity.

In time, those satellite lay associations most directly linked with the Mendicants, the brotherhoods and sisterhoods of penance, came to be regarded as a third order, as distinct from the friars and nuns who constituted the first and second orders, and their members were referred to as Tertiaries. The Franciscan penitential fraternities were the first to receive official recognition. They were approved in 1289 by Pope Nicholas IV, who prescribed a rule for them. The papal bull claimed that the fraternities had been founded by St Francis,[27] and although the claim was without historical foundation, it was to be reiterated in all subsequent papal privileges. Before the end of the thirteenth century, references are to be found in wills to 'brothers of the Third Order or Third Rule of St Francis'.[28] The Rule, in fact, bound them never to leave the fraternity, unless to join an approved religious order, to dress humbly, to avoid 'dishonourable feasts and shows', to hear mass daily if possible, to confess and receive communion three times a year, and to assemble monthly for a community mass and sermon. Those sufficiently educated are expected to recite the Divine Office, when possible attending the morning Hours in church; the others are to recite *Pater Nosters* in place of the Hours.

The so-called third orders and the other confraternities that

---

26. G. Meerseman, 'Etudes sur les anciennes confréries dominicaines': *AFP* 20 (1950), pp. 5–113. On the Laudesi and the multiplication of penitential fraternities in the fourteenth century see C.M. de la Roncière, *Le mouvement confraternel au moyen-âge, France, Italie, Suisse* (*Collection de l'Ecole Française de Rome* 97, Rome 1987), pp. 297–342.

27. *Bullarium Franciscanum* IV ed. J.H. Sbaralea (Rome 1759), pp. 94–7.

28. A. Pompei, 'Terminologia varia dei Penitenti' in *Il Movimento Francescano della Penitenza nella società medioevale* (Atti del 3° Convegno di Studi Francescani, Rome 1980), pp. 11–22.

continued to proliferate in the fourteenth century represented a response of the married laity to the revivalist preaching of the friars. They offered men and women the opportunity to adopt the evangelical life within the limits imposed by their worldly circumstances. They realised in institutional form the message of the Mendicants that personal sanctification was accessible to those living in the secular world. The confraternity was one of the most effective instruments used by the friars to instruct the urban laity, to communicate their ideals, and to direct the religious enthusiasm of the laity into orthodox channels.

. . .

THE GREAT DEVOTION

The crowded conditions of life in medieval cities made urban populations particularly susceptible to waves of religious excitement, which sometimes displayed symptoms of mass hysteria. Some of these outbursts of popular devotion, which appeared with startling suddenness and spread with the speed of a prairie fire, were stimulated by Mendicant preachers; others derived their initial inspiration from the activities of free-lance evangelists and prophetic tramps, whose links with the clerical establishment are far from clear. But if the friars did not always initiate such movements, their prestige and influence enabled them to assume control of them and link them to their own organisation.

One of these eruptions of mass fervour kindled by a freelance prophet was the Great Devotion, or alleluia movement, which convulsed many Italian cities in the summer of 1233. Salimbene saw the arrival of the movement in his native Parma and describes the leader of the huge procession as it entered the city, a man named Benedict Cornetus:

> a simple and illiterate man, of perfect innocence, whom I often
> saw at Parma and later at Pisa . . . resembling St John the
> Baptist, he had an Armenian cap on his head and he had a long
> black beard; and he was wearing an ankle-length black habit like
> a hair-sack, with a big red cross on the back of it, in the manner
> of a priest's chasuble; and he carried a small brass trumpet,
> which he blew with a fearsome din. Thus girt, he proceeded with
> his trumpet and preached in the churches and the squares,
> followed by a huge troup of boys . . . he concluded his preaching
> with the praise of God, beginning with the words 'Praised be,

116

and blessed be, and glorified be the Father', and ending with an
'Alleluia' thrice repeated, which the boys repeated after him.[29]

Seeing the huge crowds coming into the city to take part in
the devotion, carrying their regional banners and branches
torn from the trees, and the numbers that flocked to hear
sermons in the morning and evening, Salimbene was convinced that the event was divinely inspired. Whether or not,
the friars had originated it, they assumed a leading role in the
movement as preachers, drawing great crowds of participants
in all the major cities of northern and central Italy. At Parma
large crowds were drawn to the central piazza to hear a
Franciscan, Brother Gerard, who laced his sermons with demonstrations of miraculous telepathy. At Verona, the preaching
of a Dominican, John of Vicenza, attracted crowds from the
nearby cities of Padua and Mantua, and the thousands who
swarmed into the city-centre to hear him acclaimed him
rector of the city, a popular coup to which the despot Ezzelino
da Romano thought it prudent for the time being to submit.

The central theme of the Great Devotion was peace and
reconciliation. It clearly derived its popular impetus from the
miseries inflicted upon humbler people by aristocratic feuding
on the streets and by the constant warfare between city-republics; and for a short time it succeeded. In a welter of penitential
fervour personal enmities were put aside and warfare was halted.

The same problem of civic violence, aggravated by famine
and disease, fired another outburst of popular devotion in
1260 which took a more macabre form. This was the Flagellant
movement, which was inaugurated at Perugia by a layman
named Ranieri Fasani, who was a member of a penitential
confraternity. Self-flagellation was a form of mortification
practised by some austere monastic communities like the
Camaldolese. What was new in Fasani's initiative was that he
converted the practice into a public spectacle performed by
laymen. He persuaded a large company of men to process
barefooted through Perugia, stripped to the waist, lashing
themselves with leather thongs. This extraordinary form of
public masochism assumed the features of mass hysteria, as it
quickly spread to Rome, Bologna and the cities of Lombardy.
Everywhere large numbers of men and boys, led by clergy

29. Salimbene, pp. 72–3.

with banners and candles, marched two by two to assemble in front of a church, where they flogged themselves unmercifully, imploring, as they did so, God's forgiveness for their sins and relief from the scourge of war. The movement was thus both a demonstration for peace and an exhibition of public repentance. War and natural calamities were regarded as signs of divine anger with the sins of the people. The penitents sought to appease it by identifying themselves with the sufferings of Christ.

It is understandable that a dramatic peace movement evoked a huge popular response in Italy. Two decades of conflict between the Ghibellines and the Guelphs – the partisans of the Hohenstaufen empire and the papacy – had split the society of the city-republics into warring groups and had caused havoc in people's lives. In 1260 the state of the papal cause and the situation of the Guelphs looked grave, for the Ghibellines of Siena had inflicted a crushing defeat upon Florence at Montaperti. This doubtless explains the fact that the mass demonstrations of penitence were eagerly taken up by cities of the Guelph allegiance like Perugia, and also the fact that Manfred, the Hohenstaufen heir to the Regno after the death of Frederick II, forbade the Flagellants entry to the towns under his control

Although the Flagellant movement sprang up at Perugia and rapidly spread to the cities of Lombardy and the Romagna, it was not confined to Italy. In the following years Flagellants appeared in the towns of Germany and France. Some historians have seen in this epidemic of public penitence the influence of Joachite speculation about the end of the world – according to some interpretations of Joachim of Fiore, the end was destined to come in the year 1260 and, as we have seen, eschatological speculation of this kind was rife among the Franciscans. But if dread of an imminent Last Judgement imparted an element of frenzy to the movement, its roots are to be found closer to hand in the more immediate fears and miseries caused by constant war, deprivation and disease, which were the common afflictions of medieval people. Many parts of Europe had experienced famine in the year 1258 following a failure of the corn-crop, and the epidemics of the following year caused heavy mortality among the poorly nourished survivors of the great hunger.

By their call to penance and compassion with the sufferings

of Christ – favoured themes in Franciscan preaching – the friars did much to promote the outburst of Flagellant enthusiasm. At an early stage they assumed direction of the movement and guided it into narrower and more restrained channels. The mass demonstrations of half-naked and bleeding penitents disappeared from the streets, to reappear only sporadically at times of natural catastrophe such as the Black Death, the bubonic plague, which struck Europe for the first time in 1348–9. In their place, the friars sponsored newly formed or existing fraternities of penitents called *Disciplinati*. These were sodalities of lay people who included self-flagellation among other religious exercises. A rule compiled for the Congregation of *Disciplinati* of Bergamo in 1336 required its members to hear mass daily unless seriously impeded, to confess their sins monthly, and to receive communion at least twice a year. In addition, on Sundays and feasts of Our Lady, the Apostles and St Mary Magdalen, they gather at the fraternity house to don penitential garb, and then proceed through the city two by two in procession, beating themselves.[30] Participation in this ritual self-flagellation was confined to male members of the society. Presumably it was thought that the sight of women beating themselves, even if their flesh was covered, would arouse ambiguous sexual responses in the spectators. Indeed in some primitive societies in Africa, men voluntarily submit themselves to public flogging in order to demonstrate their virility. In the later middle ages associations of *Disciplinati* were to be found, alongside other pious confraternities, attached to many of the churches of the Mendicants.

How can we explain the immediate and lasting impression that the friars made upon the turbulent and volatile urban societies of the thirteenth century? Part of the explanation clearly lies in their deployment of superior pastoral skills. They were able to attract urban congregations, promote lay spirituality, and canalize volcanic eruptions of religious enthusiasm because they were highly effective as preachers and confessors. In both roles they brought to the religious scene a fresh and reinvigorating charge of energy. Before their advent, the church-going laity rarely heard a sermon. Few of the parish clergy, in fact, had enough education to be able to offer their people doctrinal or moral instruction. This dangerous

30. Lester K. Little, *op. cit.* pp. 196–9.

gap in the pastoral ministry, a failure of the *ecclesia docens* at ground level, was a cause of growing concern to the more zealous prelates. It drove one simple parish priest, Foulques de Neuilly, to put himself to school at Paris, so as to learn how to instruct his parishioners – an enterprise that turned him into a revivalist preacher famous throughout France. Maurice de Sully, when bishop of Paris, addressed himself to the problem by composing and circulating model vernacular sermons for the use of his parish clergy. The wind of renewal was beginning to blow by the time St Francis and St Dominic had come to the notice of the ecclesiastical authorities. But it was left to the friars to lead and impose their trademark upon a great revival of popular preaching throughout western Christendom.

.   .   .

THE ART OF PREACHING

In the friars' hands sermon-making became a new art, which was inculcated in their schools and through their writings. To help the preacher perform his task they produced a large body of didactic literature. There was the theoretical treatise, like *The Instruction of Preachers* composed by the Dominican Master-General Humbert of Romans, and there were more technical aids to sermon construction, such as the *Art of Preaching* by the Dominican Thomas Waleys, as well as collections of model sermons, which survive in large numbers from the thirteenth and fourteenth centuries. The early Bible concordances, which were compiled by Dominicans working at the Paris friary, belong to this class of literature; their primary purpose was to provide the sermonizer with an arsenal of appropriate Scriptural quotations. But the sermon aids that were most characteristic of the revival of popular preaching were the *Exempla* – collections of moralizing anecdotes garnered from the Lives of the saints, romances and oral tradition, which a preacher could use to enliven his sermon and catch the attention of his audience.

It has been persuasively argued that Paris was the major centre for the production of sermon literature in the thirteenth century.[31] The new art of preaching was a by-product of the university. Its peculiar rhetoric was derived from the schools.

31. D.L. d'Avray, *The Preaching of the Friars* (1985), pp. 132–79.

The new form of sermon was not, of course, like an academic disputation; but with its systematic analysis of a theme, its definitions, semantic distinctions and marshalling of authorities, it bears all the marks of the scholastic discipline inculcated in the university classrooms. Model sermons of the thirteenth century look dull stuff. This is because they offer no more than a schematic plan buttressed with suitable texts, like the scheme a student prepares before writing an essay. It was left to the preacher, speaking in the vernacular, to flesh out the skeletal argument of the model with ideas and anecdotes drawn from his own experience or culled from the anthologies of *Exempla*. It was here that the friars excelled. They had learned in the classroom the need to argue, to challenge and to entertain.

Some Mendicant preachers identified with their city audiences by using the vocabulary and imagery of commerce to make their points; but to judge from the sermons that survive, this obvious trick of the trade was not as common as has sometimes been suggested. In collections of Mendicant sermons the themes that recur most frequently are the need for repentance and contrition, reconciliation with enemies, confession of sins, and the obligation to give alms to the poor.

Lively and well argued sermons were calculated to make an irresistible impact upon congregations which contained significant numbers of literate merchants and professional people, long starved of pulpit oratory. But it was not only superior technique and lively performance that enabled the friars to grip the attention of their audiences. An even more important factor in their success was the message they brought. To lay people dissatisfied with their role as passive spectators of religious observances and hungry for guidance in personal religion, who could find no outlet for their spiritual aspirations in the existing structures of the Church, they offered new possibilities of active participation. In a sense, they pioneered the idea of the devout life for the laity both by their teaching and their example – a Christian life of prayer and sacrifice not modelled upon that of monks or dependent upon the vicarious merits acquired for them by professional ascetics, but one lived fully in the world. It was a hopeful message that contrasted with the pessimism of the traditional monastic spirituality, which regarded the monk as the only complete Christian and offered only a tenuous hope of salvation to the married laity.

The contrast between these new exponents of the evangelical life and the representatives of the old established order was frequently pointed up by attacks made by Mendicant preachers upon the wealth and pride of monks and secular prelates and nepotism among the higher clergy:

> What can loose the chains, the riches, honours and pleasures, that hold the clergy and false religious in bondage? What can tame their pride and lead them to Thee? For simony sits in the saddle in the high place of the city, that is in the seats of ecclesiastical office. . . . These men build Jerusalem in blood, that is by granting ecclesiastical benefices to their relatives, their nephews and grand children.[32]

St Anthony of Padua, the author of this denunciation, was one of the most admired and feted Franciscan preachers of northern Italy. Such attacks impugning the credibility of clerical and monastic leadership were common enough to to be made the subject of a prohibition by Bonaventure when he was Minister-General of the Friars Minor.[33] They were dangerous stratagems for the friars to adopt, but they must have gained them an appreciative hearing from their urban congregations.

Those lay people who were stirred by the teaching of the friars to ask how they could respond to the call of the evangelical life were offered fulfilment in the penitential confraternities, especially in those that were later called Third Orders: 'there are many,' observed Humbert of Romans, 'who say they cannot perform penance in the world, nor do they wish to enter religion, which they cannot do on account of being married; but lo, divine Providence has ordained so as to remove an excuse of this kind: there exists in the midst of the world a way of doing penance which has been approved by the Pope and distinguished by many graces and privileges, which is adopted by the brethren called brethren of penance . . . Many people of high birth, both men and women, most of all in parts of Italy, have adopted this kind of life.'[34]

What the friars offered was a new theology of the secular life, which had its intellectual roots in the syntheses of the school-

32. *S. Antonii Sermones Dominicales*, ed. A.M. Locatelli (Padua 1895–1913), I p. 113, II, p. 350.
33. *S. Bonaventurae Opera Omnia* VIII (Quarrachi 1898), pp. 470–1.
34. *De Eruditione Praedicatorum*, pp. 474–5.

men, who were in the process of reappraising the relationship between grace and nature. As the Dominican Aquinas was to say, 'grace does not remove nature, but perfects it',[35] Personal sanctification was within the reach of those engaged in secular occupations – even for merchants, whose calling was generally censured by ascetical theologians. The new orientation is exemplified by the popularity of a genre of sermon that had made its first tentative appearance in the twelfth century – sermons *ad status*, addressed to the particular spiritual needs of different classes and occupations: sermons for knights, merchants, scholars, masters, servants, rulers, married people, and so forth, which took full account of their state and worldly responsibilities. This was a genre in which the friars excelled. Humbert of Romans included in his *Instruction of Preachers* a series of model sermons suitable for lay people in cities, those living in rural communities, members of lay confraternities, merchants attending fairs and rulers of cities, as well as various categories of religious. An interesting feature of this preaching, which is only now receiving attention from scholars, is a more appreciative and optimistic approach to the theme of marriage and married love, a subject that in the past had often evoked virulent misogyny from ascetical writers. 'Our order,' the Dominican Henry of Provins reminded his brethren, 'is the work of a simple mortal; but it was God who himself instituted the order of marriage . . . at the time of the flood, the Lord showed his preference by saving married people.'[36]

. . .

QUESTIONS OF CONSCIENCE

It would be unjust to the friars to suggest, as some historians have done, that they ingratiated themselves with the mercantile classes by proposing a revised ethic of commerce. It is true that the expansion of international trade and the growth of a money economy provided the schoolmen, who lived and taught in urban communities, with an inducement to rethink the ethics of trading for profit. The old adage 'it is hard for a merchant to be saved' was the product of a less sophisticated economy. The schoolmen of the early thirteenth century

35. *Summa Theologica* I^a Q. 1, 8.
36. Lecoy de la Marche, *La chaire française au moyen-âge* 2nd edn (Paris 1886) pp. 429–30.

generally display some appreciation of the services rendered to society by merchants. A modification of the traditional teaching on the subject of commerce had been prepared in the Paris classrooms; and in his *Summa Confessorum* Thomas of Chobham provided a resume of it for his clerical readers:

> [The essence of] business is to buy something more cheaply, with the intention of selling it more dearly. But this is quite permissable for lay people, even if they render no compensation for the goods they have previously purchased and subsequently sold. For otherwise there would be great shortage in some areas. For merchants transport what is abundant in one area to another place where the same thing is in short supply. Therefore merchants can legitimately receive the price of their labour and carriage and the expenses over and above what they paid when they purchased the goods.[37]

This was a reassuring message for confessors to communicate to their tradesmen penitents, even if it was hedged about by the reservation that the seller's margin should not exceed fifty per cent of the just price of the goods.

Thomas was a secular clerk and a canon of Salisbury when he completed his book for the guidance of confessors shortly before the Lateran Council of 1215. His careful justification of commercial profit reflected the teaching on the subject then prevalent in the schools. It was this that the friars applied in their confessional practice. 'Fairs,' observed Humbert of Romans, 'exist by divine providence, for no country is so self-sufficient that it does not need the goods of another country.'[38] Chobham's justification of profit margins was echoed by the Dominican William Peraldus in his *Summa de Vitiis et Virtutibus*, a popularisation of moral theology that was widely read in the later middle ages.[39] Nevertheless, the prevalent note struck by

---

37. *Thomae de Chobham Summa Confessorum*, ed. F. Broomfield (Analecta Namurcensia 25, Louvain–Paris 1968), pp. 301–2. This argument was adopted by the canonists, see *c6. X iii. 17*; J.W. Baldwin, 'The medieval theories of the Just Price' in *Transactions of the American Philosophical Society* n.s. 49 (Philadelphia 1959), pp. 22–3, 43–4; see also the discussion of Lester K. Little, *Religious Poverty and the Profit Economy in Medieval Europe* (1978), pp. 177–8.
38. *De Eruditione Praedicatorum*, pp. 561–2.
39. 'Notandum est quod negotiatio bona est in se et hominibus necessaria': *Summa de Vitiis et Virtutibus* (Antwerp 1587) II p. 46. On the popularity of this work see A. Dondaine, 'Guillaume Peyraut: vie etœuvres': *AFP* 18 (1948), pp. 162–236.

Mendicant preaching to commercial communities is one of warning. Peraldus's approval of trade is qualified by the observation that merchants are much given to lying, perjury and theft. Humbert allows that trade is usually without sin, but warns his hearers against taking excessive profits out of avarice, fraudulent dealing and contracts involving usury. The friars were not apostles of a new commercial morality.

Their pastoral mission was not confined to preaching. An equally important part of it, though one less accessible to the historian, was the hearing of confessions. 'There are some preachers who totally refuse to hear confessions,' wrote Humbert disapprovingly, 'these are like farmers who are glad to sow, but are unwilling to reap any harvest.'[40] It was the aim of the evangelical preacher to move his hearers to contrition for their sins and so to confess them. This was an area in which the friars had conspicuous success. They were much in demand by the laity as confessors and spiritual directors both in the towns and in royal and aristocratic courts. Several factors explain this success. For a lay person, the ministry of a friar offered a welcome channel of escape from the embarrassment and discouragement of having to confess to his local parish priest, who knew too much about him and who might be personally hostile or perhaps simply uneducated and ignorant. Bishops' registers of the later middle ages record numerous concessions to lay petitioners of the right to resort to a confessor of their own choosing. It is probable that in most of these cases the desired alternative to the petitioner's parish priest was a friar.

The popularity of the friars as confessors can be partly explained by the fact that they received intensive training for the role. Every Dominican priory contained a lector who gave the brethren regular instruction in the theology and practice of penance, using the approved manual of Raymond of Penaforte. But the phenomenon was more complex than that. Enemies of the Mendicants accused them of letting their penitents off too lightly, especially where a generous thank-offering was to be expected:

> He was an esy man to yeve penaunce
> Ther as he wiste to hav a good pitaunce.

40. *De Eruditione Praedicatorum* II, p. 79.

Chaucer's gibe expressed a sentiment that was widespread among the secular clergy of the fourteenth century. Yet it was a half-truth, the product of misunderstandings aggravated by a century of bitter polemic between the Mendicants and their secular colleagues.

The practice of the confessional was being quietly transformed by a nascent science of casuistry or applied moral theology which was promoted in the schools. In the hands of the early thirteenth-century masters such as Robert Curzon, Thomas of Chobham and William of Auxerre, the analysis of virtue, sin and human motivation achieved a refinement that was beginning to make the old Penitentials look obsolete.[41] The superior skill of the friars in the delicate art of the confessional derived from these advances made by the schoolmen. They were the practitioners of a gentler and more humane system, which sought to escape from the strait-jacket of the traditional Penitentials with their graded tariff of sins and punishments, and gave greater weight to the circumstances and intentions of the penitent. It was a practice that was obviously well adapted to the spiritual needs of the more educated and more complex people to be found among towndwellers. But it was regarded with suspicion by traditionalists, and it easily lent itself to misunderstanding and misrepresentation.

The ministry of the friars to the towns of Europe achieved great success because they brought new and better pastoral skills to the task and because they offered lay people a fulfilment of their religious aspirations that seemed to be denied them by the traditional assumptions of monastic theology. But however welcome their message may have been, the impact it made owed much to the idealism of the messengers. The voluntary poverty and self-imposed destitution that identified the early Mendicants with the humblest and most deprived sections of the population, in loud contrast to the careerism and ostentation of the secular clergy and the corporate wealth and exclusiveness of the monasteries, moved the conscience and touched the generosity of commercial communities.

41. The analysis of virtue and motivation by the Paris masters received magisterial treatment from O. Lottin, *Psychologie et morale aux XIIe et XIIIe siècles* vol. 3 (Louvain 1949), pp. 329–535.

Chapter 7

THE CAPTURE OF THE SCHOOLS

'At the schools of Oxford, where I am at present,' wrote Brother Jordan of Saxony, 'the Lord has given us hopes of a good catch.'[1] The friars won recruits everywhere, but their favoured hunting grounds were the university towns of Europe. In the fourteenth century, the lamentations of the University of Oxford bore unwilling testimony to the success of this long-tried strategy. The Congregation of Masters complained that the rich were becoming shy of sending their children to the schools for fear of losing them to the friars: 'It is commonly said, and we have learned from experience, that noble persons of this kingdom, gentlemen, and even those of common birth desist from sending their sons or relatives or others dear to them to the university in their youth, when they would make most progress in the primary stages of learning, because they are very fearful that the friars will entice them into joining the Mendicant Orders.'[2]

A policy of recruitment from the academic population was one thing; entry to the universities was another. Dominic had recognised at an early stage that his Preachers would need a theological training that only the schools could offer; and in the decade following the death of St Francis the demands of their mission pushed the Friars Minor along the same road. Both orders were impelled by their vocation to become participants in the new scholastic world of the universities. There they attracted the intellectual élite of their age, and succeeded

1. *Beati Iordani de Saxonia Epistulae*, ed. A. Walz *MOFPH* XXIII (1951), pp. 19–20.
2. *Statuta Antiqua Universitatis Oxoniensis*, ed. Strickland Gibson (1931), p. 164.

127

so brilliantly that from the middle of the thirteenth century Mendicant schoolmen dominated the study of Western theology.

The initial problem facing both orders was how to provide lectors – teachers, that is, competent to lecture to the brethren on the Bible and give them instruction in systematic theology. If the friars were to receive the intellectual preparation needed for preaching and hearing confessions, every friary would have to be a school. But theologians were in short supply and took a long time to produce. Most of the Bachelors and Masters recruited from the classrooms in the early years were arts men. They were well equipped to embark upon the study of theology, and they brought with them in many cases an interest in natural science that became a distinctive mark of Mendicant scholarship; but they did not meet the immediate need for teachers of theology. To solve this problem the friars at Paris and Oxford at first attended lectures given by secular masters of the university who were already regent – that is, actively conducting schools – in the faculty of theology.

At Paris, the friars dispatched by St Dominic were received with enthusiasm by members of the university. In 1218 they obtained the hospice of Saint-Jacques on the left bank – the house that was to be made famous by the teaching of Aquinas and a series of leading schoolmen – and secured the services of a secular master of theology, the Englishman John of St Albans, who lectured to them on the Bible.[3] Master John held his classes in the friary, and they were open to secular students as well as to the brethren; so from the outset the school in the Dominican house was a public school of the university, being conducted by a member of the magistral corporation. He was followed after some years by another English theologian, Master John of St Giles. One of the students of the latter was Roland of Cremona, who had entered the order at Bologna as a fully-fledged Master of Arts. By 1229 Roland was ready to incept as a Master in the theology faculty. He was the first friar to do so, and he inaugurated a chair that was thereafter to be occupied by an unbroken series of Dominican theologians for the rest of the century.

We must remember that in the thirteenth century the

3. *Chartularium* I pp. 101–2: cf. P. Glorieux, *Répertoire des maîtres en théologie de Paris au XIII* siècle* (Paris 1933), p. 274.

University of Paris, like other medieval universities, had little or nothing in the way of buildings or immobile plant. The academic community was scattered in borrowed accommodation on the left bank of the Seine and on the bridges. Students lived in rented rooms in the houses of the townspeople; a mere handful had places in endowed hospices like the Dix-Huit. Congregations of the faculties, which regulated the curriculum and prescribed courses, used the churches of the town or sometimes the taverns for their meetings. Lectures were given and disputations were held in rooms hired by individual masters for the purpose. It was not until the fourteenth century that the Arts Masters of the English and Picard Nation acquired a tumble-down property in the rue du Fouarre for their schools. Thus masters using the houses of the friars for their schools were doing nothing out of the ordinary.

A year after Roland of Cremona graduated and began to teach, the school of Saint-Jacques received an academic windfall in the shape of a spectacular conversion, which gave it a second foothold in the university faculty of theology. Doctors or Masters (the terms were interchangeable) of theology were under a statutory obligation to deliver university sermons on days specified by the calendar. In September 1230 Master John of St Giles fulfilled this obligation by preaching at Saint-Jacques and chose for the theme of his sermon the evangelical counsels. In the course of it he pointed to the Friars Preachers as the best living exemplars of the Gospel teaching. At this point he interrupted his discourse, left the pulpit, and requested the Master-General, Jordan of Saxony, who was present, to admit him to the order. His request granted, he returned to the pulpit wearing the habit of a friar and finished his sermon.[4]

Whatever the impact of this carefully staged performance upon his audience, it was more than a theatrical demonstration. The General dispensed John from the period of noviciate and allowed him to take his vows immediately, so enabling him to continue teaching in the schools without a break. By this stratagem, which vividly illustrates the place of learning in the Dominican Order of priorities, the Friars Preachers

---

4. M.M. Davy, *Les sermons universitaires parisiens de 1230–31* (Paris 1931), p. 134.

gained a second chair in the faculty of theology and retained it by training a succession of masters.

The Minorities entered the universities more slowly, perhaps hindered by the warnings of their founder. 'O Paris,' Brother Giles lamented, 'thou hast destroyed Assisi.'[5] To the elders, now living in retirement, it seemed that the misgivings of Francis on the subject of higher learning had proved prophetic. Something of the innocence and humility of the primitive Franciscan fraternity had been lost in the process of converting the Friars Minor into a student order. But the leaders of a new generation, like John Parenti and Haymo of Faversham, recognised that the change was imperative if the order was to fulfil its pastoral mission. Hugh of Die, the fiery Provençal, the expositor of Joachim's vision, argued that no one was better fitted to expound the Gospel than the university master who was also a friar.[6]

The Franciscans made their first settlement in the Paris region at Saint Denis. It was only in 1230 that, with the help of the bishop and Blanche of Castile, the Queen Regent, they acquired a house within the city near the abbey of Saint-Germain-des-Prés. The new settlement was evidently intended to be a house of studies, but the early teaching arrangements there are obscure. The order already possessed at least one competent theologian in Haymo of Faversham, the future Minister-General, but there is no record of his having taught at Paris. It was not until the English theologian Alexander of Hales sought admission to the order in or about the year 1236[7] that the Franciscans had a master of their own in the faculty of theology. Alexander was already a regent master and a scholar of eminence when he took the habit. By continuing to teach without interruption until another friar, Jean de

---

5. There are various versions of this saying, cf. *Dicta Beati Aegidii Assisiensis* (Quaracchi 1905), p. 91, and *Chronica XXIV Generalium Ordinis Minorum* (*Analecta Franciscana* III, Quaracchi 1897), p. 86.

6. *Hugh of Digne's Rule Commentary*, ed. David Flood (Spicilegium Bonaventurianum XIV, Grottaferrata 1979), p. 187.

7. There is some doubt about the date of Alexander's admission to the Friars Minor. Glorieux in *Répertoire* II, p. 15, assigns it to 1231 on the strength of Roger Bacon's assertion that it occurred after the resumption of the University of Paris following the great dispersal of 1229–31; but he appears still holding the archdeaconry of Coventry on 12 August 1235: Calender of Patent Rolls 1232–47, p. 116, cited by J.C. Russell, *Dictionary of Writers of Thirteenth-Century England* (1936), pp. 13–14.

la Rochelle, was ready to succeed him, he ensured that the chair at the Franciscan school stayed in the possession of the order.

At Oxford the Dominicans obtained their first regent in theology in a similar way. A party of thirteen of them dispatched by St Dominic had made their first settlement in the city in 1221. Escorted across the Channel by the bishop of Winchester, Peter des Roches, they had declined Archbishop Langton's invitation to stay in Canterbury, and they had similarly declined the offer of a house in London; they were clearly under instructions to proceed to the university town, which was the goal of their journey. Their party included a lector. Who else provided them with teaching in the early years is unknown. It was the admission to the order of Robert Bacon, already a regent in theology, in or about 1229 that gave them their first chair in the faculty.[8] As had been done with John of St Giles, Bacon was dispensed from the noviciate so that he could continue to teach.

The first party of Friars Minor, consisting initially of two Englishmen, arrived at Oxford in late October 1224. After a brief period as guests of the Dominicans, they acquired a house in the parish of St Ebbe's in the south-west corner of the city. In the year 1229–30 they gained possession of a larger property, where the Provincial, Agnellus of Pisa, decided to open a school. This decision was probably the outcome of events at both Paris and Oxford. The Great Dispersal of the University of Paris following the riot of 1229 had forced a number of English scholars to return home. Among them were friars who had entered the order at Paris. These had to be accommodated and their theological education had to be continued. In the same year Jordan of Saxony visited Oxford, and his preaching to the university brought an influx of recruits, including some bachelors and masters, into the Franciscan community as well as into his own order. These new arrivals offered a reservoir of educated men ready to embark upon the study of theology. In time they would supply the lectors needed by the rapidly growing English province.

To begin with they were taught by a series of secular

8. On Bacon's antecedents and the Dominican school at Oxford see Beryl Smalley, 'Robert Bacon and the early Dominican school at Oxford': *TRHS* 4th ser. 30 (1948), pp. 1–19; W.A. Hinnebusch, *The Early English Friars Preachers* (Rome 1951), pp. 360–1.

masters of the university. Agnellus achieved a remarkable *coup* by securing for his new academic flock the services of Robert Grosseteste, a senior theologian and one of the greatest and most original of the schoolmen, who had some years earlier been the head of the Oxford schools.[9] Grosseteste had a profound empathy for the Mendicant ideal, and after his election to the see of Lincoln in 1235 had removed him from the schools, he continued to be a powerful friend and patron of the Friars Minor. Eccleston names three other secular masters who lectured to the Oxford Franciscans in succession after the departure of Grosseteste. This arrangement continued until the first of the friars to occupy a chair, Adam Marsh, incepted as a master in the theology faculty in 1243 or 1245.[10]

Adam had been a Master of Arts. A well-to-do cleric and a nephew of the late royal chancellor and bishop of Durham, he had thrown up a promising ecclesiastical career to join the Friars Minor in the year 1232–3. The length of time between his reception into the order and his inception as a doctor of theology reflects the length of the preparation demanded for graduation in theology. In the first half of the thirteenth century the course requirements were only gradually being formulated. The practice of Oxford closely followed that of Paris, where many of the early Oxford masters had previously studied and taught. The earliest Paris statue on the subject, which was a decree made by the cardinal legate Robert Courçon, when he visited the university in 1215, required a minimum of eight years of study before inception.[11] An Oxford statute drawn up before 1253 decreed that a student of theology must not presume to act as a respondent in the disputations of the masters – an obligatory academic exercise on the way to graduation – until he has heard lectures for at least six years. Then, having achieved the status of bachelor, he was required to have lectured on a book of the Bible and a book of

9. Not all agree about the dates of Grosseteste's headship of the schools. Some place it in 1214–16, see C.H. Lawrence, 'The Origins of the Chancellorship at Oxford' in *Oxoniensia* 41 (1976), pp. 316–23. R.W. Southern, however, assigns it to the years after 1230 in *The History of the University of Oxford* vol. I, ed. J. Catto (1984), pp. 30–6.
10. On the problem of dating Adam's inception see C.H. Lawrence, 'The Letters of Adam Marsh and the Franciscan school at Oxford': *JEH* 42 No. 2 (1991), pp. 218–38.
11. *Chartularium* I, p. 41.

Lombard's *sentences* in order to qualify for the master's licence.[12] All this presupposed a course of nine years.

Adam was the first friar to lecture to the Oxford school of his order and the first of a series of Franciscans who were at the same time lectors to the brethren and regent masters in the university. He continued to teach until 1250, when the pressure of public duties forced him to stand down. His regency, which coincided with that of the Dominican Richard Fishacre at Oxford and that of Albertus Magnus at Paris and Cologne, inaugurated an extraordinary period of intellectual history in which, thanks to a brilliant constellation of talent, the friars dominated the teaching and writing of theology in the universities of Europe. The Dominicans and Franciscans, followed after 1260 by the Carmelites, Austin Friars and Crutched Friars, founded houses of higher studies in other universities owning a faculty of theology, like Cambridge, and also in several cities that had not yet acquired a faculty of the theology such as Cologne, Toulouse and Bologna.

The early achievements had been made possible by the recruitment of numbers of men who had already graduated in the arts. For the arts course, as it had taken shape at Paris and Oxford by the beginning of the thirteenth century, had become an indispensable grounding for the would-be theologian. Literary studies had been extruded from it by the pressure of new sciences. What it offered was an intensive training in the Aristotelian logic, which supplied the vocabulary and method of scholastic theology. But the Mendicant Orders followed a well-worn monastic tradition in regarding the arts as a mundane secular diversion, a regrettable if unavoidable staging-post on the way to the study of the Scriptures, which were the proper study of those who had renounced the world and which equipped the missionary for his task: 'let them not study in the books of the pagans and the philosophers though they look at them for a time; let them not learn the secular sciences.[13] This grudging permission of the early Dominican statutes in effect debarred friars from attending the arts schools in the universities; and the other orders of friars adopted the same policy. This meant that recruits who had no yet embarked upon the arts course had to

12. Strickland Gibson, *Statuta Antiqua*, p. 48.
13. *Constitutiones Antique Ordinis Fratrum Predicatorum*, ed. H. Denifle *ALKG* I, p. 22.

be provided with the necessary instruction in the houses of their order. Initially this was one of the responsibilities of the lectors; but in the course of time all the Mendicant Orders followed the practice pioneered by the Dominicans, creating specialist schools of logic and natural philosophy for each province. The general chapter of the Carmelites, meeting at Bordeaux in 1294, decreed that special schools for the arts curriculum should be established in England and Germany, in addition to those already existing at Paris, Toulouse and Montpellier. These, though, were internal schools which did not admit secular clergy or outsiders.

. . .

CONFRONTATION IN THE SCHOOLS

This refusal to allow their men to take the arts course was contrary to established university practice, and it offered a point of attack by their secular colleagues in the faculty. The secular masters were increasingly concerned at the encroachment of the friars upon their academic preserve. The opening of more schools of theology by Mendicant masters, the originality of their teaching, and their attraction for many of the ablest students, posed a serious challenge if not a threat to their secular colleagues. At Paris this incipient rivalry for position in an important but relatively small scholastic market burst into a violent confrontation in 1252–3. At Oxford it came to a head in the spring of 1253, when the Franciscan Thomas of York, a protégé of Adam Marsh, applied for the doctoral licence in theology. The faculty sought to block his inception, ostensibly on the grounds that no man might incept in a higher faculty unless he had previously graduated in arts, which Thomas had not done.

After the chancellor had set up a committee to consider the case, the faculty permitted Thomas to incept, but it went on to enact a statute disqualifying for the future anyone from incepting in theology who had not graduated in arts.[14] The statute did not necessarily debar the friars from the doctorate, as it allowed the university to dispense from the requirement by an act of special grace. But, as was obvious to Adam Marsh who refused his assent to the rule, it provided the university with an instrument with which it could control the

14. Strickland Gibson, *Statuta Antiqua*, p. 49.

number of friars admitted to regency in theology at any one time. This démarche by the Oxford theologians was probably inspired by what their colleagues at Paris had done the previous year. There the seculars had enacted a restrictive statute, limiting each religious house to a single school and a single regent master.[15] It was a direct challenge to the appropriation of two chairs of theology by the Dominicans.

The houses of study set up by the friars in university towns and a few comparable scholastic centres were the pinnacles of the extraordinary educational edifice devised, as we have seen, by the Dominicans, and copied by the other Mendicant Orders.[16] These were the general schools, the *studia generalia*, to which was sent the intellectual *crème de la crème* from every province – the men who had been sifted through the net of the specialised provincial schools of logic, natural philosophy and theology. Among them Paris held a unique position which reflected its status as the leading theological school of the Church. Every Dominican province had the right to send three men, and every Franciscan province to send two, to Paris. It was the responsibility of the student's province of origin to supply him with the books he needed for the course. In each order the Parisian school was subject to the control of the general chapter and the oversight of the General, who reserved the right to decide which of the brethren was to be presented for the doctoral licence, and who was to proceed to the grade of bachelor to lecture on the *Sentences*.

This articulated system of advanced education with its hierarchy of schools made the order a kind of disseminated university. Under the direction of his superiors the individual friar, whether he was a student or a teacher, moved from house to house and from province to province in pursuit of learning. The general school thus housed a cosmopolitan community. Its primary and continuing function was to educate lectors for the friaries; but it quickly acquired a much wider role than that. In theology as in other disciplines,

15. *Chartularium* I, pp. 226–7.
16. See chapter 4 above. Not all the Mendicant *studia generalia* were in university towns but all were in cities with a significant scholastic tradition. Thus Cologne was designated a general school for the German province of the Dominicans in 1248, a century before the city acquired a university. The Carmelites designated London, not Oxford, as the general school for the English province of the order.

advanced teaching and original scholarship march hand in hand. Each feeds the other. The general schools of the Mendicants offered the opportunity for independent inquiry and creative scholarship. They represented the belief of the men who governed the orders that the disinterested pursuit of truth was one of the highest forms of the Christian vocation.

Their commitment to learning explains the success of the friars in attracting so many of the best minds of the thirteenth century. Compared with the schools of the seculars, the system of the Mendicants had important advantages besides those of superior organisation. In the secular schools men taught for a few years and moved on. University teaching was not regarded as a career for life. The pressing need to acquire a benefice, to repay debts to patrons, the expectation of a career in the higher echelons of church or state, constantly drew men away from the schools in early middle-life. But when a man became a friar he opted out of the race for preferment. At the schools, free from the pressures of secular ambition and the struggle for livelihood, he was able to pursue scholarship with a sense of detachment hardly open to his secular colleagues. If he was successful, he might be allowed to spend his whole life in the scholastic world, lecturing at one or another of the higher schools of his order. These were propitious conditions for original intellectual work. They go some way towards explaining the fact that in the thirteenth century, the classical age of scholastic theology, it was the friars who produced the leading scholars and the most influential books.

Normally a Mendicant master would not conduct his school as a regent in the university for more than two or three years. The limitation imposed by the faculty on the number of chairs tenable by religious, combined with the need to allow younger colleagues a chance to incept, made it desirable for him to stand down. But he would then be assigned to schools elsewhere or be involved in the government of his order. Exceptionally he might be allowed a fallow period, freed from teaching, to complete written work, or even be recalled for a second period of regency in the university where he had incepted.

This variegated and flexible pattern of academic life is illustrated by the career of Thomas Aquinas. As a young man of nineteen or twenty, he joined the Order of Preachers at Naples, and shortly afterwards he was sent to study under Albertus Magnus at Paris and Cologne. In 1256 he incepted as a master in the Paris faculty and taught at the school of Saint-Jacques for three years ending in 1259, when an English friar, William of Alton, was ready to succeed him in the chair. He then returned to the province of Rome from which he had been sent. After a period of two years, spent probably at his home priory of San Domenico at Naples,[17] he was assigned as lector to the priory of Orvieto. Then in September 1265 the general chapter directed him to set up a school in Rome at Santa Sabina for friars of the Roman province. He taught at Santa Sabina for two years and was then assigned as lector to the priory of Viterbo, and while there he served as Master of the Sacred Palace at the Curia during the papal residence in the city. In 1269 he was brought back to Paris for a second regency, which lasted until 1272. Then, after presiding over the inception of his successor, Brother Romano Orsini, he returned to Italy to set up a general school of the order at Naples.

Several items of his huge literary output were written at Paris under the stimulus of scholastic controversy, but it is significant that the two greatest of his works were completed elsewhere and over an extended period of time. Thus the *Summa contra Gentiles*, a large-scale apologia for Christianity designed to controvert the objections raised by Jews and Muslims, was begun at Paris, but completed in 1263 during his residence at Naples. Of his *Summa Theologiae*, the huge synthesis of doctrine, the most famous of his works, which was to become the classical text-book of the Dominican schools in the later middle ages, the first part was begun at Rome and continued at Viterbo, the second part was composed during his second Paris regency of 1269–72, and the third and last part was finished a year later at Naples. The text was, in fact, incomplete when he laid aside his pen on 6 December 1273. 'I can write no more,' he told his astounded secretary, 'it all seems to me like a bit of straw.' Those appointed to the office of lector were normally assigned another friar to provide secretarial assistance. The great mass of written work left by Aquinas and the other Mendicant schoolmen, the fruit of academic leisure and freedom from material anxieties, is testimony as much to the strength and stimulus of the educational system that supported them as to their own creative genius.

17. There is some uncertainty about his whereabouts in this phase of his career. I follow the chronology of his career and writings established by J.A. Weisheipl, *Friar Thomas d'Aquino, his Life, Thought and Works* (1975).

. .

AUTHORITY AND METHOD IN THE SCHOOLS

To appreciate the impact the friars made upon the world of learning we have to understand the methods used in the schools. Medieval teaching was based upon the study of authoritative texts. The master expounded the text in his lectures; problems raised by it formed the subject of disputations – formal debates presided over by the master and conducted according to recognised rules. Each faculty had its own authorities or prescribed set-books. The artists had the logical and scientific books of Aristotle; the law doctors of Bologna lectured on the Code and Digest of Justinian; and the canonists lectured on Gratian and the supplementary books of papal decretals. For the theologians the authoritative text was the Latin Vulgate Bible. The authority of the inspired text was such that Biblical exegesis was regarded as the fundamental task of theology, and the title of 'master of the sacred page' was the recognised synonym for an academic theologian.

In the course of time, the text of the Bible, like that of the Justinian corpus, acquired an adjunct in the form of a standard exposition or commentary called the *glossa ordinaria* – the standard gloss – which encrusted the text: in the manuscripts it was written in the margins and between the lines to which it referred. It too was discussed in lectures and referred to in scholastic commentaries. So the student attending lectures on the Bible needed to take to the classroom both the text of the book which was the subject of the course and its accompanying gloss. Often a written record of the master's commentary was made in the classroom by a bachelor or one of his senior pupils and this, after the master himself had corrected it, was passed to the university stationers for copying and circulation.

By the time the friars opened their schools, Paris had already established its reputation as the leading school of theology. Even the xenophobic Matthew Paris acknowledged it to be 'the first school of the Church'. In the last forty years of the twelfth century a succession of famous teachers, beginning with Peter Comestor and ending with Peter the Chanter and Stephen Langton, had made it the promised land of the Biblical theologian. These men, who have been described as the 'biblical moral school',[18] left as a memorial of their work a huge number of commentaries on both the Old and New Testaments. One of the distinctive features of their teaching was their fondness for using lectures on the Bible as a medium for practical moral instruction. In their commentaries they display an awareness of their responsibility to prepare their pupils not only for the chancellor's examination and the magistral licence, but also for their future role as pastors and rulers of the Church.

A major hindrance to further advance was the state of the Vulgate text. Centuries of unco-ordinated copying had produced as many variant readings as there were manuscripts. Students coming to Paris from all parts of Europe were bewildered by the innumerable variations between one text and another. The so-called Paris Bible was an attempt by the university stationers to remedy this situation by reproducing a standardized text for use in the classroom. Among its most useful features were the fixation of the order of the various books of the Old and New Testaments in a sequence that was logical and became permanent, and the division of each book into numbered chapters of manageable length according to their content. This arrangement of the text, originally devised for easy reference in the lecture-room, appears to have been the work of Langton in the last years of his teaching career before he was whisked away in 1206 to be made a cardinal; and with some modifications it remains that of the Bible at the present day. But the version the stationers had chosen to multiply for the sake of uniformity was a corrupt text, littered with interpolations. It was, as the Franciscan Roger Bacon complained, a purely commercial venture undertaken by 'illiterate and married men', who lacked the learning necessary to produce an accurate text. Off-the-cuff corrections made by lecturers only worsened the situation.[19]

Given the vast number of manuscripts in circulation, the establishment of an accurate version of St Jerome's translation was a monumental task. The friars embarked on the enterprise at Paris in the 1230s by producing a series of aids to textual

18. By M. Grabmann in the first place in *Geschichte der scholastichen Methode* (Freiburg) II, pp. 467ff; quoted by Beryl Smalley, *The Study of the Bible in the Middle Ages* 2nd edn (1952), pp. 197ff.

19. *Opus Minus* in *Fratris Rogeri Bacon Opera Hactenus Inedita*, ed. J.S. Brewer (RS 1859), p. 333.

study. The Dominicans led the way, prompted no doubt by their experience of Bible-punching with heretics. The general chapter of 1236 decreed that all the Bibles in use in the order should be standardized in accordance with the corrections prepared in the French province.[20] It was a co-operative effort by a group of friars working at the house of Saint-Jacques, directed in the early stages by Hugh of St Cher, who had incepted in the Dominican chair in 1230. They produced a series of *correctoria* – lists of variants from the Paris text – which became a standard part of the student's equipment. The Franciscans followed in the path pioneered by the Preachers. One of the most learned and widely used of the *correctoria* was the work of a Franciscan, William de la Mare, who was regent at Paris in the 1270s.

William was a Hebrew scholar, who compiled a lexicon of Greek and Hebrew words used in the Bible with their Latin equivalents. He was the answer to Roger Bacon's complaint that few Western scholars had any knowledge of the Biblical languages, without which it was impossible to establish an authentic text. In his characteristic fashion Bacon exaggerated. Several twelfth-century scholars had shown an interest in the Hebrew Scriptures and displayed an acquaintance with rabbinics, and in the thirteenth century an increasing number of scholars were acquiring a rudimentary working knowledge of Greek and Hebrew. The friars were at the forefront of this development. For Greek they had the advantage of contacts through their houses at Constantinople. Hebrew could be learned from Jewish converts. The Dominican team working with Hugh of St Cher had the linguistic knowledge to 'improve' or correct Jerome's Vulgate text by reference to words in the original Greek and Hebrew. It was a growing interest in ancient languages, promoted by the friars, that culminated in 1312 in the call of the Council of Vienne for the establishment of salaried chairs of Greek, Hebrew, Arabic and Chaldaic, at the universities of Paris, Bologna, Oxford and Salamanca.

Besides *correctoria* the team of Hugh of St Cher produced a Bible concordance, a useful index for both the preacher and the disputant, and the first of its kind. But the Mendicants' contribution to Biblical studies was not confined to the provision of technical aids. They lectured on the Bible, and some of

20. Reichert I, p. 9.

their commentaries acquired the status of classics. One such was Bonaventure's on Ecclesiastes, an authority quoted by all his successors. The huge commentary compiled by Hugh of St Cher, covering the entire Bible and incorporating the glosses of the masters of the twelfth and thirteenth centuries, remained in continuous use in the classrooms of the later middle ages and was among the earliest to be printed.[21]

Influential though their work on the Bible was, the most significant innovation the Mendicants made in the theological curriculum lay in a different direction. The application of the Aristotelian logic or dialectic gave rise to a form of theological inquiry which used the *Questio* as its method. The *Questio* was the record of a debate, actual or fictitious – scholastic writers generally used it as a purely literary device. It originated in the problems raised by the teacher and debated in the course of commenting on the Bible text. But with the growth of theological speculation, the lecture devoted to a particular book of the Bible seemed an unduly restrictive and inadequate framework for a systematic treatment of doctrinal questions. So independent disputations and separate lectures on doctrine took their place in the curriculum alongside Bible lectures. But for the medieval scholar, lecturing without an authoritative text to comment was unthinkable. This need for an authority was supplied by the *Sentences* of Peter Lombard, himself a schoolman, who had been elected bishop of Paris in 1159.

Among other collections of Sentences compiled in the twelfth century, Lombard's work commended itself to the masters who followed on account of its completeness, its cautious orthodoxy and the clarity of its plan. Like other such collections, it was an anthology of the thoughts or judgements (*sententiae*) of the Fathers on the dogmas of the Christian faith. It was divided into four books, the first of which dealt with the attributes of God, the second with creation, the third with the nature and work of Christ, and the fourth with the sacraments and the last things. It thus provided a coherent conspectus of Christian doctrine. It exemplified the early stages of the scholastic method: the author's preoccupation was to reconcile conflicts between his patristic and Biblical authorities by means of dialectical analysis. The work was

21. On Hugh of St Cher and his commentaries see Smalley, *Study of the Bible*, pp. 269–73. For the Bible concordance see R.H. and M.A. Rouse, 'The Verbal Concordance to the Scriptures': *AFP* 44 (1974), pp. 5–30.

unoriginal – the Lombard pillaged earlier collections of sources, including those of Abelard and Gratian, without acknowledgement[22] – and sometimes hesitant in its judgements. It lacked the speculative verve and penetration of Abelard; but its intellectual limitations themselves offered scope for magistral commentary. In the eyes of the Paris masters it had the additional merit that the Lombard's Trinitarian doctrine had received the express approval of the Fourth Lateran Council.

The adoption of the Lombard's *Sentences* as the authoritative course-book for teaching speculative theology was largely the result of its promotion by the masters of the Mendicant Orders. According to Roger Bacon, it was Alexander of Hales, while still a secular master in the early 1230s, who had introduced the practice adopted at Paris of giving public lectures on the *Sentences*.[23] The earliest Dominican masters, Roland of Cremona and Hugh of St Cher, had done the same. At Oxford the practice was introduced by the Dominican Richard Fishacre. His widely-read commentary on the *Sentences*, written 1240–5, was the first of its kind to emanate from the Oxford schools. It was followed a few years later by the first Franciscan commentary, which was the work of Richard Rufus of Cornwall.[24]

The elevation of the *Sentences* to the status of an authority, and with it the progressive application of dialectical analysis to the problems of theology, aroused misgiving in more conservative scholars. Bacon thought it compromised the unique authority of the Bible and deplored the excessive subtleties of the dialecticians. Fishacre's plan of lecturing on the *Sentences* during his regency evoked a famous remonstrance from Grosseteste. 'You are the builders of the house of God,' he reminded the Oxford masters. 'The foundation-stones of the building, of which you are the architects, are the books of the Prophets; also the Gospels and the books of the Apostles; no others than

22. For the antecedents and sources of Peter Lombard's *Sentences* see J. de Ghellinck, *Le mouvement théologique du XIIᵉ siècle* (Brussels & Paris 1948), pp. 230–9.
23. *Opus Minus*, pp. 328–9.
24. Fishacre's commentary on the *Sentences* was very influential and much quoted. It survives in several manuscripts, of which an edition is being prepared by an international team. For the commentary of Richard Rufus see P. Raedts, *Richard Rufus of Cornwall and the Tradition of Oxford Theology* (1987).

these can be used to lay the foundations.'[25] He went on to insist that the ordinary lectures delivered in the morning should be confined to commenting on the books of the Old and New Testaments. To do otherwise, he argued, was to depart from the example of the Fathers and the practice of the regent masters of Paris. For Grosseteste, theology was to be identified with exegesis of the Bible.

As bishop of Lincoln, he had jurisdiction over the university, which lay within the boundaries of his diocese. But despite his prestige as a scholar, there is no reason to think that the faculty of theology welcomed this attempt to dictate its teaching arrangements. In his belief that the Paris masters confined their lecturing to the Bible he was clearly out of date. The Dominicans, at any rate, refused to accept his prohibition without a fight. They obtained a rescript from Pope Innocent IV instructing the bishop of Lincoln to allow Brother Richard to give his ordinary lectures on the *Sentences* and urging the bishop to promote lectures of this type.[26] The new method promoted by the Mendicant masters was unstoppable. The Lombard's work became a standard part of the curriculum. At both Paris and Oxford, a bachelor was required to lecture on a chosen book of the *Sentences* in order to qualify for the magistral licence in theology. Lecturing on the Bible did not cease, but it was confined largely to exegetical comment. Questions of speculative theology were increasingly left to lectures on the *Sentences* and to the *questiones*, which circulated separately from the text. It was a form of specialisation that made possible the rise of theology as a science, based upon the rational exploration of the data of Revelation. It paved the way for the great *summas* – the compendia of doctrinal questions composed by leading schoolmen like Aquinas, Bonaventure and Giles of Rome.

25. *Roberti Grosseteste Epistolae*, ed. H.R. Luard (RS 1861), pp. 346–7.
26. G. Abate, 'Letterae secretae d'Innocenzo IV in una raccolta inedita del secolo XIII' in *Miscellanea Franciscana* 55 (1955), p. 347, no. 149; see discussion in C. H. Lawrence, 'The University in Church and State' in *History of the University of Oxford*, vol. I, p. 101.

. . .

INTELLECTUAL CRISIS

The major factor determining the activity of the schools was the new learning – the newly translated works of Greek and Arabic science and philosophy which poured into the West from Sicily and Spain in the last decades of the twelfth century. The schoolman's library, which had already included Aristotle's logical works, known collectively as the Organon, was now greatly enlarged by Latin versions of the *Metaphysics*, the *De Anima* (containing Aristotle's treatment of psychology), the *Physics*, and a wider range of lesser Aristotelian and pseudo-Aristotelian works on natural science – the so-called *libri naturales*. Besides these came the translations of the Arab commentators, Alfarabi, Avicenna and Averroes. Of these the most influential were the commentaries on the *De Anima*, the *Metaphysics* and the *Physics* by the twelfth-century Arab scholar from Cordova, Averroes, who was court philosopher to the Caliphs.

These works were gradually assimilated during the first thirty years of the thirteenth century by the teachers of the arts. Before long it became obvious that the new learning, which was of pagan origin, contained elements that were difficult if not impossible to reconcile with the Biblical account of creation and the Christian belief in divine providence and the immortality of the human soul. The first signals of impending crisis were emitted in 1210 by a synod presided over by the archbishop of Sens, Peter of Corbeil, whose ecclesiastical province contained the city and University of Paris. The synod condemned the works of Master David of Dinant to the flames, adjudging them to be heretical, and forbade lecturing on the *libri naturales* at Paris.[27] Five years later, the legate Cardinal Robert Courçon reiterated the condemnations of Sens in his statutes for the University of Paris, and forbade public lectures on the *De Anima*, the *Metaphysics* and the *libri naturales*.[28]

These early prohibitions went the way of all efforts to dam the course of independent thought and inquiry. The legate's statute appears to inhibit discussion of the problems raised by

27. *Chartularium* I, p. 70.
28. *ibid.* I, pp. 78–9.

the new science by banning the study of the essential texts. But in fact it did no such thing. In 1231 Pope Gregory IX issued two letters, one of which renewed the prohibition until such time as the offending books of Aristotle had been examined by a commission of masters and, if need be, expurgated of erroneous matter; the other letter instructed the chancellor of Paris to absolve from penalties all those masters who had in the meantime been lecturing on the books in question.[29] Nothing more is known of the expurgatory commission. Twenty-four years later all the banned texts appear among the set-books prescribed for study by students in the faculty of arts.[30]

The arts faculties of Paris and Oxford were the first to experience the impact of the new Aristotle and his Arabic commentators. The lapsing of ecclesiastical censures opened the way for the circulation of magistral commentaries and collections of *questiones* on the *Metaphysics*, the *De Anima* and the books of natural science. Among the earliest that survive are the commentaries of Roger Bacon, composed when he was teaching arts at Paris and before he took the Franciscan habit, and those attributed to Robert Kilwardby, the future Dominican head of the English province and archbishop of Canterbury. He too was regent in arts at Paris shortly before and after 1240. The commentaries of Adam of Buckfield, the harvest of his teaching at Oxford, date from the same period.

If the artists led the way, the theologians were quick to follow. Most of them had come to theology after qualifying for the master's licence in the faculty of arts, where they had been initiated into the new learning. Philip the Chancellor, William of Auvergne and Alexander of Hales, all of whom were regent in theology in the third decade of the century, all display acquaintance with the metaphysical and psychological doctrines of Aristotle.[31] But they were the pioneers. It was after the middle of the century, in the work of the great Mendicant doctors, that all the main features of Aristotle's philosophical system were absorbed into a creative synthesis with the Christian doctrines of God and Man to construct a Christian philosophy.

29. *ibid.* I, pp. 143–4.
30. *ibid.* I, pp. 277–8.
31. F. van Steenberghen, *The Philosophical Movement of the Thirteenth Century* (1955), pp. 75–8.

Beginning with Albertus Magnus and Thomas Aquinas, scholastic theologians not only employ the language and syllogistic method of the Aristotelian logic; they also accept the main features of Aristotle's analysis of the intellectual process, his metaphysical categories of being, act and potency, form and matter, and his physical model of the universe. It is also a striking fact that in the process of constructing a rational philosophy from a synthesis of Christian and pagan materials, they all use the commentaries of Averroes and Avicenna to elucidate Aristotle's texts. Aquinas, for instance, accepted without qualification Aristotle's analysis of the intellectual process. Following Aristotle, he held that the mind forms concepts by abstraction from the data of the senses – everything that exists in the mind has first existed in the senses. But in his *Summa Theologica*, when he comes to discuss cognition, his thoroughly Aristotelian analysis of the process is accompanied by a running argument with the interpretations of Averroes and Avicenna.[32]

The efforts of Aquinas and his pupils to use the Aristotelian system as the basis for a Christian philosophy, embracing both the natural order and the order of revealed truth, aroused mistrust in more conservative theologians. The Thomist synthesis was also in danger of subversion on the left by a group of more radical Aristotelians in the Paris arts faculty. These were the so-called Latin Averroists, a group of masters whose figurehead was Siger de Brabant. The term 'Averroists', which was fastened on them by Aquinas, has been criticised by modern scholars as misleading. The object of the group was to establish philosophy as an autonomous science without regard to its implications for revealed doctrine. They had drunk deeply of Aristotle and his Arab expositors to the point of drowning; there was, of course, much in both sources that was incompatible with Christian faith and which Aquinas had rejected, such as the eternity of the world, the impossibility of free will and the absence of divine providence. These and other heterodox tenets expounded by the masters were listed in a condemnation published in 1270 by the bishop of Paris, Stephen Tempier.[33]

Master Siger and his disciples had not renounced Christ-

32. *Summa Theologica* 1ª Q. 84 *passim*.
33. *Chartularium* I, pp. 486–7.

ianity. They were simply concerned to expound the natural model of the universe they found in Greek philosophy and science, and they saw no need to reconcile it with the dogmas of faith, an insouciance that brought down on their heads the accusation of 'double truth' or, as we should now say, of double-think. Several of the theses condemned by the bishop of Paris were derived from Aristotle, but one that was singled out for attack by the opponents of the school was originated by Averroes in his much quoted commentary on the *De Anima*. This was the proposition that the intellect was not a faculty of the soul, but a separate substance and that there existed only a single intellect for the entire human race, which was manifested in individuals, rather like a giant candle hidden behind a screen pierced by innumerable holes, creating an illusion of plurality where in fact there was only a single light.

The outbreak of heterodox rationalism in the arts faculty was of particular concern to Mendicant theologians. It appeared to call in question the very possibility of the synthesis between Greek philosophy and Christian doctrine that they had attempted to create. It threatened to declare a conflict between faith and reason. It was thus a challenge that brought into the field the leading exponents of the new theology, who were anxious to defend the tempered Aristotelianism that was the basis of their work. Foremost among them was Aquinas. Possibly it was the need to address this crisis that persuaded the superiors of his order to recall him to Paris in 1269 for a second period of regency. The following year he published his controversial broadside *On the Unity of the Intellect against the Averroists* attacking the thesis that Siger had taken from the commentary of Averroes. The basis of his refutation, he asserts, will be unaided reason – he will adduce no arguments from faith.[34] It was a fundamental principle of his theological system that the truths of faith and reason could not conflict. His central preoccupation in the treatise was to demonstrate that the idea of the unicity of the intellect was an error derived not from Aristotle, but from Averroes, who had misinterpreted his source.

It was evidently the same anxiety to save the essentials of

34. *Tractatus de Unitate Intellectus contra Averroistas*, ed. L.W. Keeler (Rome 1957), pp. 2–3, 80; transl. Beatrice H. Zedler, *Thomas Aquinas on the Unity of the Intellect against the Averroists* (Milwaukee 1968).

Aristotle for Christian orthodoxy that prompted him to embark in the last five years of his life upon a series of commentaries designed to cover the whole range of Aristotle's works. At his death in 1274 the plan was still uncompleted. Albertus Magnus, his master, had undertaken a similar enterprise some twenty years earlier. For both men it is probable that the primary intention was to provide an orthodox exegetical guide to the maestro for the benefit of their younger brethren who were studying the arts in the higher schools of their own order before proceeding to theology.

The Averroist crisis raised the perennial problem of the relationship between faith and reason. For the friars engaged in the controversy like Albertus, Aquinas and the Augustinian Giles of Rome, what was at stake was the possibility of a reconciliation in a rational theology, using the instruments of Greek philosophy and Greek science to explore the implications of the data provided by Revelation. By no means all their spiritual brethren approved of their method or shared their enthusiasm for Aristotle. In fact a number of the Aristotelian premisses adopted by Aquinas and his disciples came under sharp attack from more conservative theologians. Some of the most stubborn opponents of the new theology were Franciscans, but the opposition also included men of Aquinas's own order, like Kilwardby.

These scholars of the traditionalist school have been dubbed 'Augustinians', though the label over-simplifies a more complex situation. Augustine, the greatest of the Latin Fathers, was after all the common possession and the most frequently quoted authority of all schools of thought. Where the traditionalists parted company with the more thorough-going Aristotelians was in the area of epistemology and metaphysics. Thus Bonaventure, for instance, tempered the purely Aristotelian analysis of the process of knowing, which Aquinas embraced, with Augustine's neo-Platonic view that the mind apprehended universal ideas through divine illumination rather than by abstraction from the data of the senses.

The continuing spread of Averroist ideas among the Artists strengthened the rising suspicion of the traditionalists that the Aristotelian revolution was in danger of subverting Christian doctrine. The question that became the focus of particularly acrimonious debate was the nature of the association between soul and body. Aquinas explained the association in the terms of form and matter. A penny is an object consisting of matter – copper, in fact – having a specific form, namely that of a disk bearing the representation of a head and an inscription. Both form and matter are necessary to its being a penny, but it is the form that makes that particular matter what it is. In the same way, Aquinas followed Aristotle in arguing that man was a being composed of matter – his body – and form, which is his rational soul; both are necessary to his being, but it is the soul that gives the body its identity as the property of a human being. Created by God and immaterial, it informed and animated the matter of the human body. Although destined to survive the body it forms with it a single being.

As against this Aristotelian analysis of the soul and body complex, the traditionalists maintained that the soul, like all other terrestrial beings, was composed of form and matter as distinct from that of the body, which had a form and matter of its own. A man thus contained a plurality of forms. Aquinas rejected this conception on the ground that the notion of matter was not applicable to a spiritual being, which was incorruptible. Only corporeal beings comprised matter as well as form. A human being possessed only one substantial form – his soul.

The question became the subject of bitter controversy, which intensified after the death of Aquinas. The bishop of Paris, Stephen Tempier, was persuaded to intervene, and on 7 March 1277 he published an omnibus syllabus of errors containing 219 condemned propositions, which was aimed primarily at the Averroists of the arts faculty but which included a number of theses sustained by Aquinas.[35] Eleven days later, Archbishop Kilwardby visited Oxford and issued a condemnation of thirty propositions that were being mooted in the faculty of arts, and the list specifically included the doctrine of Aquinas on the unity of form.[36] Like most attempts at censoring ideas, the condemnations were counter-productive. Rather than stopping debate on the subject, they exacerbated it. The Thomist view of the unity of form in man continued to gain ground both at Paris and Oxford. The Dominicans closed ranks to defend the posthumous reputation of their foremost schoolman: the general chapter of 1278 dispatched envoys to

35. *Chartularium* I, pp. 543–58.
36. *ibid.* I, pp. 558–60.

England to seek out and punish brethren who were denigrating the works of their 'venerable doctor',[37] foreshadowing the decree of 1309 which adopted the theology of Aquinas as the official doctrine of the order.

At Paris a leading opponent of the Thomist thesis had been the Franciscan theologian John Pecham. In 1279 Kilwardby was removed from the English scene by his elevation to the cardinal bishopric of Porto, and Pecham succeeded him in the see of Canterbury. From his new eminence he determined to pursue the attack upon those who taught the Thomist doctrine of the unity of form, which he regarded as a pernicious error endangering the dogmas of faith. In 1284, in the course of a metropolitan visitation of Oxford, he reiterated the condemnation of the theses listed in Kilwardby's syllabus of prohibited propositions.[38] The provincial of the the Blackfriars, William Hothum, who shared the view of Aquinas, had intercepted the archbishop at Sonning and had tried to dissuade him from his purpose, but having failed to do so, he appealed to Rome against the prohibitions. The Dominicans, in fact, regarded this act of censorship by a Franciscan prelate as a direct attack upon the reputation of the man they were coming to venerate as their maestro, and Pecham had to defend himself against the charge of having maliciously stirred up enmity between the two orders of friars.[39]

By stigmatizing as heretical a philosophical thesis that was to be the orthodoxy of the following generation of schoolmen, Pecham had overreached himself. Neither his Oxford prohibitions nor his subsequent persecution of Richard Knapwell, a Dominican theologian who had boldly challenged Kilwardby's position on the plurality of forms, could stem the Aristotelian tide. But the controversy planted markers for the different routes to be followed by the Mendicant scholars of the next generation. While the Dominican school adhered to the essentials of Thomism, the leading masters of the Friars Minor, from Richard of Middleton to Duns Scotus, would be 'Augus-

---

37. Reichert I, p. 199.
38. *Annales Monastici* ed. H.R. Luard (RS 1864–9) IV, pp. 197–9. Rashdall, *Universities of Europe in the Middle Ages*, ed. F.M. Powicke and A.B. Emden 3 vols. (1936), III, pp. 122, 252; cf. the account of Pecham's censures in D.L. Douie, *Archbishop Pecham* (1952), pp. 272–301.
39. *Registrum Epistolarum Iohannis Peckham*, ed. C.T. Martin (RS 1885) III, pp. 868, 870–2.

tinian' in opposition to Thomist metaphysics and psychology, yet no less Aristotelian in the terminology and methods of discourse. In the thirteenth century Aristotle had been received into the Church, and his conversion was largely the work of the friars.

Chapter 8

THE COMPLAINT OF THE CLERGY

From the outset, relations between the friars and the secular clergy were fraught with ambiguity. In some places their settlement was greeted with mistrust, obstruction or even open hostility. It was to counter this that Honorius III issued a stream of papal letters commending the Friars Minor and the Preachers to the bishops of Christendom. The lead from the papacy had its effect. In Germany, France and England, the Mendicants were welcomed as helpers by a number of the more zealous and discerning prelates. When the Franciscans arrived at Hildesheim, Bishop Conrad summoned the clergy of the city to hear one of them preach. At Worms, the bishop and canons offered them the use of the cathedral to hold a provincial chapter, as the friars had no building of their own that was big enough. There were some like Grosseteste who, after he became bishop of Lincoln, wrote to the provincials of both the Dominicans and the Friars Minor, asking them to send him friars to preach and hear confessions on his diocesan visitations. But as the Mendicants expanded their pastoral activities, began building their own churches, and moved into the schools and universities, they came increasingly into collision with the interests of the secular clergy.

The bull *Nimis iniqua* of Gregory IX (1231) instructed the bishops to allow the friars almost unlimited freedom of action for the purpose of their pastoral mission. They now constituted a second force, independent of the established hierarchy, working alongside the secular clergy. Their success as popular preachers and confessors siphoned congregations away from parish churches, and with them, of course, went the flow of offerings and pious bequests, which were diverted into trust funds administered for the friars. In the cities, under the jealous eyes of the parish clergy, huge preacher churches began to rise, like S. Maria Novella in Florence and San Domenico in Bologna, built and embellished with frescoes at the expense of an enthusiastic bourgeoisie and paved with the monuments of the civic aristocracy. Many of the secular clergy now began to regard the friars as a threat to their status and livelihood. Bishops, who had at first welcomed them, felt misgivings as the shower of papal privileges emancipated the new evangelists from the control of the ecclesiastical hierarchy.

These anxieties were voiced by many visitors to the papal Curia. In 1245 the English Franciscan Adam Marsh, who had accompanied his friend Grosseteste to the Curia and stayed on for the Council of Lyons, wrote home to warn his provincial that many bishops were planning an onslaught upon the friars at the forthcoming council, with a view to curtailing their privileges or even securing their total abolition.[1] This threat failed to materialise. Probably it was headed off by Innocent IV, who favoured the Mendicants as valuable arms of papal policy.

.　.　.

ACADEMIC CONFRONTATION

Thwarted at the Council, the discontent of the secular clergy found an articulate voice among the masters of the University of Paris. Here the dispute began as a straightforward conflict of interests. Papal decree had limited the number of chairs or schools in the faculty of theology to twelve at any one time, three of which were reserved to canons of the cathedral. By the process we have seen, the Mendicants had gained control of three chairs, and the Franciscans were looking to gain a fourth by opening a second school for their members. The brilliant success of the Mendicant teachers necessarily reduced the opportunities open to the secular masters of the faculty. Even apart from the papal injunction, the length and expense of the theology course meant that the number of aspiring theologians was not big enough to sustain more than a limited number of schools. The friars were capturing too large a share of this restricted academic market.

In face of what they perceived to be a growing threat to

---

1. *Monumenta Franciscana*, ed. J.S. Brewer (RS 1858) I, p. 377.

their prospects, the regent masters in theology decided upon concerted action to curb the invasion of their territory by the Mendicants. In February 1252, they approved a statute ordaining that each religious order should be limited to a single school and a single regent master in the university. This ordinance, which would have involved the suppression of one of the schools conducted by the Dominicans, proved to be the opening salvo of a bitter struggle that continued for the following five years.

Although academic rivalry added fuel to the conflagration, the conflict, when it broke out, was more than a squabble over jobs. The Mendicant masters, teaching in their own schools on the left bank, were technically in the university, yet not of it. They tended to sit loose to their obligations towards the academic corporation. The flash-point came in the Lent of 1253. In the course of a street brawl, a student was killed by the city watch and four others were wounded and imprisoned. The university, in a hastily convened congregation, responded by a suspension of teaching and a threat to secede from the town unless it received immediate redress from the city authorities. But the friars refused to take part in the demonstration or to suspend teaching. They were therefore excommunicated and expelled from the university by their enraged colleagues. What had begun as an 'industrial dispute' now developed into a violent controversy, which brought into focus some of the deepest tensions and most revolutionary developments in the structure of the medieval Church.

The secular masters found a spokesman in William of Saint-Amour, a Burgundian scholar who had trained as a canonist before incepting in the faculty of theology and who enjoyed the security of prebends at Mâcon and Beauvais. He was entrusted with pleading the university's case against the friars at the papal Curia. To help him with this task, William was supplied with some unexpected ammunition from the opposing camp in the form of the book put out by Gerard of Borgo San Donnino, then a young bachelor at the Paris house of the Franciscans. Gerard had drunk deeply of the eschatological prophecies of Joachim of Fiore, and unlike Salimbene, he was to drown in them. His announcement that the third age of human history – the age of the Holy Ghost – had arrived, and his identification of Joachim's spiritual men of the new age with the friars, the poor, bare-footed people destined to replace the clergy of the previous dispensation, confirmed the darkest suspicions of the secular clergy. Gerard's essay in millennial fantasy dropped into the Paris dispute with the explosive force of a bomb falling into a quarrelsome duck-pond. It was passionately denounced by preachers from the city pulpits; and William and his colleagues triumphantly excerpted a list of heretical passages for delation to the Curia, to show that the Church's trust in the Mendicants had been misplaced.

The seculars had a brief success at the Curia. The sharp but legalistic mind of Innocent IV was persuaded that the position of the friars was a threat to the hierarchic structure of the Church, and despite the favour he had previously shown them, in November 1254 he published the bull *Etsi Animarum* which rescinded their privileges, including those of preaching and hearing confessions without the prior authorisation of the local bishops. But the triumph of the seculars was short-lived. Less than a month after pronouncing judgement Innocent died. His successor, Alexander IV, was none other than the Cardinal Protector of the Franciscan Order, Rainaldo di Segni, and he promptly rescinded the bull *Etsi Animarum*, and in the privilege *Quasi lignum vitae* of 14 April 1255 he restored and renewed the privileges of the Mendicants and commanded the University of Paris to readmit the Mendicants masters to their association.

In the year that followed, the attack upon the friars by William and his colleagues reached a new pitch of intensity. The masters used the pulpits of the city to enflame public opinion. Friars in the streets were pelted with mud and stones, and the Dominicans had to appeal to the king for protection of the convent of St Jacques against the threat of bombard-ment.[2] The verbal warfare was waged on parchment as well as in the pulpits and taverns of Paris. In 1256 William published a comprehensive attack upon the principles and privileges of the Mendicants in a polemical tract called *Concerning the Perils of the Last Days*.[3]

---

2. The sufferings of the friars at Paris were described by Humbert of Romans in a letter to the prior and brethren of Orleans: *Chartularium* I, pp. 309–13.

3. *De periculis novissimorum temporum*, ed. Edward Brown in *Fasciculus Rerum Expetendarum* (London 1690) II, pp. 20–2. For William's background and role in the controversy see M.-M. Dufeil, *Guillaume de Saint-Amour et la polémique universitaire parisienne 1250–59* (Paris 1972).

In this he did not confine his assault to the academic activities of the friars; he challenged their right to exercise any form of pastoral ministry. He took his stand on the theory that the diocesan and parochial structure of the Church was founded upon the mission of the Apostles, and was of divine ordinance. In this divine dispensation, the secular clergy alone were entrusted with the cure of souls, and this was something that no one, whether pope or anybody else, had authority to change. In support of his argument he appealed to the *Ecclesiastical Hierarchy* of the Pseudo-Dionysius, which divided Christians into two orders – those who perfect others (*ordo perficientium*), meaning bishops, priests and deacons, and the order of those to be perfected (*ordo perficiendorum*), being monks, lay people and catechumens. In other words, it was the exclusive role of the superior priestly order to instruct others and guide their spiritual progress; monks, including friars, belonged, like the laity, to the inferior order of those who received pastoral ministrations; they could not perform the office that belonged to their superiors.

The complaint that the privileges granted the Mendicants had overturned the hierarchical order of the Church was only half of William's case. For the rest, he challenged the legitimacy of mendicancy, which the friars had made a cardinal principle of the evangelical life. It was, he argued, contrary to the example of Christ and the express instructions of St Paul. It was all very well to abandon all one's property for the sake of Christ, but this did not mean a licence to beg; Christians who had no other source of income should earn their living by working. The friars, therefore, were false prophets, men who preached without having been lawfully sent, and in view of their begging activities, to be classed with common thieves.

In face of this attack, the friars invoked the authority of the pope, who had authorised their ministry, and took refuge behind the accumulated rampart of their papal privileges. A systematic refutation of William's propaganda was written by the English Franciscan Thomas of York. But others joined the fray, most notably Bonaventure, who at the outbreak of hostilities was a Bachelor at the Paris house of the Franciscans, waiting to incept in theology. To counter William's arguments, the Mendicant apologists expounded a different system of Church order. 'In the Church,' explained Thomas of York, 'the totality of authority and power is derived from a single person – the pope – and from that one alone it descends, and so it is in his power alone to remove or grant permission.'[4] For Bonaventure, the pope was not only the universal bishop; he was every man's parish priest. As such, he could delegate his responsibilities to any helpers he chose; and he had chosen to delegate them to the friars.

The controversy thus resolved itself into two conflicting ecclesiologies: that of William of Saint-Amour based upon a static hierarchy – which anachronistically classified monks as lay Christians – and upon the indefeasible rights of local churches within the territorial boundaries of their jurisdiction; and over and against it, that of the friars – a dynamic theory, which reflected the rising power and centralising thrust of the papacy, and regarded the Church as a single social organism emanating from the pope. It was a theory well adapted not only to developments in the organisation of the Church; it also reflected the social and economic changes of the thirteenth century, when the isolation and autonomy of local communities was being eroded by the agents of the central power, by the growth of international trade and by the rise of an international community of learning.

William's assault upon the doctrine and practice of mendicancy provoked a considerable body of apologetic literature as well as some heated debate in the schools. Besides Thomas of York, both Bonaventure and Aquinas picked up their pens to defend the principle that was close to the heart of their religious vocation. In his *Questiones* 'Concerning Evangelical Perfection' (*de perfectione evangelica*), Bonaventure argued that begging was the sign of a total voluntary destitution which constituted the imitation of Christ: 'The Lord had no temporal goods; if he was so poor that he could not pay a penny to render unto Caesar (he asked someone else to produce a penny), it is evident that he was in a state of supreme poverty; the essence of Christian perfection, therefore, is to possess nothing in the world, either individually or in common, for the sake of Christ. According to the Gloss, it is Christ who is

4. *Manus que contra Omnipotentem tenditur* in Max Bierbaum, *Bettelorden und Weltgeistlichkeit an der Universität Paris* (Munster 1920), pp. 37–168. Thomas of York's authorship of this work was demonstrated by F. Pelster, 'Thomas von York als Verfasser des Traktat Manus': *AFH* XV (1922), pp. 3–22, and by E. Longpré, 'Thomas d'York': *AFH* XIX (1926), pp. 875–930.

speaking of himself in the words of the psalmist who says "I am poor and mendicant".'(Ps.39).[5]

William's tract was condemned at Rome, and he was forced to retire from the schools. But the attack was resumed in 1269 by Gerard of Abbeville in a university sermon, denouncing the Franciscan doctrine of evangelical poverty as an implicit attack upon the property of the clergy. He followed this up some months later with a polemical treatise 'Against the Adversary of Christian Perfection' (*Contra adversarium perfectionis Christiane*),[6] which drew from Bonaventure his *Apologia Pauperum* – a more elaborate vindication of the Mendicant way of life as being the literal imitation of the pauper Christ. This doctrine of the absolute poverty of Christ, which was a shibboleth of Mendicant apologetics, long continued to be a topic of fierce debate between the friars and the secular clergy, for, as Gerard had pointed out, it implied a judgement upon clerical wealth. The topic was also becoming a source of dissension within the Franciscan Order itself.

The renewal of the controversy at Paris synchronised with a further effort by a number of prelates to get the privileges of the friars curtailed. Their anxiety had been heightened by the expansion of Mendicant church-building and the proliferation of new Mendicant Orders and their satellite lay associations. The attack that had been headed-off in 1245 was now pressed home by the bishops who assembled for the Second Council of Lyons in 1274. Pope Gregory X, who had summoned the council, was prevailed upon to frame a constitution which, in effect, suppressed several small orders of friars, and this was approved by the council.

The conciliar decree *Religionum diversitatem*[7] invoked the canon of the Fourth Lateran Council of 1215 prohibiting the foundation of new religious orders, and abolished all that had been founded since that date, unless they had been approved by the Apostolic See. The decree was specifically aimed at

5. *S. Bonaventurae Opera Omnia* V(Quarrachi 1891), pp. 117–98. On Bonaventure's part in the Paris controversy see J.G. Bougerol, 'Saint Bonaventure et la défense de la vie évangelique de 1252 au Concile de Lyon (1274)' in *S. Bonaventura Francescano* (*Convegno del Centro di Studi sulla Spiritualità medievale* Todi 1974), pp. 109–26.
6. S. Clasen, 'Tractatus Gerardi de Abatisvilla contra adversarium perfectionis christianae': *AFH* XXXI (1938–9), pp. 276–729; XXXII (1939–40), pp. 89–200.
7. Mansi XXIV, col. 134.

those orders that lacked endowments and depended upon begging for their livelihood. Those Mendicant Orders that had been founded since 1215 and had been approved by the papacy, might retain their existing members, but they were to accept no more recruits nor to acquire new houses; they were thus condemned to slow extinction; their land and buildings were reserved to the Holy See to be used for the benefit of the Holy Land and the poor. The decree, however, excepted the Franciscans and Dominicans from its application on account of their 'evident usefulness' to the Church. As more recent arrivals, the Carmelites and Augustinian Friars were clearly more vulnerable. But, with benign casuistry, the decree stated that their foundation had antedated the Council of 1215; they were therefore permitted to continue in their existing state 'until we ordain otherwise concerning them'. Whatever Gregory's ultimate intentions towards them, the favour of his successors ensured their continued existence and growth. On the other hand, the Friars of the Sack and several smaller Mendicant Orders were slowly extinguished by the operation of the decree.

. . .

A PARTIAL RESOLUTION

Gregory's decree had given the prelates some of what they wanted, but it had not satisfied their demand for the curtailment of the friars' privileges and it had left the big battalions untouched. Their pastoral activities continued to enjoy papal protection. In fact, the advent of Pope Martin IV, in 1281, added fresh fuel to the sense of grievance felt by many of the secular clergy. Determined to vindicate the mission of the friars, Martin provided them with the privilege *Ad fructus uberes*, which authorised them to perform pastoral and sacramental functions in any diocese or parish without seeking the consent of the local clergy. This represented the high-water mark of their privileged status, and it led to a prolonged and bitter struggle. In France, opposition was expressed through provincial synods. The parish clergy were told to expound to their people the canon of the Fourth Lateran Council requiring everyone to confess at least once a year to his or her parish priest; those who failed to do so (having perhaps chosen a friar as their confessor in preference to their parish chaplain or rector) were to be threatened with excommunication and to be denied Christian burial. And the Masters of Paris were invited to debate the question whether a person who had received absolution after confessing to a friar was bound to confess the same sins again to his own parish priest, as was seemingly required by the decree *Utriusque sexus* of the Fourth Lateran, which had never been rescinded. Territorial jurisdiction over sin was, after all, the logical application of the system of Church order expounded by William of Saint-Amour and the Gallican clergy.

In the hope of getting the offending bull annulled, or at least modified, the French bishops mounted a series of delegations to place their grievances before the pope. At length, Nicholas IV commissioned the cardinal legates, Benedict Gaetani and Gerard of Santa Sabina, to examine the complaints. For this purpose, the legates convened an assembly at Paris in November 1290. But the bishops got cold comfort from the cardinals: Gaetani roundly rejected the protest against *Ad fructus uberes* voiced by the bishop of Amiens, and annulled all the acts of French synods which limited the application of the bull. The Masters of the University, who had sent a delegation of their own, were rudely berated for their presumption: 'You fools! You think the world is governed by your reasonings'. The Curia, they were told, would sooner destroy the University of Paris than deprive the friars of their privileges.[8]

In the end, after a further decade of wrangling, it was Gaetani himself who, as Boniface VIII, devised the terms of a truce with his bull *Super Cathedram*, promulgated in 1300. This decreed that friars might only preach in parishes with the consent of the incumbent; that the provincials of the Mendicant Orders should present a number of their members to the bishop, who, if he approved them, would license them to hear confessions in his diocese; and that, although the friars might accept requests for burial in their churches or cemeteries, a quarter of the mortuary dues and bequests were to be reserved to the parish priest of the deceased. This outlined a statesman-like settlement which proved to be workable. Bishops' registers of the fourteenth century record the regular presentation of named friars to be licensed as confessors in the English dioceses.

Although *Super Cathedram* gave the bishops much of what they had asked for, it did not allay the sense of grievance felt by many of the lower clergy, nor did it silence the controversy,

8. H. Finke, *Aus den Tagen Bonifaz VIII* (Munster 1902), p. vi.

which was occasionally fanned into fresh flame by preachers hostile to the Mendicants. In the fourteenth century, regardless of papal privileges and bishops' licences, we still find writers of manuals of instruction designed for the parish clergy questioning whether a penitent who confessed to a friar had fulfilled the canonical requirements for absolution; he would be safer, they suggested, to repeat his confession to his own parish priest. In the 1350s the secular clergy found a new champion ready to voice their smouldering resentments in Richard FitzRalph, the archbishop of Armagh.

.   .   .

POLEMIC AND SATIRE

FitzRalph, a former Chancellor of Oxford, had played a prominent role in theological debates with representatives of the Eastern churches held at Avignon. His reputation as a theologian and preacher stood high at the court of Avignon when, in July 1350, he delivered an address to Pope Clement VI and the cardinals in consistory attacking the privileges of the Mendicants. It seems that what had prompted this renewed attack was an attempt by the friars to persuade the pope to relax the terms of *Super Cathedram* in their favour.

The curious thing about FitzRalph's broadside is that it came from a scholar who for many years previously had had a close and appreciative relationship with the friars; he had been a much sought-after preacher in their churches at Avignon. What had turned him from a friend into a relentless enemy? His latest biographer finds the answer in his experience as a diocesan in Ireland:[9] he had come to regard their unsupervised ministry, especially their practice in the confessional and their alleged readiness to grant absolution for crimes against property and persons before restitution, as a menace to the peace of a racially divided and feud-stricken community. This was certainly an issue on which he felt deeply. But the allegation that the friars let off their penitents too lightly was a commonplace of anti-Mendicant polemics, which reflected, as much as anything else, the inability of the less educated parish clergy to adapt to the new theology of penance.

His initial attack focused upon the right of the friars to preach and hear confessions – a permission that he claimed

9. Katherine Walsh, *Richard FitzRalph in Oxford, Avignon and Armagh* (1981).

was detrimental to the hierarchical structure of the Church and injurious to the ministry of the parish clergy. This was well-trodden ground. The problem for exponents of this view was how to state it without openly challenging the authority of the papacy, which had authorised the pastoral activities of the Mendicants. This was the pit William of Saint-Amour had fallen into. FitzRalph could not directly attack *Super Cathedram*; he alleged it had been abused by the way friars had exercised their prerogative. What was new in his invective was his assertion that by seeking to act as confessors they had violated their own Rule of poverty and humility – meaning specifically the Rule of St Francis – because the role of confessor was a source of honour and influence, especially when their penitents included princes and members of the aristocracy; they were moved to seek such positions, he suggested, by pride and avarice. There can be no doubt that here he was voicing the resentment of many of the lower clergy, who sourly observed the presence of friars in the courts of kings and at the tables of the nobility.

Six years later, FitzRalph adopted a more radical line of attack in his treatise 'On the Poverty of the Saviour' (*De pauperie Salvatoris*). Here he struck at the root of the Mendicant ideal. He maintained that the claim of the friars to have no property on the grounds that they only enjoyed the use of their buildings and assets, which belonged to others, was fraudulent; that the practice of mendicancy was in any case unlawful – returning here to the old controversy about the absolute poverty of Christ – and that, being in a state of unrepentant sin, the friars could not perform any valid sacramental acts – an assertion that was clearly contrary to the received sacramental theology of the Western Church. Whereas previously he had pleaded for the abolition of the friars' privileges, he now argued for the total abolition of the Mendicant Orders. Besides writing against them, he pursued his vendetta in the London pulpits.

The friars did not remain impassive in the face of this new onslaught. At Oxford, where the *De pauperie Salvatoris* had been circulated, Geoffrey Hardeby, an Augustinian friar regent in the theology faculty, wrote a refutation. And proctors of the Mendicants instituted proceedings at the papal court. FitzRalph was thus obliged to return to Avignon to defend himself against a charge of heresy. But the case, which was conducted before a tribunal of three cardinals, dragged on at a snail's pace, and had reached no conclusion when FitzRalph died in November 1360. His work proved to be seminal: in the next generation his ideas on dominion and grace and his campaign against the friars were to be taken up at Oxford by John Wyclif. At London, Paris and elsewhere, echoes of the controversy continued to reverberate for many decades to come. One fact emerged from this long and futile conflict: the position of the friars was unassailable because it could not be challenged without challenging the authority of the papacy.

Safe under the umbrella of papal approval, the friars continued to discharge their mission to the townspeople of Europe. But although they emerged victorious from each phase of the conflict, they were not unscathed. The quarrel was not confined to clerks. The bitter controversies of thirteenth-century Paris seeped from the schools into the streets, and were perpetuated in the vernacular literature of the later middle ages. The adherents of William of Saint-Amour had been defeated at the Curia, but their cause was immortalised in satire – the classical revenge of the helpless in the face of immovable power. One of William's less academic champions was the French poet Rutebeuf, a clerk turned jongleur, who set the saga of his master's defeat and the iniquities of the friars to rhyming couplets for the benefit of the tavern population of Paris. Rutebeuf was a younger contemporary of William. In the next generation, the cynical Jean de Meung included the story, for no apparent reason other than its current newsworthiness, in his chaotic continuation of the *Roman de la Rose*.

The immense popularity of the *Roman de la Rose* ensured the wide diffusion of the anti-Mendicant theme in England and Germany, as well as in France. In the poem the Mendicant ideal is savagely satirised in the person of a hypocritical and greedy friar called Fals Semblant, who expresses a preference for the company of the rich and noble and an abhorrence for the poor. The middle-English version was composed after the middle of the fourteenth century. Here, as in the French original, Fals Semblant refers to the attack upon the Franciscan belief in the poverty of Christ made by William of Saint-Amour:

> Who seith 'ye', I der sey 'nay' –
> That Crist, ne his apostles dere,

163

Whyl that they walkede in erthe here,
Were never seen her bred begging

As William Sent Amour wolde preche,
And ofte wolde dispute and teche
Of this matere alle openly
At Paris ful solempnly.[10]

In Fals Semblant we have the stereotyped lampoon which provided the model for Chaucer's friar – the confidence trickster who sold easy penances and traded on the credulity of pious women – and for the hateful figure of Friar John in the Summoner's Tale. Here too we have the link in the literary tradition that connects Langland's invective against the Mendicants with the bitter polemics of thirteenth-century Paris.

Of course, the secular vitality of the anti-Mendicant theme cannot be explained solely in terms of a literary convention. It persisted because it expressed the genuine sentiments of certain sections of medieval society. Langland, the author of *Piers Plowman*, was himself an impoverished clerk in minor orders[11] and he voiced the festering grievances of the lower clergy – the perpetual vicars, parish chaplains and hedge priests, the nameless proletariat of clerks without benefices, whose plight caused them to envy the popular success of the friars and to resent their competition in the pulpit and confessional. They saw with bitterness their richer and more educated parishioners and potential patrons drawn away by the superior pastoral skills of an intellectual *corps d'élite*.

The sense of grievance nursed by the lower clergy was sharpened by the contemptuous attitude often shown towards them by their rivals. It must be admitted that the friars were not entirely free from the institutional arrogance and self-congratulation which is a common vice of religious organisations, as it is of their secular counterparts. Disparagement of the secular clergy was a common enough feature of Mendicant preaching to be made the subject of an express prohibition by

10. *The Romaunt of the Rose* (C), 6547–66 in *The Complete Works of Geoffrey Chaucer*, ed. W.W. Skeat (1912, 1937), pp. 67, 69. Cf. the discussion by P.R. Szittya, *The Anti-fraternal Tradition in Medieval Literature* (Princeton 1986).
11. On the question of Langland's attitude to the friars see F.R.H. Du-Boulay, *The England of Piers Plowman* (1991), pp. 80–6, 134–6.

Bonaventure in a letter he wrote to the Minister of Provence.[12] The author of the thirteenth-century *Questio* on why the brothers preach in cities justified the pastoral mission of the friars by arguing that many of the parish clergy lacked the knowledge necessary to instruct their people, and that many of them were such notorious fornicators that honest women feared to approach them in the confessional for fear of being solicited. The charge was repeated with some Rabelaisian anecdotes by Salimbene. Chaucer's Friar John was harping on the theme of clerical inadequacy when he expressed contempt for the efforts of the parish priest who had heard Thomas's death-bed confession.

Ridicule of Mendicant pretensions must have evoked a sympathetic response in other social milieux besides that of the lower clergy. Anybody who claims to exemplify an ideal way of life incurs the risk of ridicule. The profession of voluntary poverty and the claim that the observance of the friars was the perfect form of Christian life because it was based upon a literal imitation of the life of Christ posed a disquieting challenge to 'possessioners' – the well-endowed monasteries and the well-to-do higher clergy. It also represented a challenge to the commercial ethos of the urban laity, especially to the *arrivistes* among them – the bourgeois families who were not prepared to allow conventional piety to conflict with their economic and social aspirations. For these groups the ridiculing of the Mendicant ideal must have been an instinctive form of self-defence. And the spectacle of friars moving in court circles and dining at the tables of the rich provided ready material for satire. So too did the compromises that were inescapable if the Franciscan ideal of absolute poverty was to be reconciled with the demands of an effective pastoral mission.

It is the nature of satire to caricature. If some individuals merited the criticism levelled at the friars by their enemies, much more of the invective was an unfair disparagement of a body of men who had committed themselves to a difficult and demanding way of life and who expended themselves in bringing spiritual nourishment to a large section of lay society, the poor as well as the rich, which would otherwise have been left without any adequate pastoral provision.

12. *S. Bonaventurae Opera Omnia* VIII, pp. 470–1.

Chapter 9

IN THE HOUSES OF KINGS

'Then were the Friars Preachers and the Minorites made councillors and special envoys of kings,' wrote Matthew Paris with more than a touch of bitterness, 'so that whereas formerly those in the houses of kings were in soft garments, now they are clothed in base attire.'[1] As a monk of St Albans with moles in the royal administration, Matthew was well placed to observe the activities of the friars at court. He voiced the misgiving and mistrust of many of the secular clergy as well as that of the monks at the appearance of these newcomers on the ecclesiastical scene and the jealousy aroused by the generous patronage they received from the king and the aristocracy. The spectacle of their growing role in public affairs evoked his rising anger: 'They build residences that aspire to the height of royal buildings; they are in the courts of kings and magnates as councillors, chamberlains, treasurers, paranymphs and negotiators of marriages.'[2]

Just as in Italy the Mendicants were welcomed and patronised by the ruling classes of the city-republics and in Germany by many of the princes, in France and England also they were warmly welcomed by the king and royal family. Louis IX's devotion towards them was notorious. Their apostolic zeal coincided with his own sense of his pastoral obligations towards his subjects, especially the poorer among them, which made him a generous benefactor of hospitals and leper-houses. He was an intensely religious man, and the Mendicant ideal, combining monastic observances with active service to the world, appealed to him as a perfect paradigm of the Christian life. He entrusted the friars with the education of his sons.

1. *Chron. Majora* III, p. 627. Cf. Matt.xi.8.
2. *ibid.* IV, p. 280.

Following his return from crusading he kept a Dominican and a Franciscan constantly in his entourage as confessors; and, according to his biographer and confessor, Geoffrey de Beaulieu, he proposed at one point in his reign to abdicate and become a friar himself, an act of fugitive piety from which he was deflected by his wife's refusal to give her consent.[3]

As patrons and benefactors, both Louis IX and Henry III led a social trend in providing the friars with sites, money for building, building materials, food and clothing. Louis, like his mother, Blanche of Castile, was a generous patron of several religious orders. Between them they founded three Cistercian abbeys, one of which, Maubuisson, was a nunnery chosen by Queen Blanche as her mausoleum.[4] Louis displayed his predilection for the Mendicants by acquiring sites for them round the outskirts of Paris and building them churches. He brought the Franciscans in from Saint-Denis, built them a dormitory and completed their church. For the Dominicans settled in the hospice of Saint-Jacques on the left bank he financed the building of a refectory and dormitory. He provided a house for the Carmelites beside the Seine near Charenton. He had a church built for the Augustinian Friars outside the gate of Montmartre; and he placed the Friars of the Sack on a site near Saint-Germain-des-Prés. The Crutched Friars were given a house in the rue Ste Croix. 'Thus,' observes Joinville unctuously, 'did the good king surround the city of Paris with men of religion.'[5] Rutebeuf, the clerk turned jongleur and a good hater of the friars, viewed the royal beneficence with a colder eye:

> Si ont ja la cité porprise.
> Dieux gart Paris de mescheance,
> Et la gart de fausse creance.[6]
> (They have already encircled the city; God keep Paris
> from harm and preserve her from false religion)

3. *Vita S. Ludovici auctore Gaufrido de Belloloco: Recueil [des historiens des Gaules et de la France]* XX (Paris 1840), p. 7.
4. For Louis' patronage of the Cistercians and other orders see Elizabeth Hallam, 'Aspects of the monastic patronage of the English and French royal houses *c.* 1130–1270': unpublished London Ph.D. thesis 1976, pp. 230ff.
5. *The History of St Louis by Jean sire de Joinville*, transl. and ed. Joan Evans (Paris 1938), p. 221.
6. *Rutebeuf. Oeuvres complètes*, ed. E. Faral and J. Bastin (Paris 1959–60), p. 323; cited by Jean Richard, *Saint Louis, roi d'une France féodale* (Paris 1983), p. 399.

In England Henry III declared himself to be as devoted to the Mendicants as his French brother-in-law. 'The king,' the canons of Dunstable were warned when they objected to a settlement of the Friars Preachers in their town, 'holds them in special devotion as men of the Gospel and ministers of the Most Holy King.'[7] The chancery clerk who penned that phrase was clearly not using language of his own. All the same, Henry's donations were less lavish in scale than those of Louis. He acquired a number of sites for the friars. The church of the Dominicans at Canterbury and the chapter-house and dormitory of the Franciscans at Reading were built largely at the king's expense; but elsewhere royal contributions to Mendicant building were more modest. The London Carmelites received no more than a 100 shillings for their fabric fund,[8] and the Crutched Friars were given a mere 20 marks to help them build their London church.[9] As founder and builder the king was but one among a host of lay benefactors.

Henry's assistance for the friars mostly took the form of regular gifts in cash or kind to help them meet ordinary running expenses, the major beneficiaries of which were the London and Oxford houses. There were periodic gifts of timber from the royal forests for fuel, and grants of money to provide clothing. The clothing allowances, which were paid directly to the suppliers, were evidently based upon the number of friars in each community. Thus in 1260 and again in 1261 the Friars Minor of London were allocated 100 shillings from the farm of the city to provide them with new habits for the approaching winter, whereas the Dominican community was allotted 100 pounds for the same purpose.[10]

A form of subvention Henry particularly favoured was a contribution to the expenses involved in holding provincial chapters of the friars, when the provisioning of large numbers posed special problems for the house chosen to be the venue for the assembly. In 1247 the sheriff of Lincoln was instructed to provide food and other necessities out of the revenue of the

---

7. *Calendar of Patent Rolls 1258–66*, p. 20.
8. *Calendar of Liberate Rolls 1267–72*, p. 113.
9. *ibid.* p. 81.
10. *ibid.* p. 70.

shire for the chapter of the Friars Preachers meeting at Stam-
ford.[11] The following year, money was allocated to feeding
those attending chapter-meetings of the Franciscans and Carmelites.[12] The record of these regular disbursements is, in fact,
a main source of our knowledge of these provincial assemblies
which are otherwise poorly documented. At Whitsun in the
year 1250, when a general chapter of the Dominican Order
met in the Holborn house of the Blackfriars, Henry went to
unusual lengths to show his interest. Matthew Paris records
that the king entered the chapter on the first day and requested the prayers of the assembly, and that on that day he
provided food and ate with the brethren; the food on subsequent days was provided by the queen, the bishop of London,
and the royal minister John Mansel.[13]

Perhaps there was an element of emulation in these demonstrations. Henry was sensitive to the risk of being upstaged
by the court of France, and Louis was known to take pleas-
ure in personally attending chapter-meetings of the friars
and Cistercians. The same year that Henry attended the
Dominican chapter at Holborn, Louis presented himself at
the provincial chapter of the Franciscans at Sens dressed
humbly as a pilgrim and accompanied by his three brothers.
He asked the friars for their prayers and paid for a feast,
which he shared with them in their refectory. Salimbene,
who saw it all, trailed the court as it proceeded on its way,
and recalled almost with incredulity an extraordinary scene
at Vézelay, where the king visited the house of the Friars
Minor. Calling them together, he addressed them sitting on
the floor in the middle of them, in the dust and dirt of the
unpaved church.[14]

Both in England and France, Franciscan and Dominican
friars were retained in constant attendance at court. To ensure
their continued presence King Henry got an indult (a special
permit) from Innocent IV dispensing them from those of their
statutes that required the brethren at all times to travel on

---

11. *Cal. Liberate Rolls 1245–51*, p. 136.
12. *ibid.* pp. 163, 169. For a list of known meetings of the English provincial
    chapters of the Friars Minor and royal subvention see A.G. Little,
    Franciscan Papers, Lists and Documents (1943), pp. 209–16.
13. *Chron. Majora* V, p. 127.
14. Salimbene, pp. 222–5.

foot and permitting them to ride horses, so that they could keep up with the court as it moved on its itinerary through the king's continental dominions.[15] Both orders required a friar travelling outside his own house to be accompanied by a brother-friar – a *socius*. Thus the friars living at court were not on their own. They formed in fact, a small community apart, with their own establishment. Money disbursed to London merchants in April 1250 for cloth to make a habit for the king's confessor, the Dominican John of Darlington, also covered the cost of material for John's fellow friars residing at court.[16] In some places they were assigned their own quarters in the royal palace, like the 'Friars Chamber' in the castle of Guildford. In September 1268 the sheriff of Wiltshire was ordered to see to the construction of a room adjoining the queen's chamber in the court of Clarendon, for the use of the Friars Minor serving the queen. Where accommodation was not available under the royal roof, a house might be hastily erected for them in the precinct. In 1270 the sheriff was commanded to build a dwelling twenty-four feet long by twelve feet wide, to house the Friars Preachers close to the royal palace at Clarendon, and a similar building was ordered for the Friars Minor.[17]

.   .   .

THE PASTORAL ROLE OF THE FRIARS AT COURT

The primary role of the friars residing at court was, of course, a pastoral one. They provided the king and the royal family with confessors. It was the practice of Louis IX to confess every Friday, and his chaplains attested the fact that he insisted on flagellation for his penance. He also wore a hair-shirt throughout the penitential seasons of Lent and Advent, despite his confessor's remonstrations. Louis was a monk *manqué*, and it is improbable that Henry III imitated such masochistic practices. But the thirteenth-century Church

---

15. T. Rymer: *Foedera et acta publica inter reges Angliae et alias quoque reges* I (1816), p. 274.

16. *Cal. Liberate Rolls 1251–60*, p. 282.

17. *Cal. Liberate Rolls 1267–72*, pp. 45, 138.; on the Friars' Chamber at Guildford see H.M. Colvin, *The History of the King's Works* II (HMSO 1963), p. 953.

laid increasing stress upon the need for contrition and the obligation of every Christian to examine his or her conscience and confess everyday failings as well as big and heinous sins. Contrition and penance were major themes in the piety of the later middle ages. A confessor was therefore an indispensable member of every royal entourage and noble household. Henry chose Dominicans as his confessors, and he was followed in this by his successors. Brother John of Darlington, Henry's confessor, continued to provide this service in the early years of Edward I's reign, to be followed after his death by another Dominican, Walter Winterborne. The tradition was not broken until the end of the fourteenth century with the accession of Henry IV and the Lancastrians, who relied upon the Carmelites for these spiritual services.

Besides supplying the king and the royal family with confessors, the friars were frequently called upon to provide court preachers. Louis IX was much given to hearing sermons and liked to seek out famous preachers. Bonaventure, as Minister-General of the Franciscans was much in demand. Of 113 recorded sermons he preached at Paris in the years 1257 to 1269, nineteen were delivered in the royal chapel before the king.[18]

The task of a court preacher was not always a grateful one. The sermon was a form of communication designed to touch the conscience of its audience and provide moral instruction. A Mendicant preacher with a strong sense of his spiritual mission undiluted by personal ambition or the need to gratify a royal patron, could be tempted to sail close to the political wind. The Dominican theologian Robert Bacon, preaching before the court in 1233 at a time of crisis, angered the king by his outspoken criticism of the royal council. The political situation was tense that summer. A brusque resumption of personal rule through the office of the Wardrobe and a revival of lapsed royal rights had aroused baronial fears and brought the country to the brink of civil war. Discontent focused upon the king's chief adviser in the business, Peter de Roches, the grandee Bishop of Winchester, and the bishop's nephew, Peter des Rievaux, a rather maligned royal bureaucrat who had been the agent of the administrative reconstruction. In his sermon Bacon took the opportunity to denounce the king's

18. Lester K. Little, 'St Louis' involvement with the friars': *Church History* 33 (1964), p. 130.

advisers and urged him to make changes in his council. It was either he or a wag who was present at the sermon who, according to Matthew Paris, made a daring pun on the name of Roches – the rock on which the ship of state was in danger of foundering.[19]

Possibly it was a similar piece of presumption that caused the Franciscan Adam Marsh to fall temporarily from royal favour. A theologian with an international reputation, Adam was one of the first fruits of the recruitment drive made by the friars in the Oxford schools. He was a fierce advocate of ecclesiastical reform, a tireless flayer of abuses and a passionate believer in the messianic mission of the Friars Minor. His advice was widely sought by the leaders of church and state and by the officers of his own order. Queen Eleanor was devoted to him and constantly pressed him to stay at court. But early in 1253, when Archbishop Boniface tried to persuade him to join the archiepiscopal household, one of the reasons he gave for refusing the invitation was that the king had forbidden the archbishop to co-opt him 'as I am a traitor and enemy of the king'.[20]

How Adam had incurred this fearsome censure, which would have made a lay magnate tremble for his life and property, is not altogether clear. He had previously reported arousing the king's displeasure 'on account of the words of life' – a euphemism he commonly used to describe preaching, but the context is obscure. It was probably his advocacy in the cause of Simon de Montfort that had provoked King Henry's fury. Adam was the friend and spiritual director of the earl and his countess. He had been present at court the previous summer during the trial of Montfort over his steward-ship in Gascony, and wrote a vivid account of the proceedings to his friend Robert Grosseteste, the bishop of Lincoln. He made no secret of his view that the earl had been treated with monstrous injustice.

Henry's vehement language was a typical effluent of his volatile personality. King Louis, too, experienced an abrasive frankness from some of the friars he invited to preach to the

19. *Chron. Majora* III pp. 244–5; see the context in C.H. Lawrence, *St Edmund of Abingdon* (1960), p. 131.
20. *Monumenta Franciscana*, ed. J.S. Brewer (RS 1858) I, pp. 342–3, 335; on Adam see C.H. Lawrence, 'The Letters of Adam Marsh and the Franciscan school at Oxford': *JEH* 42 No. 2 (1991), pp. 218–38.

court, but he was in better control of his tongue and tempera-
ment. Arriving at Hyères in Provence on his way to embark
for the crusade, he requested a sermon from the Franciscan
Hugh de Digne. A Provençal from Barjols, Hugh was famous
as an exponent of the prophecies of Joachim of Fiore and a
preacher noted for his fiery eloquence and personal austerity.
Having been invited by the king to preach, he used the
occasion to denounce members of the regular clergy – men
bound by monastic vows – who resided at court and in the
king's entourage: the court was no place for monks. He
ridiculed their claims that they could combine fidelity to their
rule with the royal service; by continuing in the king's service
they were in peril of their souls. He ended by admonishing
Louis to do justice lest God should deprive him of his kingdom.
Louis' response to this jeremiad was as characteristic as
Henry's in similar circumstances. Instead of expressing the
irritation he probably felt, he joined Joinville in begging the
preacher to stay at court. But Hugh would have none of it,
nor would he make any concessions to majesty. He roughly
rejected Louis' invitation: 'Faith, Sir, I will not; but will go to
a place where God will love me better than in the king's company.'[21]

.   .   .

THE FRIARS AND GOVERNMENT

Although Hugh's invective was not directed primarily at
members of his own order, it was obviously relevant to the
position of friars in the royal service. In practice it was hard to
draw a line between pastoral service and political activity;
and it was not a line that either Louis or king Henry wanted
to draw. The attractiveness of the friars for rulers who used
them lay in their unique combination of piety, education and
detachment. Having opted out of the race for ecclesiastical
preferment, they sought neither wealth nor patronage. They
offered all the advantages of conscientious and sagacious man-
agement consultants who were completely disinterested and
who would accept no fee. Thus friars in the royal service
found themselves involved, not always willingly, in administrative and political activity.

Louis constantly associated Dominicans and Franciscans in

21. *The History of St Louis*, transl. and ed. Joan Evans, p. 201.

government. Their presence at council meetings and parlements was taken for granted, and they were used as commissioners of inquiry on the regional inquests set up to investigate administrative abuses, which were a regular feature of government in the later years of the reign. Sometimes they were associated with lay commissioners; sometimes they comprised the entire body. In January 1247, for instance, royal letters addressed to the people of the dioceses of Meaux, Troyes, Auxerre and Nevers, named four commissioners – two of whom, Brothers Peter Chotard and Theobald de Columbariis, were Dominicans and the other two, Brothers Nicholas de Troyes and John de Sancto Lugo, were Friars Minor – to hold inquiry into complaints of injury, exaction or unlawfully procured services, by royal agents in the area.[22] For an investigation of this sort friars were obviously ideal agents because they were beyond the reach of bribery or most forms of intimidation; and their work among the lower orders of society made them approachable to complainants who might have been afraid to testify before a more exalted body.

In England, as in France, friars were pervasive in many areas of government. The Dominicans John of St Giles and John of Darlington, the king's confessor, were both members of Henry III's increasingly professional council, and in that capacity the latter was to play an active role in the political turmoils of the years 1258 to 1265. Brother Walter Winterborne, Edward I's confessor, served on the king's council until his elevation to the cardinalate in 1304 took him from the country. These men were permanent residents at court, whether the king was in England or visiting his overseas dominions in Gascony.

Friars of both major orders were in frequent use as royal envoys and confidential agents. In 1233 Agnellus of Pisa, the provincial minister of the Franciscans, was sent on a mission of pacification to Richard the Earl Marshal, who had raised war against the king in the Welsh Marches. According to Eccleston, the journey in late December to Margam Abbey, where the earl was staying, contributed to Agnellus's early death from cold and exhaustion.[23] Adam Marsh, despite his protests and lamentations over his interrupted studies, was

---

22. *Recueil* XXIV, p. 4.
23. *De Adventu Fratrum Minorum in Angliam*, ed. A.G. Little (1951), p. 76.

inexorably drawn into public life. In 1247 he was sent together with the Dominican provincial, Brother Matthew of Bergeveney, on a diplomatic mission overseas; and by 1257, whatever the cause of his fall from favour, the king's trust in him had been sufficiently restored to entrust him with a political mission of the highest importance: together with Hugh Bigod and Walter Cantilupe, the bishop of Worcester, he was appointed a member of a triumvirate that was sent to negotiate a peace treaty with Louis of France.[24] The following year, as the political crisis of Henry's central years came to a head, he and the queen pressed for Adam to come and join the deliberations of the assembly summoned to consider the insolvency of the crown.[25]

Many qualities besides personal trustworthiness commended friars as ambassadors. Those that were chosen for these important and delicate missions were highly educated men, practised in logical analysis, who had travelled in pursuit of learning or in the service of their order. Being members of an international organisation, they had contacts abroad; some of them had unusual linguistic skills. They were thus much in demand, as Matthew Paris had noticed, as negotiators of marriages between members of royal families of different kingdoms. In treaty negotiations they were the trusted communicators of the king's personal wishes as well as keepers of his conscience. The discussions terminating in the Treaty of Paris of 1259, for which the embassy of Cantilupe and Adam Marsh had prepared the way, were led on the French side by another Franciscan, Odo Rigaud, a former regent in theology of Paris and one of Louis' most trusted councillors, who since 1247 had been archbishop of Rouen. The evangelical zeal of the Mendicants and their lack of worldly impedimenta made them a suitable choice for missions that were thought too dangerous to engage the services of other people. It was a French Dominican, André de Longjumeau, who was chosen to represent King Louis' views to the Great Khan of the Mongols in 1247. And it was two friars, a Dominican and a Franciscan, who in 1294 were assigned the ungrateful task of conveying to Philip IV the information that Edward I repudiated his overlordship in respect of Gascony.

24. *Cal. Liberate Rolls 1245–51*, p. 133; *ibid. 1251–60*, p. 416; *Cal. Pat. Rolls 1247–58*, p. 594.
25. Brewer, *Monumenta Franciscana*, pp. 387–8.

This involvement with affairs of state posed a moral di-
lemma for friars attending court. The discharge of their pastoral mission as confessors and spiritual counsellors to princes
and the trust they enjoyed depended upon their independence
and their reputation for impartiality and incorruptibility.
Their vow of poverty was a guarantee of their independence
and a pledge of their disinterested advice, which made them
widely acceptable as negotiators and mediators. But their
standing as impartial counsellors could easily be compromised
by the king's reliance upon them to maintain his interests or
by their involvement in the political plans of the papacy. So,
for instance, the services rendered to Henry III by the Dominicans has caused some historians to suggest that they were
royalist partisans in the period of baronial war and reconstruction between 1258 and 1265, in this differing from the Friars
Minor, whose populist sympathies are alleged to have aligned
them with the forces of rebellion and reform. The historian of
the English Dominicans has been at some pains to refute this
suggestion, which he evidently regarded as a slur on the
honour of his order.[26]

The allegation that the Friars Preachers supported the
king's cause against the baronial reformers is based upon
flimsy evidence – no more, in fact, than a malicious aside by
the Westminster chronicler[27] and the conspicuous presence of
John of Darlington, the king's confessor, in the royal council
during the period of conflict. Clearly Darlington enjoyed
Henry's complete confidence. He was nominated as one of the
twelve representing the king's interests on the committee of
twenty-four, which was set up by the crisis parliament of 1258
and which drafted the Provisions of Oxford. Later he attested
the oaths of the Montfort group to abide by the arbitration of
Louis IX on the issues between them and the king.[28] The
value Henry placed upon his services is indicated by a letter
he wrote to the Dominican provincial after Montfort's defeat
at Evesham, requesting John's immediate return to court and

26. W.A. Hinnebusch, *The Early English Friars Preachers* (Rome 1951),
    pp. 465–9.
27. The Westminster continuator of the *Flores Historiarum*, ed. H.R. Luard
    (RS 1890) III, p. 266. The writer, who is strongly royalist in sympathy,
    accuses the Friars Minor of disloyalty to the king after the battle of
    Lewes.
28. *Documents of the Baronial Movement of Reform and Rebellion 1258–67*, ed. R.F.
    Treharne and I.J. Sanders (1973), pp. 100, 284.

referring to his loyal friendship and his sagacity in affairs of state.[29]

The director of the king's conscience possessed great potential for influencing royal policy. As Henry's confessor and trusted councillor, Darlington cannot wholly escape the suspicion that he prompted, or at least complied with the king's foolish plan of underwriting the debts of the papacy as part of a bid for the crown of Sicily. But it would overstep the evidence to depict him as an eminence grise behind the throne. Here and elsewhere his political judgement may have been weak, but there is no reason to think that he represented the views of his religious brethren. Possibly his election to the headship of the London priory in 1261 signified a desire of his order to withdraw him from the political arena.

In reality both the charge of partiality and its refutation are based upon liberal assumptions about the events of the years 1258 to 1265 which are anachronistic. Whether they were in the royal service or not, friars shared the common belief that royal authority was a divine vicariate. Most of them would probably have subscribed to the judgement of Louis IX at Amiens that the seizure of executive powers by the magnates and the imposition of administrative restraints upon the king were a violation of natural and divine law. Darlington's loyalty to his royal master does not seem to have impaired the reputation of the Mendicants as disinterested mediators and peace-makers. At the close of the battle of Lewes, Dominicans and Franciscans were to be seen together, scurrying to and fro between the exhausted combatants, endeavouring to negotiate terms of peace between Montfort and the royalists.

.   .   .

THE PROBLEMS OF POLITICAL NEUTRALITY

Yet even if the Mendicants as a whole succeeded in walking the tightrope of political neutrality, the prominence of individual friars in government service associated them with the exercise of political power in the minds of the people and exposed them to attack by radical movements of protest. The risks of their position were apparent from the tumultuous events that occurred in France in the summer of 1251, while Louis IX was absent on crusade. The alarming news of the

29. Hinnebusch, *Friars Preachers*, pp. 463–4.

king's defeat and surrender to the Muslims in Egypt touched off an anarchic populist movement calling itself the Crusade of the Shepherds. It seems to have originated in Picardy. A swelling mob of peasants, armed with pitchforks, clubs and axes, marched south, picking up recruits from the villages on their route and terrorizing the people of the towns where they gained admittance. Their leader, a renegade monk called Jacob, managed at first to ingratiate himself with Queen Blanche, but as the mob, now some thousands strong, turned to preaching and mayhem against the clergy and the looting of churches, the authorities and townspeople organised a counter-attack. At Bourges Jacob and several of his followers were killed by the citizens' militia; and a section of the rag-tag army that descended on Gascony was dispersed by Simon de Montfort. A remnant that landed at Shoreham in Kent was scattered by the posse of the sheriff on the king's instructions.[30]

Contemporaries who report what seemed to them an apocalyptic event are agreed that the violence of the shepherds – the pastoureaux – was directed against the clergy. Adam Marsh received a horrified letter from the custodian of the Friars Minor at Paris describing the mayhem in the city and the vandalizing of churches, where clerks were beaten or thrown into the Seine.[31] But the friars seem to have been singled out for particularly vicious attack. Some houses of the Franciscans were wrecked and the friars driven out. At Tours the mob smashed the choir-stalls of the Dominican church and dragged eleven of the Preachers, stripped of their habits, through the town beating them, and were only stopped from killing them by the intervention of the townspeople. Salimbene thought these attacks on the Mendicants were provoked by the fact that the friars had preached the failed royal crusade;[32] in any event, it was clearly their identification with power and official policy that made them targets of mob fury.

---

30. A detailed account is given by Matthew Paris: *Chron. Majora* V, pp. 246–54. Royal letters warning the Keepers of the Cinque Ports and the sheriffs of the landing were issued on 8 July 1251: *Close Rolls 1247–51*, p. 549.
31. The letter is reproduced by the Burton annalist: *Annales Monastici*, ed. H.R. Luard (RS 1864–9) I, pp. 290–3. The mayhem at Paris, Orleans and Tours was described in further detail by the chronicler of Metz: *Chronica Universalis Mettensis*, ed. I. Heller *MGH SS* XXIV (1879), p. 522.
32. Salimbene, pp. 444–45.

In Germany, as in France and England, the Mendicants were warmly welcomed by the secular aristocracy and enjoyed the patronage of the Hohenstaufen imperial house. The Ascanian margraves of Brandenburg provided sites for Franciscan and Dominican friaries in their territories and chose friars as their chaplains and confessors. The margrave Otto III had himself buried in the Dominican priory at Strausberg, which he had founded.[33] The Provincial of the German province of the Blackfriars authorised the prior of Rostock to accompany the court of Prince Nicholas von Werle of Rostock-Werle when it moved outside the boundaries of his jurisdiction.[34] The Mendicants, in fact, established close personal ties with the households of several of the princes east of the Elbe.[35]

In the Spanish kingdoms also the Mendicants were closely associated with the ruling dynasties. Both Dominicans and Franciscans were retained at court as confessors to Alfonso the Wise of Castile-Leon (1252–84), his queen, Violante, and his turbulent son, the future Sancho IV.[36] It was a Dominican who helped smooth the path of Sancho's uncanonical marriage with Maria de Molina, and her understandable devotion to the order was expressed by her decision to be buried in a Dominican habit. In the kingdom of Aragon, Jaime I (1213–76) showed himself to be a generous patron of the Franciscans. Throughout the peninsula the friars received the steady support of the kings in the face of hostility from the bishops and cathedral clergy of the unreformed secular Church.[37]

The ambiguity of the position of friars at court was thrown into sharp relief by events in Germany. They had at first been made welcome by the Emperor Frederick II and his son Henry VII, who was left in charge of the German kingdom while his father was occupied in Italy. But Frederick's conflict with the papacy, culminating in the announcement of his

33. *Chronicon Principum Saxoniae*, ed. O. Holder-Egger *MGH SS* XXX (1896), p. 34.
34. *Ungedruckte Dominikanerbriefe des XIII Jahrhunderts*, ed. H. Finke (Paderborn 1891), p. 97.
35. Freed, *The Friars and German Society in the Thirteenth Century* (Cambridge Mass. 1977), pp. 57–60.
36. A. Lopez, 'Confessores de la familia real de Castilla': *Archivo Ibero-Americano* 16 (1929), pp. 5–75.
37. P. Linehan, *The Spanish Church and the Papacy in the Thirteenth Century* (1971), pp. 223–9.

deposition by Innocent IV at the Council of Lyons in 1245, made their position at the Hohenstaufen court untenable. Any hopes they may have entertained of adopting a stance of benevolent detachment were swept away by a torrent of papal madates instructing them to preach a crusade against the Hohenstaufen and rally public opinion behind the anti-king William of Holland.[38] They were thus, through their obedience to the pope, involved as partisans in the civil war that racked Germany for two decades; and they were treated as enemies by Frederick and the adherents of the Hohenstaufen interest. Jordan of Giano laments over the sufferings of the Friars Minor, many of whom were ejected from their friaries, some were imprisoned and some killed 'because they adhered to the mandates of the Church', a loyalty, adds Jordan sadly, that was displayed by no religious other than the Friars Minor.[39]

Understandably the Dominican provincial, Ulrich Engelberti, wrote to the brethren in ecstatic terms to report the advent of peace with the election of Rudolf of Hapsburg to be King of the Romans, a choice the Dominicans had helped to procure.[40] Here as in other areas the friars proved themselves a formidable arm of papal policy in obtaining rulers compliant with the interests of the Church.

38. Freed, *Friars and German Society*, pp. 138–67.
39. Salimbene, p. 61.
40. Finke, *Ungedruckte Dominikanerbriefe* pp. 87–8.

Chapter 10

IN THE SERVICE OF THE PAPACY

. . .

PROTECTION AND SERVICE

By the time the friars came on the scene, the claim of the papacy to possess plenitude of power over the Church had behind it a long period of evolution. In the course of the thirteenth century the doctrine of papal sovereignty material-ised in a multitude of different ways – papal provision to benefices, the taxation of clerical incomes, and an ever-grow-ing flood of petitioners and litigants to the papal Curia. The canonists taught that as heir of St Peter the pope was 'the universal ordinary' – everyman's bishop, to whose tribunal all men, even the humblest clerk or layman, might have immedi-ate access. But the care of all the churches could not be effectively concentrated in the Apostolic hands without the help of a central bureacracy and a corps of devoted and well-instructed agents. As international organisations, dedicated by their founders to the papal obedience and the service of orthodoxy, the Mendicant Orders were perfectly fitted for this role. The fact that they possessed a mobile and highly educated corps of schoolmen made them ideal agencies of the papacy in its efforts to integrate the Western Church into a single centralised administrative and legal system.

From an early stage the position of the friars was secured at the Curia by having patrons at the highest level to look after their interests. In Ugolino, the cardinal bishop of Ostia, St Francis found a powerful friend and counsellor who com-mended the order to the pope and nursed it through the problems of its infancy. It was at the request of Francis himself that Honorius III designated Ugolino the Protector and Governor of the Friars Minor, and this office was perpetuated when, on becoming pope in 1227, Ugolino appointed his nephew, Cardinal Raynald of Segni, to succeed him as the Cardinal Protector. Primarily the Protector's role was to provide the order with a permanent voice at the Curia, to help it secure privileges and to oversee its welfare; but equally he served as a channel through which the demands of papal policy could be intimated to the leaders of the order.

The official status of Cardinal Protector seems to have been an innovation made in response to the petition of St Francis, and for a long time it had no counterpart in other religious orders. The Dominicans had no Protector, officially designated as such, until the fourteenth century.[1] But other orders of comparable size had representatives at the Curia, who in practice performed a similar function. The acts of the general chapters of Cîteaux reveal that the Cistercians habitually depended upon the services of one of their number in the sacred college – a 'white cardinal' – to obtain privileges and promote their interests at Rome. One of their most active and influential patrons was the English Cistercian John of Toledo, who was appointed cardinal-priest of St Laurence-in-Lucina in 1244. The chapter acts in fact refer to him as Protector of the Order.[2]

If the Friars Preachers were at first without an official Cardinal Protector, they never lacked members of the order who were in a position to represent their interests at the Curia. Ugolino, both as cardinal and pope, showed as much concern for their welfare as he did for that of the Franciscans. According to Celano, it was he who brought about the meeting between Francis and Dominic in his house. As Pope Gregory IX, he brought a number of Dominicans into the service of the Curia as chaplains and penitentiaries. One of them was the Spanish friar Raymond of Penaforte, whom Gregory employed to compile the great collection of decretals or papal judgments to supplement the work of Gratian, the so-called *Liber Extra*, destined to become one of the classical canon law books of the Western Church.

The function of a papal penitentiary was to deal with the

1. Hinnebusch *HDO*, pp. 210–11.
2. J.-B. Mahn, *L'ordre cistercien et son gouvernement* (Paris 1951), p. 166.

cases of penitents whose sins had been reserved for absolution by the pope. By the beginning of the thirteenth century the canonists had established the rule that three offences came into this category of 'reserved sins'. These were striking or assault upon a member of the clergy or a religious, the forging of papal letters, and incendiarism. Those who committed such offences could be absolved only by the pope, unless they were at the point of death, and they were required to go to Rome, or at any rate to the Curia, for confession and absolution. In response to a rising flood of petitioners seeking absolution or requesting dispensations, Innocent III created the office of Cardinal Penitentiary to deal with them, and before long it was necessary to provide him with assistants or minor penitentiaries. The Cardinal Penitentiary was one of the three major offices of the papal administration. When the Dominican theologian Hugh of St Cher was appointed to the office with the title of cardinal-priest of S. Sabina, the Friars Preachers acquired a powerful advocate at the Roman Curia.

The majority of the men commissioned to act as minor penitentiaries were friars. The instruction in moral theology and the art of the confessional, which they received in their friaries, equipped them better than most of their contemporaries for this task. Gregory IX and his successors appointed both Dominicans and Franciscans alongside others to serve in this capacity. One of the earliest Franciscans to be chosen was the English brother Henry of Burford. According to Eccleston, he had entered the order at Paris, where as a novice he enlivened the brethren with light-hearted verses about the temptations that beset a poor Minorite, but later he was to be a pillar of strengths to four successive Ministers-General.[3]

Of necessity the friar penitentiaries followed the papal Curia. At Rome, they made themselves available to penitents and petitioners in the Lateran basilica attached to the palace of the popes, and lived in an adjacent house allocated to them.[4] Under Nicholas III, who moved the papal residence to the Leonine city, they operated in St Peter's. In the fourteenth century they continued to act as penitentiaries at Rome as well as providing the same service at Avignon. The penitentiaries were privileged persons, who enjoyed direct access to the

---

3. *De Adventu Fratrum Minorum in Angliam* ed. A.G. Little (1951), p. 31 & n.
4. P.L. Oliger, 'I penitenzieri Francescani a San Giovanni in Laterano': *Studi Francescani* 22 (1925), pp. 495–522.

papal presence, and as such they enjoyed exemption from the jurisdiction of their own religious superiors.

That 'protection draweth allegiance and allegiance draweth protection' is an old adage of the English common law. The protection and patronage the friars received from the popes, often in the face of protests from the secular clergy, were rewarded by their devoted service in many areas of papal government. They were appointed as nuncios or financial emissaries to supervise the collection of papal taxes; and we find both Dominicans and Franciscans commissioned to act as papal judges-delegate to hear cases that had been referred to the court of Rome in their country of origin. Sometimes they were designated as special visitors with the delicate task of investigating monasteries whose affairs were causing the pope concern.

The academic reputation of many of the Mendicant school-men made them the chosen agents of the popes in furthering their scholastic plans. Gregory IX entrusted the Dominicans with the task of erecting a faculty of theology in the university he sought to create at Toulouse, where it was to serve as a cell of orthodoxy in a heretical countryside. In or shortly after 1245, when the Curia was residing at Lyons to shelter from the armies of Frederick II, Innocent IV set up a Curial university to provide instruction in theology and law at the papal palace. This rather shadowy school of higher studies, the *studium curiae*, which followed the migrations of the papal court, was staffed on the theology side mainly by a series of friars, who were styled Lectors of the Sacred Palace.[5] Its first recorded master of theology was Bartholomew of Bregenz, a Dominican. The office of lector at the Curia was not a monopoly of the Mendicants – secular masters were also appointed – but the dominance of Dominican, Franciscan and Augustinian friars among the successors of Bartholomew of Bregenz reflected the eminence of the friars in the theology faculties of the universities.

5. R. Creytans, 'Le studium Romanae Curiae et le maître du sacré palais': *AFP* 12 (1942), pp. 5–83. In the thirteenth century the Mendicant lectors at the Curia included such famous names as Aquinas and John Pecham.

. . .

PREACHING THE CRUSADE

One of the most cherished projects of the thirteenth-century popes was the crusade. It was directed in the first place at the recovery of the Holy Land from the Muslims; and even after the fall of Acre in 1291 and with it the last foothold of the Latin principalities in the East, the possibility of regaining Jerusalem continued to haunt the minds of Western Christians. But crusading was not confined to warfare in the Islamic East. Crusades were also declared against the pagan Lithuanians of the Baltic; and beginning with Innocent III, the popes invoked crusades against heretics and against Christian leaders, such as the ministers of the Hohenstaufen empire in Italy and disobedient city communes that threatened the Papal State.

Following the proclamation of a crusade, the first stage in mobilising the necessary army and raising the required funds was the announcement of indulgences for participants and the appointment of preachers specially commissioned by the pope to preach the cross. Numbers of secular clergy, especially schoolmen, were designated for this task, but among those chosen the friars had pride of place. Their mobility and their training in the arts of popular preaching obviously fitted them for the role. In 1225 the Dominican John of Wildeshausen, later to be Master-General of his order, was commissioned to preach in South-West Germany to drum up recruits for Frederick II's crusade to the Holy Land.[6] Dominicans and Franciscans were repeatedly called upon by Gregory IX to preach the cross, both for the relief of the Holy Land and for the Baltic crusade against the pagan and aggressive Lithuanians.

Some of these commissions were addressed to named individuals; others were addressed to provincials of the Mendicant Orders, instructing them to select suitable brethren to preach the cross in their area. One of these was a mandate sent to the provincial prior of the Dominicans in Germany by Innocent IV in September 1243. The letter instructs the provincial to command priors and brethren of his order in the provinces of Magdeburg and Bremen to preach a crusade in support of the Teutonic Knights who are fighting the pagans in Prussia and

---

6. For this and the following paragraph see C.T. Maier, 'The Friars and the preaching of the Cross in the thirteenth century': London Ph.D. thesis, 1990.

Livonia. Besides accepting recruits, the preachers have the power to absolve from their vows any who have already taken the cross but are prevented from going by sickness or poverty. They may also promise an indulgence of one year to those who take the cross, and an indulgence of twenty days for all those attending the solemn preaching. The same mandate was addressed to the Dominican provincials of Poland, Bohemia, Pomerania, Denmark, Norway and Sweden.[7]

The offer of indulgences for attending the preaching and an elaboration of ceremonial were expedients used to boost the size of audiences at a period when popular enthusiasm for crusading was on the wane. An important part of the preacher's job was to raise funds by allowing those who were unable to go on the expedition or who simply had cold feet to redeem their rashly taken vows. Matthew Paris, who observed the friars of both orders preaching Gregory IX's summons to a crusade in 1234–5, accused them of self-promoting pomp and sharp practice over the redemption of vows: 'they take care to be received in monasteries and towns in solemn procession, with banners, lighted candles and festive vestments – they who have chosen humility and voluntary poverty – and those they sign with the cross today, they absolve from their vows tomorrow in return for a gift of money'.[8] Whether or not the charge was true, Matthew's snide censure identified a genuine problem. The constitutions of the Mendicants expressly forbade the collection of money on the occasion of preaching or the use of friaries to store money. Through their involvement in preaching the crusades, the friars were obliged to breach both these prohibitions.

The friars were vowed by their Rule to the obedient service of the papacy; but the diversion of the crusade against Christian rulers tested their loyalty to breaking-point. Their standing as disinterested peace-makers was compromised by their use as Innocent IV's propagandists and agents in his struggle against the Hohenstaufen. They had at first been welcomed by the German princes and the ruling dynasty, but following Innocent's announcement of Frederick II's deposition in 1245, they were commanded to preach a crusade against him in Germany and Italy and to muster support for his rival,

7. *Les Registres d'Innocent IV*, ed. E.B. Berger (Paris, Ecole Française d'Athènes et de Rome 1884) I Nos. 162–3.
8. *Chron. Majora* III, p. 287.

William of Holland. They thus found themselves forced into the position of partisans in the civil war in Germany and were treated as enemies by the adherents of the Hohenstaufen.

In the same way, in the 1280s Mendicant preachers were used as the propaganda arm of the popes in the War of the Vespers over the succession to the Sicilian Regno; and in the 1320s the Curia relied upon the Dominicans and to a lesser extent upon the Franciscans and Augustinians to preach crusades against the Ghibelline cities in northern and central Italy.[9] After 1323, when a section of the Franciscans rebelled against the authority of John XXII, he depended almost exclusively upon the Dominicans to mobilise support for the papal cause against the Visconti of Milan and the Ghibelline party. The depth of the Dominican commitment to the struggle is indicated by the acts of the chapter of the Roman province which met in 1324. The chapter not only ordered preachers at public sermons to expound the papal case against the rebels; it bade those who heard the confessions of the laity to use the occasion in order to induce suitable persons to help the papal cause, drawing their attention to the generous indulgences that could be secured in this way.[10]

Apart from occasional protests at the misuse of crusading taxes, the diversion of the crusade to fighting Christians who had been declared enemies of the Holy See seems to have been generally accepted by the leaders of Western society, other than those who were the targets of the campaigns.[11] Making war against heretics was thought to be meritorious; and the Ghibellines, who rejected the power of the keys, were easily tainted with heresy. Nevertheless there were clearly some among the friars who had misgivings about the use of the pulpit and confessional to defend the Papal State and to further the political aims of the papacy. The protest of the Franciscan radicals against the corruptions of the carnal Church is well known. That the Dominicans also harboured a few dissidents is suggested by the fulminations of the Roman provincial chapter against 'any brother who uses a derogatory

9. Norman Housley, *The Italian Crusades. The Papal-Angevin Alliance and the Crusades against Christian Lay Powers, 1254–1343* (1982), p. 117.
10. *Acta Capitulorum Provincialium Provinciae Romanae*, ed. T. Kaeppeli and A. Dondaine (Rome, Istituto Storico Domenicano, 1941), pp. 230–1.
11. Norman Housley, *The Later Crusades, 1274–1580: from Lyons to Alcazar* (1992), pp. 234–40.

word or writes against the papal case, or lets slip his tongue and utters any irreverent or derogatory word about the Holy Father, or worse, offers help to the Church's rebels by speech or writing.'[12]

. . .

THE INQUISITION

The theological training of the friars and their superior pastoral skills made them the chosen instruments of the papacy for the task of extirpating heresy. It was a role that made them the object of popular hostility in some quarters and it has not won them much appreciation from modern students of the medieval world. The repression of dissent by totalitarian regimes of the twentieth century has reminded us that religious toleration is a late and fragile growth of liberal democracy. The violent repression of religious dissent, of which the Inquisition was the symbol and agent, can only be understood in the context of a society where church and state were so closely entwined that they were in effect two aspects of a single commonwealth.

As Christianity became the official cultus of the late Roman Empire, the Church gradually ceased to be a voluntary society. People were baptized into it in infancy, just as they were born members of the state, and they could not leave either without incurring the penalties of *lèse-majesté*. Religious dissent was a rebellion against the system, an attack on the polity, and it was the recognised duty of emperors and kings to repress it. In medieval Europe this ancient tradition was reinforced by popular fear of the outsider. In Western Europe, where Catholic Christianity was the universal religion, the Jew and the dissenter were objects of suspicion and popular hatred, which sometimes erupted into violence. The First Crusade was disfigured by a series of pogroms as it made its way southwards through the Rhineland. This collective mentality underlay the draconian penalties enacted against heretics by rulers of the thirteenth century. It was still implicit in the famous declaration *cuius regio eius religio* (the religion of a country is determined by its ruler) enunciated at the Peace of Augsburg in 1555.

The Inquisition was an apparatus of repression that was

12. Kaeppeli and Dondaine, *Acta Capitulorum*, pp. 23–31.

developed slowly out of various measures designed to combat the dualist heresies that were rampant in France and in northern and central Italy by the middle of the twelfth century. In the early middle ages the detection and punishment of heresy was a duty incumbent on the bishop within the area of his jurisdiction. Bishops were goaded into a more active pursuit of heretics by the decree *Ad abolendam* published by Pope Lucius III at the Council of Verona in 1184. This required them to tour their dioceses twice a year to seek out alleged heretics and examine them, using for the purpose the secular procedure of the sworn inquest or inquisition – an interrogation of the accused based upon statements made by local witnesses under oath. Those convicted and obdurate were to be handed over to the secular authorities for 'condign punishment', and their property was to be confiscated. The pope's decree, which was reiterated by the Fourth Lateran Council of 1215, squeamishly avoided elaborating the expression 'condign punishment' which was to be administered by the secular arm, but a long tradition declared that it meant death by fire. This was how it was understood by the Emperor Frederick II who made it the mandatory penalty for impenitent heretics in the Ravenna decrees of 1232.

The manifest inability of diocesan bishops to make any impression upon the rising tide of heterodoxy persuaded the papacy to assume direction of the campaign through a variety of agencies. Innocent III commissioned the Cistercians to engage in a preaching mission to the people of the Languedoc in the hope of recovering the sectaries for the Church. His appeal to the king of France and the northern aristocracy to undertake a crusade against the Albigenses was part of a strategy to coerce or supplant rulers, like the Count of Toulouse, who protected the Cathars, and to replace them with secular princes who were willing to collaborate with the efforts of the Church in repressing heresy.

As we have seen, it was the crisis of orthodoxy in the Midi that called St Dominic's Order of Preachers into existence. The defence of Catholic orthodoxy and the conversion of heretics had been the primary aim of their fraternity. After the Albigensian war had ended with the Treaty of Paris in 1229, the Dominicans of Toulouse played a leading part in the pursuit of people accused of heresy by their neighbours. One of the community, Brother William Pelhisson, chronicled with macabre relish their proceedings against those accused posthumously. The theologian Roland of Cremona, whom the Toulousain friars had acquired as their lector, hearing that a canon of St Sernin had received heretical rites before his death, led a party to exhume the corpse, which was dragged through the town and burned outside the walls. Roland organised the same treatment for the body of a deceased Waldensian, and oversaw the demolition of his house, which was made into a refuse pit.[13]

Bishops engaged in prosecuting heretics increasingly sought the assistance of Dominican friars because their theological training and their dialectical expertise were valued assets when it came to interrogating those accused. Sometimes individual friars were appointed by bishops to master-mind the whole operation, like the Dominican Brother Ferrier who was commissioned by the archbishop of Narbonne to seek out and examine heretics throughout the province. The Franciscans too were drawn into the enterprise, though at first on a more limited scale. A first step towards the creation of a standing papal Inquisition was taken by Gregory IX in 1227, when he gave a general commission to prosecute heretics in Germany to the monk Conrad of Marburg, whose ruthlessness in sending people to the stake created a reign of terror in the Rhineland and made his name a byword for fanaticism and cruelty.

The ubiquity of the problem evidently convinced Gregory that local diocesan courts were not adequate to deal with it without the reinforcement of some permanent and professional apparatus. So, after the issue of a number of *ad hoc* commissions like that of Conrad of Marburg, in April 1233 the pope set up the permanent papal Inquisition. This was a standing tribunal of judges-delegate empowered to investigate and adjudicate cases of heresy in a specified region. It was appointed for the Languedoc in the first place, and the conduct of the Inquisition was entrusted to the Dominicans. The provincial of the Friars Preachers of Provence was instructed to select friars qualified to act as Inquisitors for the provinces of Narbonne, Auch, Bordeaux and Bourges. About the same time the pope authorised the notorious Robert le Bougre – himself a former convert from the Cathars and now a Dominican – to act as

13. W.L. Wakefield, *Heresy, Crusade and Inquisition in Southern France, 1100–1250* (1974), p. 210. On the origins of the Inquisition in Provence see also C. Thouzillier, 'La répression de l'hérésie et les débuts de l'inquisition' in A. Fliche and V. Martin, *Histoire de l'église* vol. 10 (Paris 1950), pp. 291–340.

Inquisitor in northern France, a commission that led to a mass holocaust of heretics at La Charité-sur-Loire.

In the following years the Inquisition was extended to Italy, and here too the tribunal was initially in the hands of the Dominicans. The prior provincial of Lombardy was given power to act in the north, and the head of the Roman province of the order was appointed for central Italy. Individual friars like Peter of Verona – the Peter Martyr of Dominican hagiography, who was murdered in 1252 – distinguished themselves by the zeal with which they mobilised the secular authorities of the cities in the pursuit and punishment of heretics.

Although individual Franciscans were sometimes co-opted to assist Dominican Inquisitors and the Friars Minor were active in preaching against the sectaries, Gregory IX seems to have been reluctant to draw upon the resources of the order to staff the Inquisition. Possibly the large lay element that prevailed among the Minorites in the early stages made him think them less reliable for the purpose than the clerical order of the Preachers who, in any case, were specifically dedicated to the work by their founder. It was not until the pontificate of Innocent IV that the Franciscans were assigned a significant role in conducting the papal Inquisition.

On his return from Lyons, Innocent set about reactivating and reorganising the Inquisition in Italy. In 1254 he appointed the provincial minister of the Friars Minor an Inquisitor for the province of the Romagna; and the same year, six months before his death, he divided Italy into eight inquisitorial provinces, of which two – Lombardy and the Regno – were assigned to the Dominicans and the remaining six to the Franciscans.[14] In this way the Friars Minor were given the responsibility for the pursuit of heretics in central Italy and the Veneto region, but it is not until 1258 that we have first information of a Franciscan Inquisitor at work. This was John Oliva, who was feeding the fires of orthodoxy with human fuel at San Gimignano and other cities of Tuscany.[15] The choice of friars for the office of Inquisitor was delegated by the pope to the General and the provincial ministers.

The decision of Innocent IV and his successors to use

14. M. d'Alatri, *Eretici e Inquisitori in Italia: Studi e Documenti* (Rome 1986–7) I, pp. 127.
15. *ibid.* p. 130.

Franciscans as well as Dominicans to run the Inquisition has been the subject of some speculation. Raoul Manselli believed the move was prompted by the hostility the Dominican Inquisitors had aroused through the ruthlessness with which they pursued their victims. Their activities had provoked outbursts of popular violence at Bologna, Parma and Milan. It was as Inquisitor of Milan that Peter of Verona was waylaid and assassinated by a group of peasants who were said to be Cathars.[16] On the other hand, Franciscan Inquisitors were no more popular than their Dominican brethren. Stephen of Saint-Thibéry who assisted the Inquisition in the Languedoc was murdered at Avignonet in 1242; and Oliva was stopped from preaching at Florence and ignominiously expelled from the city. The co-optation of the Franciscans for the struggle against heresy was merely a response to changes that had overtaken their organisation: by the time of Alexander IV they had become a learned and clerical order, boasting some of the leading theologians of the scholastic world.

Hostility to the activities of the Inquisition was widespread and brought odium on the friars who operated it. Pelhisson complained that the nobles and burghers of the Toulousain sheltered heretics and obstructed efforts to arrest them. These people were their neighbours and friends.[17] In any case, the inquisitorial procedure, which allowed secret accusations by unnamed witnesses, and allowed no right of appeal, showed scant concern to protect innocent people who had been falsely accused. 'I have a wife and I sleep with her,' shouted John the weaver as he was led through the streets of Toulouse protesting his innocence, 'I have sons; I eat meat; I lie and swear and I am a faithful Christian.'[18] Pelhisson, who recorded John's protest without a trace of irony, noted that the crowd intervened to stop the weaver being burned. It was at Toulouse that the Dominican Inquisitor William Arnold overreached himself and brought reprisals on his brethren by citing some of the city's ruling families before his tribunal. The consuls reacted by ordering his expulsion and then by invading the cloister of the Friars Preachers and herding them ignominiously out of the town.

16. He was appointed Inquisitor for Milan in 1251 by Innocent IV, who canonized him eleven months after his murder. A. Dondaine in 'Saint Pierre Martyr': *AFP* 23 (1953), pp. 66–162, observed that his legend has been greatly 'improved'.
17. Wakefield, *Heresy, Crusade and Inquisition*, p. 212.
18. *ibid.* p. 213.

An inquiry that followed a riot at Bologna in May 1299 revealed the intensity of popular aversion for the Inquisition and for the Dominicans who operated it. The angry voices of the streets were faithfully recorded by the notaries: 'I heard it said that the Inquisitor was a heretic, that he was the Anti-Christ come to slaughter men, that heresy came from the friars. The Inquisitor and the friars are doing it for money. The friars are evil men and thieves, and since they came into the world, faith has been lost. It would be a good thing to go to the house of the friars and set fire to it and burn the Inquisitor and the friars with him.'[19]

It was only possible for the Inquisition to operate where it had the active co-operation of secular rulers. Such co-operation was in fact demanded by the papal edicts under threat of excommunication. In France the Capetian kings showed themselves more than willing to collaborate in repressing heresy, especially in the Midi, where the triumph of orthodoxy went hand in hand with the extension of royal authority over the newly conquered territories. James I of Aragon welcomed the Inquisition and showered favours upon the Dominicans. Elsewhere the compliance of the secular arm was less easily obtained. In Germany the activities of the Inquisition were virtually halted by the interregnum and the political strife that followed the death of Frederick II in 1250.

. In Italy co-operation depended upon the shifting kaleidoscope of communal politics. The friars mobilised public opinion through the medium of the more militant confraternities like the Society of the Faith and the Society of the Cross; and they persuaded the city councils to incorporate the anti-heretical decrees of the pope and the emperor in their statutes. The Franciscan Henry of Milan himself composed the relevant statutes for the commune of Vercelli. But the amount of assistance the Inquisitors could get from the civic authorities depended upon the attitude and allegiance of the dominant party in the commune. The struggle between the partisans of the Hohenstaufen imperial dynasty and the supporters of the papacy offered a serious impediment to the free functioning of the Inquisition.[20] In many cities the Ghibelline party made common cause with the Cathars and other dissidents. Ezzelino

19. L. Paolini, 'Gli Ordini Mendicanti e L'Inquisizione' in *Les ordres mendiants et la ville en Italie centrale* (Rome 1979), p. 708.
20. d'Alatri, *Eretici e Inquisitori in Italia* p. 137.

da Romano, Frederick's son-in-law, who ruled as a tyrant over Verona, Padua and Vicenza, was a notorious patron and protector of heretics. Some cities of northern Italy offered sanctuary to numbers of refugees from the holocaust in the Languedoc. When the Guelf party was in the ascendant, the friars had greater freedom to pursue the campaign against the sectaries, but even here the *podestàs* of the cities were often unenthusiastic in supplying the forces needed to execute the mandates of the Inquisition.

One by-product of the struggle was a new genre of literature designed to provide guidance for the friars who operated the Inquisition. The majority of these text-books or manuals were composed by friars. The earliest of them are little more than formulary-books – collections of model letters, papal mandates, formulas of abjuration and reconciliation for heretics who confessed and repented, and so forth. One of the earliest of these compilations was one written up by the Dominican canonist Raymond of Penaforte in 1242 at the instance of Pedro d'Albalat, the archbishop of Tarragona. It was intended for the instruction of friars acting as Inquisitors in Pedro's diocese.[21] In time the manuals became more elaborate. They incorporated orders of procedure and accounts of the distinctive doctrines of the heretical sects for the guidance of uninitiated friars who had the task of interrogating suspects. One of these *summae* that was widely distributed was the *Summa de Catharis et leonistis seu de Pauperibus de Lugduno* by the Italian Dominican Raynier Sacconi. Raynier was an authority on the subject: he had been a Cathar himself before he had seen the light, and in the 1240s he was engaged as an Inquisitor hunting down his former brethren in Florence.[22] The genre achieved its classical form in the famous *Practice Inquisitionis* compiled by the Dominican Inquisitor Bernard Gui in the fourteenth century.

. . .

ROME AND CONSTANTINOPLE

One of the services the friars rendered the papacy was that of representing Rome in a series of negotiations aimed at restoring unity with the Eastern Church. The long-standing breach between Rome and Constantinople, rooted less in any deep theological divergence than in cultural antipathy between

21. A. Dondaine, 'Le manuel de l'inquisiteur': *AFP* 17 (1947), pp. 85–174.
22. *ibid.* pp. 91–3, 170–4.

Greeks and Latins, had been made almost irreparable in 1204 when the Crusaders from the West had sacked the ancient Christian capital of the Eastern Empire. The diversion of the Fourth Crusade against Byzantium, which had been engineered by the Venetians, had been followed by the coronation of Baldwin of Flanders in Hagia Sophia as head of a new Latin empire and the colonization of parts of Greece and the islands by Frankish adventurers. All this was viewed with horror by Greek-speaking Christians, who continued to regard the refugee Basileus at Nicaea as the only legitimate emperor and looked for the recovery of Constantinople. The capital was in fact to be regained in 1261 by Michael Palaeologus VIII.

Unfortunately the sins of the Latins, who had raped and plundered the holy city, were compounded in Greek eyes by an attempt to Latinize the Greek Church in the conquered territories. The chief abettor, if not the instigator of this misconceived policy was Innocent III. He had not anticipated the attack on the eastern capital, but he seems to have regarded the outcome as a providential chance to end the schism, subordinating the eastern churches once more to the primatial authority of Rome. He thus ratified the appointment of the Venetian Thomas Morosini as Latin patriarch of Constantinople and proceeded to designate Latin archbishops of Greece, while leaving in place those Greek prelates who made their submission to the papacy.

The fierce hostility these proceedings aroused in the Greek clergy foredoomed plans for any formal reunion of the Church to failure for the foreseeable future. Nevertheless, the pressure of the Seljuk Turks upon Anatolia, the desire to recover their ancient capital, and the subsequent threat to Byzantium posed by the ambitions of Charles of Anjou, persuaded the Basileus and Greek patriarch to swallow their pride from time to time and seek a *rapprochement* with the West. The first of these overtures came from the Patriarch Germanos II, who addressed an irenical letter to Pope Gregory IX in 1232 suggesting negotiations for the restoration of communion between the churches. The bearers of this missive were, as the patriarch explained, five Friars Minor, lately escaped from Turkish captivity, who had enjoyed his hospitality at Nicaea. While there, they had discussed with him the question of healing the breach with the Roman Church. So he is sending them to his holiness, 'all of them without staves, each with only a single garment, and without shoes, though I reckon their feet are as beautiful as those who bring good tidings of peace between the Greeks and the Latins'.[23]

In response to this plea Gregory wrote a letter expounding the papal view of the case, and the following year he dispatched a delegation to Nicaea consisting of two Franciscans, Haymo of Faversham and Ralph of Reims, both of whom had been masters of theology at Paris, and two French Dominicans, Peter of Sézanne and Hugh. The tone of the pope's letter boded ill for the success of the mission. Gregory took the occasion to expound the papal doctrine of the Roman primacy in the most uncompromising terms fortified by reference to the full panoply of Petrine texts from the Gospels; he blamed the Greeks for having seceded from communion with the see of Rome, adding, by way of a gratuitous clout, that the enslavement of their church to the secular power was a divine judgement on them for refusing to acknowledge the primacy of Peter.[24]

The four friars arrived at Nicaea on 15 January 1234. It seems that Ralph of Reims was the only member of the party who could speak Greek, and the report of the conversations that followed was probably the work of his hand.[25] The first round of talks took place at Nicaea in the imperial palace in the presence of the patriarch and the emperor, John III Vatatzes, who presided and took an active role in the discussion. The main agenda was determined by the Greeks and was concerned with the question of the *Filioque* – whether the Holy Spirit proceeded from the Father and the Son or, as the Greeks insisted, from the Father alone. They pressed the Latin party to justify the fact that the Latin church had added the phrase 'and the Son' to the original version of the Nicaean creed. After ten days of unfruitful argument about this abstruse

23. *Les Registres de Grégoire IX*, ed. L. Auvray (Ecole française de Rome, 1896–1910). I, p. 502. Text in Matthew Paris, *Chron. Maj.* III, pp. 448–55. On Germanos and the Franciscan mission see M. Roncaglia, *Les Frères Mineurs et l'Église Grecque Orthodoxe au XIIIᵉ siècle: Biblioteca Bio-bibliografica della Terra Santa e dell'Oriente Francescano* serie IV, Studi II (Cairo 1954), pp. 34–42.
24. Auvray, *Les Registres de Grégoire IX* I p. 523; text in *Chron. Maj.* III, pp. 460–6.
25. H. Golubovich, 'Disputatio Latinorum et Graecorum': *AFH* 12 (1919), pp. 418–70.

topic, it was decided to adjourn the conversations until March.

The disputants reassembled at Nymphaeum in Lydia, Germanos having now brought up reinforcements in the shape of the patriarchs of Jerusalem, Antioch and Alexandria. The discussion now moved on to the sacrament of the altar and the Latin practice of using unleavened bread in the mass, and it became increasingly acrimonious. The friars accused the Greeks of denying the validity of the Latin sacraments and reproached them with having erased the pope's name from the diptychs – the altar tablets bearing the names of those to be commemorated during the eucharist – thereby implying he was a heretic and an outcast from the communion of the Church. Finally, despite a last-minute attempt by the emperor to save the situation, they stalked out of the meeting with mutual recriminations: 'You have no excuse for your sins. And since we have found so many abominations among you, and no will to emend your errors, we are returning to him who sent us.'[26] We catch here a far-off echo, doubtless unnoticed by the writer of the narrative, of the parting words of that other disastrous mission of Cardinal Humbert nearly two centuries earlier, which had precipitated the rift with Constantinople.

The language of the report displays the dialectical skill the Mendicant masters had deployed to confute the Greek spokesmen, which had evoked a remonstrance from the emperor: 'It is not for you to proceed by syllogisms. Such a method is a source of contention and dispute . . . better you proceed with simplicity.'[27] It is apparent that the chief motor-force behind the discussions on the Greek side was the emperor. 'How then can we make peace?' he asked the Latin delegation despairingly as the talks looked like foundering. But the friars responded to this appeal with an uncompromising demand for acceptance of the Catholic formularies.

John Vatatzes had turned the empire of Nicaea into a strong and prosperous state, but the incursion of the Mongols close to his eastern borders made him anxious to establish friendly relations with the West, and in 1248 he took the initiative in trying to break the deadlock and resume the

26. *ibid.* p. 452.
27. *ibid.* p. 436.

discussions with Rome that had been broken off in 1234. Here too the agents he chose were two Greek-speaking Franciscans, one of whom, Thomas, was lector to the Friars Minor at Constantinople. His overtures persuaded Pope Innocent IV to dispatch a mission to Constantinople the following year led by the Minister-General of the Friars Minor, John of Parma. These discussions also proved abortive.

The friars were chosen for these negotiations by the popes not only for their theological expertise and dialectical skill; the settlements of the Mendicants in the eastern capital had given them a unique value as channels of communication between the two cultures as well as equipping them to act as mediators between the Greek and Latin Churches.[28] It was thus the Greek-speaking friars of Constantinople who played a significant role in the resumption of discussions that led in 1274 to a formal if short-lived act of reconciliation between the churches. They were chosen as mediators and interpreters because their empathy for the spirituality and rites of the Orthodox Church had won them the respect of the Greek clergy.

The initiative to reopen negotiations came from the emperor Michael VIII Palaeologus. Michael was indifferent to the finer points of theology, and his motives for seeking a *rapprochement* with the papacy were political. He had regained possession of Constantinople and had expelled the Franks from the capital, to find his position threatened a decade later by a new crusading project from the West. The promoter of this was Charles of Anjou, the brother of King Louis IX, who had been left the undisputed king of Sicily by the defeat and execution of Conradin, the last Hohenstaufen claimant to the throne. Charles's restless ambition now sought an outlet in the creation of a Mediterranean empire. He was encouraged in these plans by the deposed emperor Baldwin II, who offered him large territorial gains in return for an army to help him reconquer Constantinople. With this in view, Charles set about forming alliances and assembling an armada at Palermo for the attack on Byzantium.

In face of this mounting threat Michael Palaeologus turned

---

28. H. Golubovich, *Biblioteca Bio-bibliografica della Terra Santa e dell' Oriente Francescano* I (Quarrachi 1906), pp. 128–9. The Franciscan house at Constantinople, founded after the Latin conquest of 1204, was until 1263 part of the Franciscan province of Romania, which included the Holy Land.

to the pope as the only power capable of stopping Charles. He was fortunate as his overtures coincided with the aspirations of Pope Gregory X. Tebaldo Visconti had been elected pope in September 1271 while he was absent with the Crusaders in Syria, and as pope one of his most cherished ambitions was to organise a crusade for the recovery of the Holy Land from the Turks. It was obvious to him that this could not be accomplished without the co-operation of Byzantium, and he was therefore eager to resume efforts to heal the breach between Rome and the Orthodox Church.

The man Michael chose to carry his message to the pope was Brother Parastron, a Greek member of the Franciscan community at Constantinople, who had gained popularity with the Orthodox clergy by participating in their liturgy, but who was Latinist in sympathy and a strong advocate of reunion.[29] Parastron reached the Curia, then residing at Orvieto, in October 1272. In response to the emperor's request for renewed negotiations, Gregory dispatched a delegation of four Friars Minor chosen for him by Bonaventure, the Minister-General. These four friars, Jerome of Ascoli, Raymond Berengar, Bonaventura di Mugello and Bonagratia, accompanied Parastron back to Constantinople. The burden of the discussions, which were chiefly with the emperor, must have been borne by Jerome of Ascoli, the only member of the delegation who spoke Greek, and Parastron.

The papal envoys remained at Constantinople for fifteen months, in the course of which they persuaded Michael Palaeologus to accept the propriety of the *Filioque* clause in the creed, the validity of the Latin sacraments, and the divinely appointed primacy of the pope. The emperor agreed to include these articles of faith in a written confession and agreed to send representatives to the forthcoming ecumenical council which the pope had summoned to meet at Lyons in May 1274. Having succeeded in their mission, the Franciscan envoys re-embarked for the council in the company of the emperor's delegation, which consisted of the grand logothete George Acropolites, a lay theologian and diplomat, the ex-patriarch Germanos III, and the metropolitan of Nicaea. It was not a strong embassy from an ecclesiastical point of view;

29. D.J. Geanakoplos, 'Bonaventura, the two Mendicant Orders and the Greeks at the Council of Lyons' in *The Orthodox Churches and the West* (Studies in Church History 13, 1976), ed. D. Baker, pp. 183–211.

the most conspicuous and ominous absentee was the patriarch Joseph, who was opposed to the reunion.

Pope Gregory had made elaborate preparations for the council, in which the friars played a major part. Among the preparatory papers commissioned by the pope one of the most significant was the *Opus Tripartitum* by the former General of the Dominicans, Humbert of Romans.[30] Humbert's treatise was irenical in its tone, urging the retention of the Greek rite and pleading for a study of the Greek Fathers by the Latins. Another Dominican helper the pope sought to co-opt was Aquinas. He was summoned to the council and requested to bring with him the treatise he had written against the errors of the Greeks, but he died *en route* at the abbey of Fossa Nuova. The Dominicans also provided one of the theologian-interpreters to the council in the person of Brother William of Moerbeke, the translator of Aristotle's *Politics*, who had learned Greek in his early days as a friar at the convent of the Preachers in Constantinople. Bonaventure, the former General of the Franciscans, who had been made a cardinal the year before, had helped to formulate the agenda of the council, but he died before its business was completed.

The council met in Lyons cathedral. The first of its enactments dealt with the controverted procession of the Holy Spirit, but there is no record of any public debates between the Greek envoys and the Latin prelates. The act of reunion, which was only part of the business before the assembly, was accomplished by a solemn but simple ritual. It was preceded by the reading of the emperor's confession of the Latin formularies and a reading of a letter from the Orthodox synod; and it was consummated by the singing of the Nicaean creed, first in Latin and then in Greek, including the *Filioque* clause, which was thrice repeated by the Greek envoys. Pope Gregory then concluded this part of the proceedings by intoning the Te Deum. The absence of public debates indicates that the outstanding issues had already been settled at Constantinople between the Mendicant delegates and Michael Palaeologus.[31] The role of the council was simply to give public ratification to the union.

Michael's primary aim in forcing through the agreement

30. *ibid.* p. 96.
31. *ibid.* pp. 208ff.

had been to secure the pope's help to ward off the impending attack by Charles of Anjou, and in this respect his *démarche* was successful. Gregory, in fact, forbade Charles to proceed with his plans, which were eventually shattered by the rising of Sicily against the Angevins. But not surprisingly the reunion, which had been dictated largely by political expediency, proved ephemeral. It was repudiated by the patriarch, the Greek monasteries and a large part of the Greek clergy. Despite the emperor's efforts to coerce his subjects, the Byzantine church as a whole could not be induced to accept the *Filioque* or the universal and overriding power of the papacy as it had by then been formulated by the Latin canonists.

Chapter 11

AFAR UNTO THE GENTILES

'Not the least of my heart's desires,' said Humbert of Romans, 'is that through the ministry of our order schismatic Christians should be recalled to ecclesiastical unity, and the name of Jesus Christ be taken to the faithless Jews, to the Saracens – so long deceived by their pseudo-prophet – to the pagan idolaters, barbarians, and all peoples, so that we are His witnesses to bring salvation to all peoples to the ends of the earth. Two things,' he added, 'stand in the way of accomplishing this. One is lack of languages. The other is love of one's native soil, a natural affection not yet transformed by grace.'[1] In 1255 when Humbert wrote that to the brethren, Franciscan missionaries had already reached the court of the Great Khan in outer Mongolia, and from the reports of their journey Western Christians were beginning to learn that the ends of the earth were more distant than they had realised.

The missionary enterprise was the *raison d'être* of the Mendicant Orders. The evangelization of heretics, non-Christians and those who were simply lapsed or indifferent, was the primary task assigned them by their founders. They were well equipped for it by their freedom from worldly impedimenta and by their structure, which allowed the individual friar mobility within the supporting framework of an international organisation. Many of their men were accustomed to leaving their own country for the sake of learning, teaching or administration.

The language problem that Humbert alluded to had al-

---

1. *Litterae encyclicae Magistrorum Generalium Ordinis Praedicatorum*, ed. B.M. Reichert *MOFPH* V (Rome 1900), pp. 16–20.

ready been addressed by the Dominican general chapter. In 1236 it had commanded the brethren of all priories to learn the languages of foreign provinces adjacent to their own.[2] The same concern was voiced by Innocent IV, when he instructed the Chancellor of Paris to find maintenance for ten youths from Outremer with competence in Arabic and other oriental languages. The pope's plan was to have them study theology at the university, so that they could become missionaries of the Gospel to their homelands.[3] The solution Humbert proposed in his encyclical was to allow any friar who felt moved to learn Arabic, Hebrew or Greek, a transfer to a house of the order in Constantinople or the Holy Land. For Arabic, one of the best places was, of course, the Spain of the *reconquista*, and in 1259 the Dominican chapter ordered the prior provincial to set up a school of Arabic language at Barcelona, open to friars from other areas.[4]

The pressure for Arabic linguists reflected the preoccupation of Western rulers and churchmen of the early thirteenth century with the threat posed by the militant Islamic states round the frontiers of the Latin world. Concern had been intensified by the failure to recover Jerusalem after the victories of Saladin and the collapse of Byzantine power. To some, including the popes, it seemed that the best hope of defending Western Christendom lay in converting the Muslims to Christianity rather than in crusading. 'War,' wrote Roger Bacon, 'is of no avail against them, because the Church is sometimes compromised by the wars of Christians, and this makes it impossible to convert the Saracens.' He went on to point an accusing finger at the knights of The Temple and the Hospitallers as people who 'much disturb the conversion of unbelievers'.[5]

The first Rule of St Francis commended friars who were

2. Reichert I, p. 9.
3. *Chartularium* I, p. 212. The arrangement was confirmed by Alexander IV in 1258 and in 1286 by Honorius IV, who doubled the number of beneficiaries: *ibid.* pp. 372, 638. Cf. J. Richard, 'L'enseignement des langues orientales en occident' in *Croisés, missionaires et voyageurs* (Variorum reprints 1983) xviii, pp. 149–64.
4. Reichert I, p. 98.
5. *The Opus Maius of Roger Bacon*, ed. J.H. Bridges (1897) I, p. 121. He also castigates the violence of the Teutonic Knights 'without which the natives beyond the frontiers of Germany would have long since been converted'.

inspired to work as missionaries to the Saracens; and Francis had himself shown his disciples the way by his audacious exploit of following the Crusaders to Damietta and obtaining an interview with the Sultan of Egypt, Al-Kamil. But the cruel fate of the brethren sent to preach in Morocco indicated that the possibilities of this approach were limited. Christian preachers endeavouring to proselytize in territories occupied by Muslim rulers were liable to be killed. It was the Muslim population in the Latin principalities that offered a free field to the missionary. In order to preach to them and to minister to the Frankish settler population, the Franciscans quickly established settlements at Jerusalem, Acre, Antioch and other cities of the crumbling Latin Kingdom, to be followed a little later by the Dominicans. The Dominican William of Tripoli claimed to have converted and baptized more than a thousand Muslims. Probably the main hindrance to missionary enterprise in these areas was the cynical attitude of the Latin settlers: Jacques de Vitry, who viewed the scene from the bishop's palace of Acre, complained that they refused to allow their Muslim slaves to receive baptism.[6]

For much of the thirteenth century, the popes pursued an ambivalent policy in dealing with the Muslim leaders. They continued to bless the crusade, while at the same time endeavouring to convert them to Christianity through the agency of Mendicant missionaries. In 1233 Gregory IX, the devoted patron of the Friars Minor, sent a party of them to expound the central articles of the Christian faith to the Caliph of Baghdad and the Sultans of Damascus, Aleppo and Cairo.[7] A similar attempt was made by Innocent IV in 1245, using a mission of Dominican friars led by Brother André Longjumeau. Coming under the umbrella of diplomatic privilege, from a prelate who was widely regarded in the Muslim world as the overlord of the West, these parties of missionaries were courteously received, but their message failed to make any impression.

Besides making these overtures to Islamic rulers, the popes displayed an active concern for reconciliation with the separated eastern churches, many of which had fallen under the political lordship of Muslims. Here too the friars were the

6. *Lettres de Jacques de Vitry*, ed. R.B.C. Huygens (Leiden 1960), p. 88.
7. J. Richard, *La papauté et les missions d'orient au moyen-âge* (Rome, Ecole française 1977), pp. 40–50.

chosen agents of the papacy on account of their linguistic skills and their acquaintance with the oriental liturgies gained at Constantinople and in the Holy Land. Longjumeau, who headed the mission to the Sultans, also had a message for the spiritual head – the Catholicos – of the Syrian Jacobite Christians. He was a fluent speaker of Arabic and Syriac. In 1246 Innocent IV sent one of his penitentiaries, the Franciscan Laurence of Portugal, with an appeal for reunion with Rome addressed to the patriarchs of the Jacobite, Maronite and Nestorian Christians in Armenia, Syria and Egypt. Both these preoccupations of the thirteenth-century popes – the conversion of Islam by the sword or the word, and the recovery of schismatic churches for the Roman obedience – were given a new complexion by the sudden irruption of the Mongols upon the states of eastern and central Europe.

The Mongols or Tartars, as they became known in the West, were a warlike nomadic people of Asia. Before they appeared in the West, they had been launched on a career of world conquest by their leader Ghengis Khan (died 1227). Moving eastward, they had conquered Mongolia and north China; then turning west, they destroyed the Muslim empire of central Asia and carried fire and slaughter into northern India. The sons and successors of Ghengis Khan subjugated Persia and Armenia and the Seljuk Sultanate of Rum and occupied the land from the lower Volga to the Caucasus known as the Golden Horde. In 1240–1, under the command of Batu, the grandson of Ghengis Khan and ruler of the Golden Horde, they invaded eastern Europe, at first devastating Kievan Russia, and then advancing into Poland and Hungary, plundering, burning and slaughtering, driving herds of terrified refugees before them. To Western observers the onslaught looked like the fulfilment of the Apocalypse. It seemed that these savage hordes riding out of the Asian steppes were unstoppable. 'Like demons released from Tartarus,' wrote Matthew Paris with a shudder, 'they cover the earth's surface like locusts.'[8] At Wahlstatt they routed an army of Poles and Teutonic Knights hastily assembled by duke Henry of Silesia, whose severed head they carried about as a trophy. They defeated Bela, the king of Hungary, and turned his territory into a shambles.

8. *Chron. Majora* IV, pp. 76–7.

Western leadership was bewildered and paralysed by the speed and ferocity of the onslaught. By the summer of 1241 the barbarians were within striking distance of Vienna and it seemed that nothing, short of divine intervention, could save Western Europe. The Mongol advance was halted, in fact, not by military action but by the death in December 1241 of their emperor, the Great Khan Ogodai. The news of his death caused Batu's army to withdraw from the newly conquered lands of central Europe to the territory of the Golden Horde east of the Carpathians. Ogodai left a vast empire ruled by under-kings or subordinate khans, the descendants of the sons of Ghengis, extending from northern China to the lower Danube.

The great Mongol invasion of 1240–1 added an incalculable new dimension to the Christian missionary task of evangelizing all peoples. The immediate concern of the popes was to organise the defense of Western Europe, in the expectation that the incursion of that dreadful winter would be renewed. Gregory IX called for a crusade, and the summons was renewed by Innocent IV. But the momentum of the Mongol advance had been stayed by the partition of the empire among the descendants of the Great Khan; and the prolongation of peace suggested to Pope Innocent and Louis IX of France that diplomacy in the service of the Gospel offered a better hope of freeing Europe from the Tartar menace. The conversion and baptism of the Tartar rulers would not only protect Christendom from renewed attack; it might even provide a new and powerful ally against Islam.

It was Innocent who took the initiative. In the spring of 1245 he addressed two letters to the king and people of the Mongols. The first expressed his dismay at the violent incursion into Europe and proposed a peace treaty; the second set out a summary of the Christian faith and accredited the papal envoys who would expound the doctrines of Christianity.[9] For the hazardous task of penetrating the inner regions of the Mongol empire and delivering these letters the pope chose two parties of friars, who set out separately. The first party consisted of an Italian Franciscan, John de Piano di Carpini and his companion, Brother Benedict of Poland; the second

9. *Les Registres d'Innocent IV*, ed. E. Berger (Paris 1884–1918) I Nos. 1364–5. For the papal missions to the Mongols see Richard, *La papauté*, pp. 65–166. I am especially indebted to this book.

mission was entrusted to the Dominicans, Ezzelino of Cremona and André de Longjumeau.

The Dominicans took ship to Syria, travelled north of Tiflis, where the order already had a priory, and from there crossed the Caucasus and made contact with the Mongol leader Baiju, the commander of the Caucasian army. His response to the papal message was hostile, and the friars began to fear for their lives. All the same, they were allowed to leave without molestation, and at the end of an expedition that had taken two years, they returned to the Curia to report the failure of their mission.

Carpini, the Franciscan, was made of sterner stuff. Travelling to Kiev, he came to the court of Batu Khan, who had conquered and occupied Russia. Carpini asked him to convey the pope's twofold message to the Great Khan, Kuyuk, but this he refused to do. Instead, he commanded Carpini to take it to Kuyuk himself. After an interminable journey through the Steppes and the inhospitable mountains of central Asia, the party reached Mongolia, and after three weeks of hard riding they arrived at the court of the Great Khan, in time to see Kuyuk enthroned as emperor, 'in a vast tent of white and purple, great enough, as it seemed to us, to hold more than two thousand men, round the circumference of which was a wooden structure painted with various images.'[10] The envoys were hospitably treated. They were assigned a tent and, pending the formalities of electing and enthroning the Khan, they were ceremoniously received by his mother.

When the friars were eventually admitted to the presence and delivered their message, the response they received was no more encouraging than the one Ezzelino had taken home. Kuyuk, who believed that the pope was the suzerain of the Western kings, rejected the plea for a pact of non-aggression; instead, he asserted that heaven had conferred on him a universal sovereignty, and demanded the pope's submission to his authority. The invitation to accept baptism was dismissed with contempt. Nevertheless, the fruits of Carpini's mission were not all bitter. He was a keen observer, and he took back with him to Lyons a store of information about the settlements and social customs of the Mongols and details of their methods

10. *Historia Mongalorum*, ed. A. Van den Wyngaert in *Sinica Franciscana* I (Florence-Quarrachi 1929), pp. 116–19.

of warfare, which he wrote up on his return. His report – the so-called History of the Mongols – circulated rapidly. It provided readers with a first written eye-witness account of the unknown lands and peoples beyond the frontiers of the Western world. In the years that followed, it was to be filled out by further reports from Franciscan missionaries and by the traveller's reminiscences of the Venetian merchant Marco Polo.

One of Carpini's most surprising discoveries was the fact that there were Christians serving as ministers and clerks in the household of the Great Khan. These were apparently Nestorians from the church of Persia, who had been displaced by the Mongol invasions. Carpini observed that they had a chapel in a tent, close to the great tent of the Khan, where they rang the Hours and chanted the Divine Office 'according to the custom of the Greeks'.[11] They told him they were convinced that the Khan would become a Christian. This optimistic prognosis, which Carpini disseminated back home, was to form the basis of several unsuccessful overtures made by Western leaders in the years that followed.

The next attempt to reach an understanding with the Mongol emperor was prompted by an unexpected approach from the Great Khan himself. In December 1248 Louis IX, who was in Cyprus mustering his crusading army for the attack on Egypt, received an embassy sent by Kuyuk. News of Louis's impending expedition had reached the Mongol court, which was planning an attack on the Caliphate of Baghdad. The Khan's envoys were two Nestorian Christians of his secretariat. Brother André de Longjumeau acted as their interpreter. The gist of their message was that the Great Khan, ruler of the world by the divine will, was a protector of Christians and their churches throughout his empire. Accordingly he sent greetings to King Louis and wished him victory in his war against the enemies of the Cross.[12] This message, which Joinville believed to be an offer of help to reconquer the Holy Land from the Mamelukes, evoked an immediate response from Louis. He commissioned Longjumeau, his brother William, and a third Dominican, to carry his reply to the Khan and explore the possibilities of a military alliance.

11. *Historia Mongalorum*, pp. 124–5.
12. J. Richard, *Saint Louis, roi d'une France féodale* (Paris 1938), pp. 493–4.

The gifts Louis provided for the ambassadors to take with them indicate his belief that Kuyuk was ready to embrace the Christian faith – a tent of scarlet cloth to serve as a chapel with hangings, on which were embroidered the annunciation and incidents of the life of Christ, a relic of the True Cross, chalices, and the service books required for singing the mass. The mission left Cyprus for Antioch in January 1249, and after a journey of nearly a year reached the Mongol court in Mongolia, only to find that Kuyuk had died. They were received by his widow, who, after the exchange of gifts, gave them a disobliging reply to take back to the king of France: he was to submit to the universal lordship of the Great Khan and send a tribute of gold, failing which, he would be attacked and destroyed. 'And, be it known to you,' observed Joinville, who noted down the text of this message, 'that the king repented sore that he had ever sent envoys thither.'[13]

Despite the disappointing outcome of this embassy, there remained cogent arguments in favour of mounting another mission. The Dominicans had discovered large numbers of displaced Christians living in central Asia, and both Louis and Pope Innocent were concerned for their pastoral needs. Hopes of an alliance with the Mongol leaders against Islam had not been abandoned and were made keener by the defeat of Louis' crusade. And for the friars surrounding Louis, the realisation that Christians were free to preach and proselytize in Mongol lands fired their missionary zeal. A new opportunity was presented by the news that Sartaq, the son of Batu and great-grandson of Ghengis Khan, had been converted and had received baptism. This, as well as strategic considerations, persuaded Louis to sponsor a fresh mission led by William de Rubrouck, a Flemish Franciscan, who had accompanied the king on the disastrous expedition to Damietta.

William set out early in 1253, armed with letters from the king and gifts, which included a Bible from Louis and an illuminated Psalter offered by Queen Margaret. He took with him as his companion an Italian friar, Brother Barthlomew of Cremona, a clerk named Gosset, and a Turkoman interpreter. At Constantinople they used Louis' money to purchase a slave named Nicholas and to hire two men to drive the carts and

13. *The History of Saint Louis*, transl. and ed. Joan Evans (1938), p. 148. Joinville's account, though confused, is a major source for this mission.

tend the horses. We know the details of William's saga because he recorded them in a diary, which he subsequently wrote up in a report he presented to the king.[14] He was a schoolman, who had served as a lector in his order, and he was a man of boundless curiosity, a passionate sightseer and a sharp observer. His account of his journey is one of the most vivid pieces of reportage the thirteenth century has to offer. It was rapidly circulated on his return, and it provided Western readers with a mass of new information about the geography, as well as the ethnic and social structure of central Asia.

The party sailed from Constantinople to Sebastopol in the Crimea, and from there they proceeded overland into the land of the Golden Horde occupied by the Tartars. They had two carts, one of which they had loaded with fruit, biscuits and muscat wine to offer their hosts, for, as the Greek merchants had warned him, 'the Tartars do not look with favour upon anyone who comes empty handed'. It took them two months to reach the court of Sartaq in southern Russia because the carts were drawn by oxen which determined the pace – 'with horses I could have done it in a month', grumbled William. 'We never slept in a house or a tent, but either in the open or under our carts; we saw no trace of a town.'[15] They were made uneasy by the continuous escort of Tartar horsemen, who surrounded them with a cloud of curiosity and suspicion.

After a precarious crossing of the Don, each cart being carried athwart two boats – 'the river at that place is as wide as the Seine at Paris' – they arrived at Sartaq's court. They were taken under the wing of a chamberlain, a Nestorian Christian named Coiac. William explained apologetically that they brought no gifts except books as he was a monk and had no property, but prudently sweetened the chamberlain with a flagon of Muscat. The following day they were summoned to meet the Khan. Having been warned by Coiac to dress up for the occasion, they processed into the presence wearing vestments and chanting the *Salve Regina*, carrying the Bible and Psalter on a cushion, preceded by their clerk swinging the thurible. Sartaq examined the thurible and slowly thumbed

14. Edited by A. Van den Wyngaert in *Sinica Franciscana* I pp. 164–332; cf. French transl. and commentary by Claude and René Kappler, *Guillaume de Rubrouck: voyage dans l'empire mongol, 1253–55* (Paris 1985).

15. Kappler, *Guillaume de Rubrouck* p. 107.

over the queen's gorgeously illuminated Psalter. William then presented the king's letters, which had been translated into Arabic and Syriac, and the party bowed out of the presence.

William asked permission to stay in Sartaq's territory to evangelize his people. As he had publicly proclaimed in Constantinople, he regarded himself as a missionary sent to preach to the infidels, not as an ambassador. But the king's letters adumbrated the possibility of an alliance against the forces of Islam, and this involved political decisions too far-reaching for Sartaq to take on his own. He therefore instructed the envoys to seek out and obtain the opinion of his father, Batu. So the party set off once more on their travels across the Steppes. Batu received them courteously in his great tent, proffered them the customary drink of mare's milk, which William had learned to consume without a shudder, but told them they could not reside in his territory without getting the consent of the Great Khan, Mongka. Moreover they were warned that only the two friars and their interpreter would be allowed to proceed to Karakorum, the residence of the emperor in Mongolia; the rest of the party was to be sent back to Sartaq.

Winter was now approaching as the three men set off on their long journey. Their hosts had given them sheepskins to keep out the cold. They rode continuously eastward for weeks. William faithfully recorded the miseries of their passage, the cold, fatigue and hunger. Their guide procured them food, but they had to make do with only a drink or a little millet at morning and a shoulder of mutton at night, less than half-cooked for want of firewood. But cold and hunger did not blunt William's powers of observation. As they rode past the Caspian Sea to their south, he noted that the Blessed Isidore of Seville had been in error in asserting that the Caspian was a gulf of the northern Ocean: 'nowhere does it touch the Ocean; it is surrounded on all sides by land.'[16] At various points along their route they encountered communities of Muslims and groups of eastern-rite Christians, and, as they approached the frontiers of Mongolia, Buddhist temples and statues of the Buddha. At one point they came upon a village entirely peopled by Nestorians, and went into their church and sang the *Salve Regina*. At length they reached the court of

16. *ibid.* p. 137.

the Great Khan near Karakorum on 27 December, some four months after leaving the camp of Sartaq.

William describes the grand palace of the Khan on the outskirts of the town 'like a church, with a nave and two aisles supported by arcades.' The town itself was encircled by a wall of earth pierced by four gateways. No more than an arrow's flight from the palace, he saw a church surmounted by a cross, and on entering it, the friars found it well furnished with an altar and a great silver cross and images of Christ and the Blessed Virgin. Here they encountered an Armenian monk, who told them that the Great Khan particularly favoured Christians. It turned out, in fact, that one of Mongka's wives was a Christian; she brought her children to church on the feast of the Epiphany. But despite this encouraging news, William eventually concluded that the Great Khan had no religious convictions of his own. The friars were surprised to discover that he presided over a pluralist religious society in his capital, which contained, besides a church, twelve Buddhist temples and two mosques, where the faithful were publicly called to prayer.[17]

Ten days after their arrival, the party was taken in charge by the Grand Secretary, himself a Nestorian Christian, who ushered them into the presence of the Great King. They entered bare-footed, despite the intense cold, chanting the hymn, *A solis ortus cardine*, and knelt in front of the Khan, who was seated with his wife beside him on a bed covered with striped skins. Addressing him through a Nestorian interpreter, they explained that the king of France sent a message of peace, and they asked permission to stay in the land and minister to the Khan's Christian subjects.

They were, in fact, allowed to stay for over five months. At Easter the two Franciscans were allowed the use of the baptistery belonging to the Nestorians, which contained an altar, and William celebrated mass and heard the confessions of a motley crowd of Christians – Hungarians, Alans, Ruthenians, Armenians and Georgians – who had been captured and enslaved by the Mongols. Finally, at Whitsun, which in the year 1253 fell on 8 June, William was summoned to meet the Khan again and was once more asked the reason for his

17. Kappler, *op. cit.* p. 201. William calls them twelve 'temples of the idolaters'. In view of the spread of Buddhism in Mongolia, it seems probable that these were Buddhist temples.

coming. He explained he had come to preach the word of God, and using the interpreter, he endeavoured to expound the central tenets of the Christian faith. But his efforts were cut short by Mongka, who countered with a syncretistic statement that has a curiously modern sound: 'we believe there is only one God; as God has given the hand several fingers, in the same way he has given several ways.'[18] Following this unsatisfactory dialogue – 'one can only speak in his presence as far as he wishes' – the friars were given their *congé*.

From a diplomatic point of view, Rubrouck's mission had proved a failure. Before leaving, he was given a letter from the Great Khan to deliver to king Louis which, while not excluding the possibility of an alliance, renewed the demand for Louis' submission and threatened war in the event of non-compliance. In his report to the king William advised that the prospects of peace were poor and events justified his pessimism. In 1258 the Mongols took Baghdad and massacred its inhabitants, and the following year the army of the Golden Horde again invaded Poland and burned Cracow before retiring to its camp in southern Russia. Yet the king and the pope continued to receive assurances of the Khan's benevolence to Christians, and in 1269 a message from Kublai, the Great Khan who had succeeded his brother Mongka, suggested the time was ripe for a new effort to convert the Mongol leaders.

The bearers of this message were two Venetian merchants, Nicolo Polo (the father of the more famous Marco Polo) and his brother Maffeo. In pursuit of fresh trading outlets they had sailed to the Crimea and ventured into the territory of the Golden Horde. While staying at Bokhara, they encountered envoys returning to the court of the Great Khan, which had now been moved to Peking in the wake of his conquering armies. Indomitable in the cause of profit, the two Italians attached themselves to the embassy and accompanied the party across Asia to the distant capital of Kublai Khan in Peking. They were graciously received and generously entertained and sent home with a message for the pope: Kublai requested the pope to send him a hundred learned men to instruct his people, and some oil from the lamp that burned before the tomb of Christ in the church of the Holy Sepulchre at Jerusalem. Possibly this relic from Jerusalem was a request

18. *ibid.* p. 214.

from the Khan's Christian mother. It may have been responsible for starting the rumour that Kublai had himself been baptized a Christian.

It was these rumours that persuaded Pope Nicholas III to dispatch a mission to the Khan consisting of three Italian Franciscans, led by Gerard de Prato. They took with them papal letters, congratulating the Khan on his baptism and expounding the doctrines of the Christian faith. The friars were at the same time authorised to reconcile with the Roman Church any prelates of the separated eastern churches they encountered in Asia. But this mission misfired. In Asia Minor the friars learned from the Mongol leader that the Great Khan had not embraced Christianity; he had in fact adopted Buddhism – the first of his dynasty to do so. The party therefore abandoned their mission and returned to the Curia.

A decade elapsed before the papacy made another and, as it proved, final attempt to convert the Great Khan. This was the object of the legation dispatched by the Franciscan pope Nicholas IV in the year 1289. It was a response to an inquiry from Kublai Khan, who had already learned much about Western ways from the Venetian Marco Polo. The Polos, father and son, had returned to the court of the Khan in 1275, and the younger man had been retained in Kublai's service. The man chosen to lead the papal mission was another intrepid Italian Franciscan, John of Montecorvino, who was already fifty when he embarked on the adventure. Like his predecessors, he was given letters for both the Mongol rulers and the patriarchs of the eastern churches situated within the Mongol empire. In many ways Montecorvino's expedition was the most remarkable of the missions to the Far East undertaken by the friars. It was not only the last attempt by the popes to proselytize the Mongol emperors; it also, unlike previous missions, led to the plantation of a Latin church and episcopate in Cathay.

The party set out in July 1289.[19] Before leaving Italy, Montecorvino recruited a Dominican friar, Nicholas of Pistoia,

19. On Montecorvino's mission see Richard, *La papauté*, pp. 145–66; and the same author's 'Essor et déclin de l'Eglise Catholique de Chine au XIVe siècle': *Orient et Occident au moyen-âge* (Variorum reprints 1976), pp. 285–95.

and a layman, a merchant named Peter of Lucalongo, to accompany him. Having reached Persia, they decided to attempt the sea route to China. From the Persian Gulf their perilous voyage took them first to southern India, where they delayed some months. While there Brother Nicholas fell sick and died, and Montecorvino and Lucalongo proceeded alone on their way through the Indian Ocean. It was not until nearly the end of the year 1293 that they arrived at Peking, after an odyssey lasting more than four years. It was now apparent that Kublai Khan had embraced Buddhism, but the missionaries were graciously received. They were given freedom to pursue their apostolate in the Khan's territories and were even provided with an allowance out of the royal treasure.

The progress of Montecorvino's mission was described by him in a letter he wrote from Cathay in January 1305.[20] He built a Catholic church in the city of Peking with a campanile in which hung three bells, 'and therein I have baptized up to the present day, I think, about six thousand persons'. He had also constructed a Franciscan friary, with residential buildings and oratory, close to the Khan's residence, and peopled it with slaves purchased from their Mongol owners. These were taught Latin and instructed in the chant: 'we sing the Offices solemnly, and our voices are audible to the Lord Cham in his chamber'. Lucalongo, who had remained faithful, had been a tower of strength, using his own resources to buy land for the mission and supervising the construction of buildings.

For many years Montecorvino worked in China without the assistance of another priest: 'I was alone on this pilgrimage without a confessor for eleven years, until the arrival of Brother Arnold the German'. This Arnold was a Franciscan from the province of Cologne, who reached Peking in 1306. The loneliness of the missionary far from home breaks through in a reproachful letter Montecorvino wrote to the Generals of the Friars Minor and the Dominicans in February 1306: 'I expect you were astonished, not without cause, at not receiving any letters from me, I having been so many years in such a distant place. But I am equally astonished that I have never, except this year, received a letter or a greeting from any brother or friend; nor does it seem that anyone has remem-

---

20. Edited by G. Golubovich in *Sinica Franciscana* I, pp. 345–51.

bered me. I believe rumours had reached you that I was dead.'[21]

He had to wait another seven years before he received the long delayed recognition of his achievement. In 1307 the news that a colony of the Latin Church had been established in Cathay prompted Pope Clement V to designate Montecorvini its first archbishop. The pope also named bishops to serve under him as suffragans, three of whom at last reached Peking in 1313. They consecrated him a bishop and presented him with the pallium – the yoke-shaped scarf of wool that symbolised archiepiscopal jurisdiction conferred by the successor of St. Peter.

Letters from two of the newly arrived bishops, Andrew of Perugia and Peregrino of Castello, reveal that they found a thriving Catholic community of many races at Peking. Under the benevolent patronage of the Great Khan, Montecorvino had had much success in preaching to the Mongols – he claimed to have baptized ten thousand of them. As archbishop he also ministered to the numerous Christians of the eastern churches in the area. Among these were the Alans, Christians of the Byzantine rite, who had been deported from their Caucasian homeland by the Mongol armies. They now attached themselves *en masse* to the Latin Church of Peking. There were also Armenians in the archbishop's flock, and a growing number of Western merchants. The Nestorians, on the other hand, who had long been settled in central Asia and had their own clergy, were less friendly towards the rising Latin Church in their midst; nor does Montecorvino seem to have made any impact upon the Chinese, as opposed to the people of Mongolian race.

The mission of Cathay continued to be a Franciscan enterprise. The suffragan bishops had no territorial dioceses; they were based upon communities of Friars Minor. In September 1333, when news of Montecorvini's death had eventually reached the Curia at Avignon, Pope John XXII appointed another Franciscan, Nicholas, to succeed him as archbishop. But it is doubtful whether Nicholas ever got to Peking, for three years later the heads of the Alan community and the Great Khan were writing to the pope to request a replacement.

---

21. *G. Gobolovich, op. cit.* p. 351. The letter is in fact addressed to the vicars of the Generals of each order.

The last Franciscan incumbent of the see of whom we have any news is William du Pré, who was appointed in 1370 by Pope Urban V. He accomplished the journey, to find on his arrival that the Chinese Ming dynasty had expelled the Great Khan and the Mongols from Peking and that the Catholic community had been dispersed.

The missions to the Orient are a heroic episode in the history of the friars. In an age when the globe has been shrunken by modern transport and communications, it is hard to recapture the courage and fortitude of men who were driven by the apostolic ideal to journey 'to the end of the world towards the East, which rocks no man hath ever crossed, wherein are enclosed the peoples of Gog and Magog, who shall come at the end of the world, when Antichrist shall come to destroy all things'.[22] To the hazards and physical hardships that beset all medieval travel was added in their case the likely expectation of death at the hands of a savage tribe which had terrorized the peoples of eastern Europe. Those who returned, and the Venetian merchants who followed them, brought back with them a load of tales and strange information which transformed medieval knowledge of the geography and peoples beyond the frontiers of the Western world.

22. *The History of Saint Louis*, transl. and ed. Joan Evans, p. 143.

EPILOGUE: LOSS AND GAIN

When the fathers assembled in the Lateran basilica for the opening of the council on 11 November 1215, the task Innocent III placed before them in his allocution was 'the reformation of the universal Church'. It was his awareness of a crisis that had prompted him to summon the council. The problems that beset the Church at the outset of the thirteenth century were, as we have seen, the outcome of economic and social changes in western Europe that had been gaining momentum for more than a hundred years. The expansion of urban communities producing a society that was more affluent and more mobile than before, the emergence of a more educated laity critical of clerical privilege and clerical failings, the spread of heresy, and the rise of an international scholastic community following a common curriculum of secular studies, all presented the Church with a challenge it was poorly equipped to meet.

Under Innocent's guidance, the council proceeded to enact a comprehensive programme for the eradication of abuses and the improvement of pastoral standards. Its seventy decrees represent, in fact, the high-watermark of the reform programme sponsored by the post-Gregorian papacy. The object was to put an end to the secularisation of ecclesiastical appointments, to promote bishops who could be expected to devote themselves to the spiritual needs of their flocks and be more responsive to the demands of Rome, and to produce a better educated and more conscientious parish clergy, able to meet the demands of the new age.

The programme of reform had its successes. Although the ranks of the thirteenth-century episcopate continued to include prelates who were little more than mitred barons or royal ministers, they also included a growing proportion of school-men and former bureaucrats who devoted themselves unstint-ingly to the care of their dioceses. In France and England, at any rate, diocesan synods were convened with a fair degree of regularity and were used by bishops to instruct the parish clergy in their duties; visitations took place; and rectors of parishes were encouraged, or in some cases required, to attend the schools. But much reform was defeated by the stubborn realities of power and patronage.

The problems of the Church were deeply rooted in the structure of medieval society. The earlier world that was passing was one in which services were supported by gifts and territorial endowments. The wealth of the Church in land and tithes was forced to bear the cost of many of the services that fall to the charge of the modern state. The endowments of parishes were used as a means of supporting royal administra-tors, ecclesiastical lawyers, cathedral clergy and university teachers. The clerks who staffed the chanceries and household offices of kings were not as a rule paid a salary; they were remunerated by being appointed to parish rectories and preb-ends in cathedral churches. Such men were necessarily non-resident in their parishes and many of them were pluralists. They provided for the administration and spiritual care of their people by hiring a chaplain who was paid an annual wage.

One of the commonest ways by which income from parish endowments was diverted from the pocket of the resident priest was by the appropriation of the church to a monastery, hospital or collegiate body. The Lateran Council required the appropriator in these cases to allocate a fixed portion of the income from tithe and offerings to a vicar who would reside in the parish and perform the duties; but the appropriator usually got the lion's share of the endowment. The Council lamented that in some areas greedy appropriators had left priests with less than enough for subsistence, drawing the obvious and well-founded conclusion that 'hence in these areas there is seldom found a parish priest who possesses even a modest knowledge of letters'. The same problem was identified by Grosseteste in an excoriating address he delivered to the pope and cardinals at Lyons in 1250. He blamed monastic appropriation for the perpetual problem of unworthy and inadequate priests – 'substitutes and hirelings, who themselves receive from the property of their churches barely enough to support life'.[1] His attack was well directed. For the papacy continued to maintain the system by issuing dispensations for plurality and by providing clerks to parish livings and prebends at the request of rulers and other petitioners.

Benefice hunting and pluralism were among the most ineradicable abuses of the medieval Church. They drew their defensive strength from a widespread acceptance of the idea – an idea shared by popes, kings and bishops alike – that government and nobility and even learning were a legitimate charge upon the property of the Church. Preachers and moralists, like Grosseteste, who questioned this assumption were felt by many people to be dangerous revolutionaries. In consequence the pastoral care at parish level, both in country and town, was left mainly in the hands of a clerical proletariat, for the most part recruited locally, barely literate, poorly paid and, with the exception of the fortunate few installed in a perpetual vicarage, without security of tenure.

One of the most debilitating weaknesses of the medieval Church arose from the failure of its leaders to create any system of training for priests. The diocesan seminary was a product of the Counter-Reformation. The expansion of educational opportunity that occurred in the twelfth and thirteenth centuries only touched the fringe of the parochial clergy. The proliferation of cathedral schools and the rise of the universities created an educated clerical élite, but its products were quickly snapped up by kings and bishops to serve the swelling bureaucracies of church and state. Those who emerged from the schools were burdened with the need to repay patrons – for education cost money – and to satisfy the high expectations of parents. They looked for a lucrative career; few of them would be prepared to accept employment as a low-paid parish chaplain.

The need for a well-informed and devoted clergy, made all the more pressing by the emergence of an articulate and

1. S. Gieben, 'Robert Grosseteste at the papal curia, Lyons 1250': *Collectanea Franciscana* 41 (1971), p. 359.

critical laity, was met by the Mendicant Orders. They offered a solution to the problems besetting the Church by providing a second force – a new body of pastors parallel to that of the secular clergy and highly trained for the task. They did not change or renew the ecclesiastical structure; they simply by-passed it. As we have seen, they included in their ranks men like Adam Marsh, Hugh of Die and St Anthony of Padua, who were among its fiercest critics. Their adoption of personal and corporate poverty as the basis of their institution emanci-pated them from the socio-economic structure of the secular Church. The man who became a friar opted out of the race for preferment. It was this that made them the trusted counsel-lors of princes and prelates; it is impossible to suborn a man who has no possessions or worldly ambitions. Thus they became the chosen agents of those popes and more zealous bishops who could see no way of changing the system, but who were anxious to pursue the cause of reform and to organise the defence of orthodoxy.

Increasingly the popes relied upon the friars rather than the secular clergy to overcome institutional inertia, to meet the pastoral demands of the new age and to reinforce papal sovereignty over the Western Church. It was they, not the secular bishops and clergy, who were used to mount the counter-attack upon heresy. The value placed upon the friars as instruments of papal policy was indicated not only by the steady flow of privileges issued in their favour, but also by a marked preference for choosing Mendicants as bishops where circumstances brought an appointment within the range of papal jurisdiction.

According to Celano, when Francis and Dominic met in Rome in the house of Cardinal Ugolino, he suggested recruit-ing bishops from the brethren as they were the best expositors of the apostolic life. But both saints demurred. Dominic replied with a brief refusal to allow it. Francis objected that his brethren had chosen a humble station in life, which was why they were called Minors, and pleaded with the cardinal not to permit them to be made bishops lest prelacy should make them arrogant. But despite the misgivings of the founders, Ugolino, when he became Pope Gregory IX, appointed a Franciscan, Brother Agnellus, to the see of Fez in Morocco; and Franciscans continued to supply bishops for the Islamic lands of North Africa, probably because the assignments were too dangerous for those who did not court martyrdom. The appointment of friars to vacant sees became increasingly common in Western Europe after 1240.

Some of these appointments represented the enthusiastic choice of cathedral chapters; others reflected the influence of kings who appreciated the political and spiritual services rendered by friars at court. It was the patronage of Louis IX that raised the Franciscan schoolman Odo Rigaldi to the archbishopric of Rouen in 1248. A year earlier, Henry III had expressed his appreciation of friar Adam Marsh by making an unsuccessful attempt to get him appointed to the see of Ely in place of the candidate elected by the chapter. The right of the papacy to adjudicate contested elections and to confirm the election of metropolitans gave the Curia scope to designate friars, sometimes without regard to the wishes of the secular ruler. Both the Dominican Kilwardby and the Franciscan Pecham owed their appointment to Canterbury to direct papal nomination. With Innocent IV's designation of Hugh of St. Cher, the Dominican theologian, to be cardinal-priest of S. Sabina in 1244, the Mendicants took their place among the princes of the Church.

The gradual absorption of the friars into the ecclesiastical establishment they had criticised was accompanied by a slow relaxation in their observance of poverty. The harrowing of the Spirituals by John XXII and the rebellion of the Minister-General, Michael Cesena, threw the Franciscan Order into disarray, but eventually left the more relaxed Conventual party, representing the majority of the brethren, in possession of the field. Voluntary poverty is a difficult ideal to sustain. In middle age religious organisations, like individuals, naturally succumb to the biological urge to seek security. By the fourteenth century, the compromises over poverty that had disrupted the Franciscans had affected the other Mendicant Orders. The complaints of the general chapters indicate a general relaxation of discipline and a slippage from the observance of poverty in the Dominican Order. Common dispensations from attendance in choir and refectory undermined community life. Ascetical ideals were enfeebled by the corrosive balm of social success. Individuals were permitted to receive a regular income from personal bequests and the proceeds of the quest for alms. A great many lesser folk imitated the example of King Philip the Fair, who bequeathed his Dominican confessor, Brother Nicholas de Goran, an income of 40 livres tournois for life.[2]

Many of the disciplinary problems were aggravated by the catastrophes of the fourteenth century. Their urban location and their ministry to the sick and the dying of all classes made the friars particularly vulnerable to the Black Death. The bubonic plague, which swept through Western Europe in 138-9 and recurred at intervals until the seventeenth century, almost wiped out many Mendicant communities. These had to be painfully rebuilt by the survivors. On the spiritual level, the Great Schism, which began with the election of a rival to Pope Urban VI in 1378, dealt a damaging blow to the morale of the friars. As international organisations devoted to, and protected by the papacy, they were directly affected by a dispute over the headship which split the Church into contending factions. The Dominican Order was temporarily divided by the papal schism, as a number of provinces declared their allegiance to the Avignon pope, Clement VII. But Raymond of Capua, who was elected General of the Preachers in 1389, rallied the support of his brethren behind Urban VI and his Roman successor.

In response to the general dilution of the founders' ideals, all the Mendicant Orders produced revivalist groups bent on restoring primitive observance. In the Friars Minor the condemnation of the Spirituals had driven the reform movement underground; but it re-emerged a decade later at Foligno, where a group of enthusiasts led by Giovanni della Valle obtained the permission of the Minister-General to form a separate community dedicated to strict observance of the Rule. In 1334 these first Observants settled in a mountain hermitage at Brugliano, for Giovanni seems to have accepted the belief of the outlawed Fraticelli that the absolute poverty enjoined by the Rule and Testament of St Francis was really practicable only in the desert. After twenty years the experiment fell victim to the hostility of the unreformed Conventuals; but it was revived in 1368 under a new leader, Paolucci dei Trinci, and by his death in 1391 there were twenty-two Italian houses following the reformed observance and the movement was gaining adherents north of the Alps.

2. A. Mortier, *Histoire des maîtres-généraux de l'Ordre de Frères Prêcheurs* (Paris 1903-20) III, p. 548.

The papal Schism, so debilitating to the Church in other respects, proved of some assistance to reform within the Mendicant Orders. The claims to obedience made by rival popes split the Franciscan Order as it had the Dominicans, but it enabled Observant congregations to get the blessing of popes who were anxious to reward the loyalty of their supporters. The Franciscan Observants continued to gain ground in the fifteenth century, when their prestige and popularity with the townspeople was enhanced by having in their number fervent evangelical preachers like St Bernardino of Siena and John Capistrano. But at every stage the expansion of the reform was fiercely opposed by the Conventuals. In the end, the long feud among the followers of the *poverello* was terminated by a legal separation decreed by the pope. In 1517 Pope Leo X recognised the existence of the Observants as a distinct Franciscan Order and authorised them to elect a Minister-General of their own.

Among the Dominicans a reform movement was set on foot by the General, Raymond of Capua, who had had the bracing experience of being both confessor and disciple of St Catherine of Siena. In 1388 he embarked upon a plan to establish at least one priory in each province following the observance of the primitive Dominican constitutions. As he explained in a subsequent encyclical to the brethren, he intended the Observant houses to be dynamic centres from which friars trained in the primitive observance would go out and reform the other priories of their province; they would be exempted from provincial jurisdiction and would be under the supervision of their own vicars. Provincial priors everywhere put up a tenacious resistance to the setting up of Observant houses outside their control. But Raymond showed himself willing to invoke papal assistance against recalcitrants, and the reform made progress in Italy, Germany and Spain. The emergence of two congregations within the Order of Preachers led to much internecine controversy, but the reform succeeded without leading to the legalized schism that split the Franciscans.

The Augustinian Friars also had their Observant congregations, the earliest of which had its centre at the famous forest hermitage of Lecceto, a few miles from Siena. This reform also attracted notable recruits. It was a house of the Observant congregation of the German Augustinian Friars, at Erfurt, that had the distinction of producing Martin Luther. In time, like most such movements, the reformed observance within the Mendicant Orders was diluted, as the reputation of its adherents for austerity and fervour brought fresh endowments; and in practice the difference between Observants and Conventuals became less apparent.

These internal disputes over observance did not diminish the standing of the Conventuals with the laity or reduce their ability to attract recruits. In the years following the Black Death, they continued to be showered with legacies from grateful penitents – many of them people of modest means – and the generosity of donors enabled them to erect or complete spacious preaching churches, where their aristocratic patrons sought burial. The decadence the reformers strove to arrest was only apparent when measured against the austere and exalted standards of ascetic destitution set by their founders. The friars may have been inclined, as their critics said, to pander to the rich and to be too eager for legacies and donations, but they never became possessors of great estates, like the monasteries; nor did they accumulate corporate wealth. Their vices, such as they were, and the occasional scandals, were accidents of a religious life spent ministering to lay society and lived among the people.

The impact of the friars upon the history of Western Christendom must be measured against the problems of the thirteenth-century Church with which we began. They were a revolutionary answer to a potentially revolutionary situation. For the spiritual and intellectual turbulence of the twelfth century, which had accompanied the growth of towns, had not only given birth to new forms of monastic life and new kinds of scholastic organisation; it had also awakened the religious aspirations of a more articulate laity, which the traditional monastic theology and the existing apparatus of the Church seemed unable to satisfy. It was the achievement of the friars, through their teaching and example, to satisfy this quest for personal sanctification and to direct it into orthodox channels. At the same time, in the schools they succeeded in reconciling the dogmas of faith with the new sciences. It can hardly be doubted that the success of their ministry checked the spread of heresy and averted widespread disaffection.

At the heart of the message the friars brought was a belief that the Christian life was not a monopoly of a professional

élite, but was accessible to all; that the interior life of the
spirit, even the higher experience of the contemplative life,
could be pursued in the secular world through the sanctification of common tasks and the faithful performance of ordinary
duties. This was the message the Dominican Meister Eckhart
communicated with passionate fervour in the sermons he
preached to the people of Cologne in the early years of the
fourteenth century. Those who were drawn to a more devout
and ascetical observance without abandoning their worldly
responsibilities were offered the exercises and more structured
life of the religious confraternity. Some of the most remarkable
spiritual teachers of the later middle ages were lay people, like
the Dominican tertiary St Catherine of Siena, who were
members of these organisations. Many of the forms taken by
the exuberant lay piety of the fourteenth and fifteenth centuries – devotion to the passion of Christ and a sympathetic
concern with his human sufferings, the use of the rosary and
the cult of the Holy Name – are clearly traceable to the
revivalist preaching of the friars.

'As Christ entered the immortal Jerusalem riding upon an
ass,' said Robert Holcot, 'so the school of theology is carried
for the most part not by the great and powerful or the rich,
but by the poor religious.'[3] Holcot was a Dominican, writing
probably at Oxford in the year 1334. He was alluding to the
fact that the faculties of theology in the universities were still
dominated both numerically and qualitatively by the Mendicants. Secular students of theology were a relatively small élite
destined for high preferment. By Holcot's time the friars had
been joined at the universities by the Benedictines and Cistercians, who had been persuaded by the example of the Mendicants to establish colleges of their own. In the fourteenth
century, the Mendicant doctors of the faculty continued to
provide lectures on Scripture alongside the courses of dogmatic
theology based on the *Sentences*, and through the lectors they
taught, a Biblical culture was transmitted to the preachers and
their lay audiences.

The secular clergy profited more directly from the teaching
of the Mendicant schoolmen. Beginning with the decree *Cum
ex eo* published by Pope Boniface VIII in 1298, papal policy

3. Quoted by Beryl Smalley, *English Friars and Antiquity in the Early Fourteenth
   Century* (1960), p. 31 & n.

encouraged bishops to dispense rectors of parishes from residence so that they could attend the schools, and a small but increasing number of rector and vicars availed themselves of this permission.[4] At the level of the local friary or conventual school many of the classrooms of the Mendicants were open to members of the secular clergy, allowing them to hear the lectors discoursing on the Bible and the Biblical *Histories* of the Comestor and to receive instruction in the principles of moral theology alongside the brethren. Some, we cannot tell how many, attended the lectures of the Mendicant doctors at the universities without staying long enough to graduate themselves. Federico Visconti, archbishop of Pisa (1257–77), exhorted his clergy to take advantage of these facilities and frequent the schools of the friars at Pisa to learn some theology, especially since, as he pointed out, the friars made no charge for their teaching.[5] By opening their doors to outsiders the friars clearly made a significant contribution to the improved educational standards of the parish clergy that has impressed students of the fourteenth-century Church. Here too Innocent III's desire for theologically instructed pastors was at least in part fulfilled.

The economic structure of the medieval Church proved resistant to the reformation that Innocent had desired. But much had been achieved through the ministry of the friars. The urban poor as well as the rural peasantry had the Gospel preached to them. The clergy as well as the people had been offered religious instruction. The devout life, hitherto regarded as the exclusive occupation of clergy and enclosed religious, had been made available to the laity. The enthusiasm for the Apostolic Life had been channeled into new religious institutes and had been largely contained within the Church. Heresy had retreated before the well-equipped forces of militant ortho-

---

4. L.E. Boyle, 'The constitution *Cum ex eo* of Boniface VIII and the education of the parochial clergy' in *Mediaeval Studies* 24 (Toronto 1962), pp. 263–302. For the English evidence see Jean Dunbabin, 'Careers and Vocations' in *The History of the University of Oxford* I: *The Early Schools*, ed. J. Catto (1984), pp. 568–9.
5. C. Piana, 'I sermoni di Federico Visconti, arcivescovo di Pisa' in *Rivista di Storia della Chiesa in Italia* 6 (1952), p. 239, cited by M. d'Alatri in *Le Scuole degli Ordini Mendicanti* (Convegno del Centro di Studi sulla Spiritualità Medievale 17, Todi 1978), p. 52; see also J. Vergier, 'Studia et universités', *ibid.* pp. 175–203.

doxy. The Mendicant schoolmen had given fresh life and a new orientation to Western theology and philosophy. Through their efforts, the intellectual crisis precipitated by the reception of pagan philosophy and science into the schools had terminated in a Christian synthesis.

These achievements amply justified the sagacity and innovative spirit of the popes and bishops who had patronised and protected the early Mendicant movement. It was in no small measure through the ministry of the friars that the Latin Church met the many-sided challenge that confronted it in the thirteenth century and remained the unique vehicle of salvation for Western Christians of the middle ages. Celano has a story that Innocent III had a dream the night after his first encounter with St Francis. In his dream he saw that the Lateran basilica (the mother-church of the West and in medieval eyes a symbol of the Church Universal) was tottering on the point of collapse, when a beggar-man, wearing a habit of sackcloth secured with a cord, crossed the piazza and shored up the crumbling edifice with his shoulder. The anecdote, which Giotto or another depicted in a fresco on the wall of the upper church at Assisi, was a parable with a strong base in reality.

GENERAL BIBLIOGRAPHY

The following is a brief guide to further reading on topics covered by each of the chapters, confined as far as possible to works in English. Place of publication is given only for works published outside the United Kingdom.

Chapter 1: The Medieval Church in Crisis

The impact of the social changes of the twelfth century upon Christian thought and the search for new modes of religious and ascetical life were brilliantly expounded in a series of seminal studies by M.-D. Chenu, *Nature, Man and Society in the Twelfth Century*, transl. J. Taylor and Lester K. Little (Chicago & London 1968). On the same theme see the stimulating studies of Lester K. Little, *Religious Poverty and the Profit Economy in Medieval Europe* (1978), and Caroline W. Bynum, *Jesus as Mother: Studies in the Spirituality of the High Middle Ages* (University of California Press 1982). Much has been written about medieval heresy. The best general guide to the subject is M. Lambert's *Medieval Heresy. Popular Movements from Bogomil to Hus* (1977). Stephen Runciman's *The Medieval Manichee* (1947) provides a good account of Dualism, but most scholars no longer follow him in deriving western forms of it exclusively from the Balkans. For a lively and learned discussion of the roots of western Catharism see R.I. Moore, *The Origins of European Dissent* 2nd edn (1985), and for a balanced account of Cathar organisation in the Languedoc, Walter L. Wakefield, *Heresy, Crusade and Inquisition in Southern France, 1100–1250* (1974); a useful selection of sources in translation will be found in W.L. Wakefield and A.P. Evans, *Heresies of the High*

Middle Ages (New York-London 1969). An excellent brief account of the *vita apostolica* and the new evangelism is provided by Brenda Bolton's *The Medieval Reformation* (1983). For the Waldenses see the works cited under notes 12 and 13; and for the Humiliati see Brenda Bolton, 'Innocent III's treatment of the Humiliati' in *Studies in Church History* 8, ed. D. Baker and G.J. Cuming (1972), pp. 73–82, and D. Flood, *Poverty in the Middle Ages* (Franziskaner Forschungen 27, Werl 1975). On the rise of the universities *Rashdall's Universities of Europe in the Middle Ages*, ed. F.M. Powicke and A.B. Emden 3 vols. (1936) remains the fundamental work. For contemporary criticism of the schools see Stephen C. Ferruolo, *The Origins of the University* (Stanford, California 1985).

Chapter 2: St Francis of Assisi and the Origins of the Friars Minor

There is a huge literature on this subject. The best guides in English to the problem of the sources are J.R.H. Moorman, *Sources for the Life of St Francis* (1940), and Rosalind Brooke, *Early Franciscan Government* (1959). A convenient collection of the Lives and writings of St Francis in translations of an uneven quality will be found in Marion A. Habig, *St Francis of Assisi: Writings and Early Biographies* 3rd edn (Chicago 1972). Modern biographies of St Francis are legion. Among those in English Father Cuthbert's *Life of St Francis of Assisi* (1912) deserves to be singled out as a careful and scholarly study, which stays close to the sources. For the beginnings of the order see Moorman *HFO* and K. Esser, *Origins of the Franciscan Order*, transl. A. Daly and I. Lynch (Chicago 1970). On the origins of the Second Order founded by St Clare see, besides the documents translated by R.A. Armstrong and I.C. Brady, *Francis and Clare, the Complete Works* (1982), the study by Rosalind and C.N.L. Brooke, 'St Clare' in *Medieval Women*, ed. D. Baker (*Studies in Church History, Subsidia* 1 (1978), pp. 275–87).

Chapter 3: The Growth of the Friars Minor, Crisis and Change

The best general guide to the history of the order is J.R.H. Moorman's *A History of the Franciscan Order from its Origins to 1517* (1968). The author's standpoint on the question of Franciscan poverty is not far removed from that of the *zelanti*. For the early development of the order see K. Esser, *Origins of the Franciscan Order*, transl. A. Daly and I. Lynch (Chicago 1970). The author seeks to show that the Franciscan movement was conceived from the beginning as a religious order in the traditional sense. An excellent account of the formation of the constitution of the order and the early crisis over the regime of Brother Elias will be found in Rosalind Brooke's *Early Franciscan Government* (1959); the same author's *The Coming of the Friars* (1975) provides a translation of a number of documents. The many studies of A.G. Little on English Franciscan history are of lasting value; among those of particular usefulness to the general student are *Studies in English Franciscan History* (1917) and the papers collected under the title *Franciscan Papers, Lists and Documents* (1943). The question of Franciscan observance and the poverty of Christ is studied by M. Lambert, *Franciscan Poverty* (1961), and by David Burr, *Olivi and Franciscan Poverty: the Origins of the* usus pauper *Controversy* (University of Pennsylvania Press 1989). For the schism within the order see Decima Douie, *The Nature and Effect of the Heresy of the Fraticelli* (1932) and D. Nimmo, *Reform and Division in the Franciscan Order, 1226–1538* (Capuchin Historical Institute, Rome 1987). On Joachim of Fiore and the Joachite controversy see Marjorie Reeves, *The Influence of Prophecy in the Later Middle Ages* (1969) and *Joachim of Fiore and the Prophetic Future* (1976).

Chapter 4: St. Dominic and the Order of Friars Preachers

The best account of St Dominic and the foundation of the order is that of M.H. Vicaire, *Saint Dominic and his Times*, transl. K. Pond (1964). The earlier work of P.S. Mandonnet, *Saint Dominique, l'idée, l'homme et l'oeuvre* 2 vols. (Paris 1937) covers a wider field and still repays study. The standard modern account of the history of the order is by W.A. Hinnebusch, *The History of the Dominican Order* 2 vols. (New York 1966, 1972). Much material relating to the affairs of the whole order as well as those of the English province will be found in the same author's *The Early English Friars Preachers* (Rome 1951). A good account of the order's constitutional arrangements is provided by G.R. Galbraith, *The Constitution of the Dominican Order* (1925). For an up-to-date discussion of the academic organisation of the Preachers see Maura O'Carroll, 'The educational organisation of the Dominicans in England and Wales, 1221–48: A multi-disciplinary approach': *AFP* 50 (1980), pp. 23–62. The generalate of Humbert of Romans is studied by E.T. Brett, *Humbert of Romans: his Life and Views of Thirteenth-Century Society* (Studies and Texts 67, Toronto 1984).

Chapter 5: New Brethren

The best accounts of the early Austin Friars in English are those of F. Roth, *The English Austin Friars* 2 vols. (New York 1961) and B. Rano, *The Order of St Augustine*, transl. P.A. Ennis (Rome 1975), being a translation of Rano's article 'Agostini' in *Dizionario degli Istituti di Perfezione* I (Rome 1974), cols. 278–381. Aubrey Gwynn, *The English Austin Friars in the time of Wyclif* (1940) is a classical study of Giles of Rome and a group of friar theologians of the fourteenth century.

There exists no satisfactory general account of the early history of the Carmelites in English. For the Friars of the Sack see R.W. Emery, 'The Friars of the Sack' in *Speculum* 18 (July 1943), 323–34; and for the Crutched Friars H.F. Chettle, 'The Friars of the Holy Cross' in *History* 34 (1949) see also R.W. Emery, 'The Friars of Blessed Mary and the Pied Friars' in *Speculum* 24 (April 1949), pp. 228–38.

The only full account of the Trinitarian or Mathurin Friars is that of Paul Deslandres, *L'Ordre des Trinitaires* 2 vols. (Toulouse–Paris 1903). A modern work is much to be desired.

Chapter 6: The Mission to the Towns

The changing social and economic background as it affected the Mendicant movement is examined in a stimulating study by Lester K. Little, *Religious Poverty and the Profit Economy in Medieval Europe* (1978); see also R.W. Southern, *Western Society and the Church in the Middle Ages* (1970). Scholastic attitudes to trade and commerce are analysed by J.W. Baldwin, *Masters, Princes and Merchants, the Social Views of Peter the Chanter and his Circle* 2 vols. (Princeton 1970), and by J. Gilchrist, *The Church and Economic Activity in the Middle Ages* (New York 1969). A seminal article on the distribution of Mendicant settlements was published by J. le Goff, 'Ordres Mendiants et urbanisation dans la France médiévale' in *Annales* 25 (1970), pp. 924–65.

Religious confraternities are receiving increasing attention, especially by continental scholars. G.G. Meerseman's *Dossier de l'Ordre de la pénitence au XIIIe siècle* (Spicilegium Friburgense 7, Freiburg 1961) is of fundamental importance. An excellent account of the social role of an Italian urban confraternity is provided by Lester K. Little, *Liberty, Charity, Fraternity: Lay Religious Confraternities at Bergamo in the Age of the Commune* (Smith College Studies in History 51, Northampton Mass. 1988). The best study of Mendicant preaching is now D.L. d'Avray's *The Preaching of the Friars* (1985).

Chapter 7: The Capture of the Schools

For the universities in general see *Rashdall's Universities of Europe in the Middle Ages,* cited above under chapter 1, and for the Mendicants at Paris, *ibid.*, pp. 344–97; see also G. Leff, *Paris and Oxford Universities in the Thirteenth and Fourteenth Centuries* (New York 1968), and A.C. Cobban, *The Medieval Universities* (1975). For the friars at Oxford see M.W. Sheehan, 'The Religious Orders 1220–1370' in *The History of the University of Oxford* vol. 1: *The Early Schools*, ed. J.I. Catto (1984), pp. 193–221, and for the Franciscan school at Oxford A.G. Little, 'The Franciscan School at Oxford in the 13th Century': *AFH* 19 (1926), and C.H. Lawrence, 'The Letters of Adam Marsh and the Franciscan School at Oxford': *JEH* 42 (1991), pp. 218–38. The best introduction to the work of the friars in Biblical studies is Beryl Smalley's *The Study of the Bible in the Middle Ages* 2nd edn (1952), pp. 264–355. An up-to-date and lucid account of the reception of Greco-Arabic learning and the ensuing controversies will be found in Michael Haren's *Medieval Thought; The Western Intellectual Tradition from Antiquity to the Thirteenth Century* 2nd edn (1992) and in F. van Steenberghen, *The Philosophical Movement of the Thirteenth Century* (1955); the latter author's *Maître Siger de Brabant* (Louvain 1977) represents his last word on Latin Averroism. New light was thrown on the reception of Aristotle by the Oxford schools by the researches of Fr. Daniel Callus, whose paper 'The Introduction of Aristotelian Learning to Oxford' in *Proc. of the British Academy* 19 (1943), pp. 229–81 was an important seminal study. For the role of Aquinas in the controversy see J.A. Weisheipl, *Friar Thomas d'Aquino* (1974) and D.A. Callus, *The Condemnation of St Thomas at Oxford* (Aquinas Society

233

THE FRIARS

Papers No. 5, 1946). The best study of Bonaventure is J.G.
Bougerol's *Introduction to the Works of St Bonaventure* (Paterson,
New Jersey 1964).

Chapter 8: *The Complaint of the Clergy*

The fullest account of the conflict at Paris in the thirteenth
century is provided by M.-M. Dufeil, *Guillaume de Saint-Amour
et la polémique universitaire parisienne 1250–59* (Paris 1972). For a
shorter account see Decima Douie, *The Conflict between the
Seculars and the Mendicants at the University of Paris in the Thirteenth
Century* (Aquinas Society Papers No. 23, 1954); see also *Rashdall's Medieval Universities*, vol. I. The structural implications
of the controversy are examined by Y. Congar, 'Aspects
ecclésiologiques de la querelle Mendiants-Séculiers': *AHDL* 28
(1961), pp. 35–151. On Bonaventure's role see J.G. Bougerol,
'Saint Bonaventure et la défense de la vie évangelique de 1252
au Concile de Lyons' in *S. Bonaventura Francescano* (Convegno
del Centro di Studi sulla Spiritualità Medievale 1973: Todi
1974), pp. 109–26. On Gerard of Borgo San Donnino and the
Everlasting Gospel see Marjorie Reeves, *Joachim of Fiore and
the Prophetic Future* (1976). The fourteenth-century phase of
the controversy is described by Katherine Walsh, *Richard
FitzRalph in Oxford, Avignon and Armagh* (1981). The hostile
stereotype of the friars in the vernacular literary tradition is
traced by R. Szittya, *The Anti-fraternal Tradition in Medieval
Literature* (Princeton University Press 1986).

Chapter 9: *In the Houses of Kings*

The role of the friars as confessors and councillors of kings,
ambassadors and administrative assistants is touched upon in
general histories of the thirteenth century, notably for England
in F.M. Powicke, *Henry III and the Lord Edward* 2 vols. (1947),
and for France in Jean Richard, *Saint Louis, roi d'une France
féodale* (Paris 1983). Princely patronage of the friars in Germany is examined by J.B. Freed, *The Friars and German Society
in the Thirteenth Century* (Cambridge Mass. 1977). The role of
the Blackfriars at the English court is described by W.A.
Hinnebusch, *The Early English Friars Preachers* (Rome 1951),
and in greater detail by Bede Jarrett, *The English Dominicans*
(1921). A useful study of the employment of the friars by

234

Louis IX is provided by Lester K. Little, 'St Louis' involvement with the friars' in *Church History* 33 (1964).

Chapter 10: In the Service of the Papacy

A general account of the governing apparatus of the medieval Papacy will be found in W. Ullmann, *A Short History of the Papacy in the Middle Ages* (1972). The various roles fulfilled by the friars in the papal service are referred to in Moorman *HFO* and Hinnebusch *HDO*. For the use made of the friars in preaching the Crusade see Norman Housley, *The Italian Crusades. The Papal-Angevin Alliance and the Crusades against Christian Lay Powers, 1254–1343* (1982) and the essays of Jean Richard, *Croisées, missionaires et voyageurs* (Variorum Reprints 1983). On the Cathars and the work of the friars in administering the papal Inquisition see the works of Lambert and R.I. Moore cited under chapter 1, and W.L. Wakefield, *Heresy, Crusade and Inquisition in Southern France, 1100–1250* (1974). An excellent brief introduction, with bibliography, is provided by B. Hamilton, *The Medieval Inquisition* (1981). A valuable collection of documents in translation will be found in W.L. Wakefield and A.P. Evans, *Heresies of the High Middle Ages* (Records of Civilization, New York 1969). For the relations between Rome and Constantinople and the role of the friars as mediators see the general study of J.M. Hussey, *The Orthodox Church in the Byzantine Empire* (1986) and S. Runciman, *The Eastern Schism* (1955) The standard work on the Franciscan contribution is by M. Roncaglia, *Les Frères Mineurs et l'Eglise Grecque Orthodoxe au XIIIᵉ siècle (Biblioteca Bio-bibliografica della Terra Santa e dell'Oriente Francescano serie 4, Studi* II (Cairo 1954)). The mission of the friars leading to the reunion of 1274 is described by D.J. Geanakoplos, 'Bonaventura, the two Mendicant Orders and the Greeks at the Council of Lyons' in *The Orthodox Churches and the West* ed. D. Baker (*Studies in Church History* 13, 1976), pp. 183–211.

Chapter 11: Afar unto the Gentiles

The Tartars were originally a tribe of South-West Asia who were conquered by the Mongols, but medieval writers apply the name 'Tartar' to all the Mongol peoples. Good modern accounts of the rise of the Mongol empire and its impact upon the West will be found in D.O. Morgan, *The Mongols* (1986), now the standard work, and E.D. Phillips, *The Mongols* (1960). The missionary activity of the Friars Minor is described by Moorman *HFO*. For a pleasing introduction to Western relations with the Great Khan see Eileen Power, 'Marco Polo' in her *Medieval People* 7th edn. (1939), chapter 2. The standard modern work on the missions to Islam and the Far East is Jean Richard's *La papauté et les missions d'Orient au moyen-âge* (Rome, Ecole française 1977); see also the same author's important studies in *Orient et occident au moyen-âge* (Variorum Reprints 1976). An excellent commentary with French translation of the narrative of Rubrouck is provided by Claude and René Kappler, *Guillaume de Rubrouck: voyage dans l'empire mongol, 1253–55* (Paris 1985). Translations of the narratives of Carpini and Rubrouck and the letters of Monte Corvino, with an introduction, will be found in Christopher Dawson, *The Mongol Mission* (1955).

INDEX

The following abbreviations have been used: abp = archbishop; bp = bishop; d = duke; emp = emperor; kg = king; qn = queen. Membership of the Mendicant Orders has been indicated as follows: OAE = Augustinian; OC = Carmelite; OFM = Franciscan; OP = Dominican; and for office holders, prov = minister or prior provincial; gen = minister-general or master of his order.

Abelard, Peter, 11–12
ad abolendam of Lucius III, 22, 189
Adam of Buckfield, 145
Adam Marsh OFM, 55, 132–3, 134, 153, 173, 174–5, 178, 221, 222
ad fructus uberes of Martin IV, 159
Agnellus OFM, bp of Fez, 221
Agnellus of Pisa OFM, prov of England, 45, 47, 131, 174
Alain of Lille, 20
Alans, 212, 216
Albertus Magnus OP, 133, 136, 146
Albert of Pisa OFM, prov of Germany, 45
Albert of Vercelli, patriarch of Jerusalem, 95
Albert of Villa d'Ogna, 18
Albigenses: crusade against, 8, 69 *and see* Cathars
Alexander IV, pope, 56, 90, 93, 99, 155
Alexander of Hales OFM, 49, 52, 130 & n., 142, 145
Alexius, St, legend of, 19
Alfarabi, 144
Alfonso the Wise, kg of Castile-Leon, 179
Al Kamil, Sultan of Egypt, 37, 204
Alleluia Movement, *see* Great Devotion
Amiens, the Mise of, 177
André de Longjumeau OP, 175, 204–5, 208–9
Andrew of Perugia OFM, bp of Cathay, 216

Angelo OFM, companion of St Francis, 28
Annibaldi, cardinal Richard, 98–9
Apostolic Life (*vita apostolica*), the idea of, 15–17, 34, 68
appropriation, of churches, 219
Aquinas, St Thomas, OP, 123, 146, 157; his career, 136–7; his *Summa contra Gentiles*, 137; *Summa Theologica*, 137, 146; commentaries on Aristotle, 148; the Averroist controversy, 146–50; his condemnation at Paris and Oxford, 149–50; on the Greek Church, 200
Arabic, study of, 140
Ardingo, bp of Florence, 107
Aristotle, reception of by the schoolmen, 10–11, 144–6; Paris prohibitions of, 144–5; scholastic commentaries on, 147–8; and unity of form, 149
Arles, Franciscans at, 45
Arnaud-Amaury, abbot of Cîteaux, 8, 67
Arnold of Cologne OFM, 215
Arnolfo di Cambio, 110
Assisi, town of, 28, 30; church of S. Giorgio, 30; church of S. Damiano, 32, 41–2; basilica of St Francis and *sacro convento*, 40; church of S. Chiara, 42; bishop of, *see* Guido
Augsburg, Franciscans at, 44; Peace of, 188; bishop of, *see* Siegfried
Augustine of Hippo, St, the Rule of, 65–6, 71, 90, 93, 148

Augustinianism, 148, 150-1
Augustinian Friars Hermits (Austin Friars); eremitical origins, 98-9; Rule of, 98; schools of, 99-100; hermitages, 101; Observants, 224
Averroes, 144, 146, 147
Averroism, at Paris, 146-8
Avicenna, 144
Avignon, papal curia at, 63, 161, 162-3, 216
Aylesford, Carmelite hermitage, 95; general chapter of, 96

Bacon, Robert OP, 131, 171
Bacon, Roger OFM, 140, 141, 145, 203
Baghdad, Caliph of, 204, 208
Baiju, Mongol commander, 207
Baldwin of Flanders, Latin emp of Byzantium, 195
Baldwin II, emp of Byzantium, 198
Barcelona, school of Arabic, 203
Bardi, of Florence, 109
Barons' Wars, in England, 176
Bartholomew of Bregenz OP, 184
Bartholomew de Castell, 111
Bartholomew of Cremona OFM, 209
Batu khan, 205 206, 207, 209, 211
Beguines, 76-7
Bela, kg of Hungary, 205
Benedict Cornetus, 116-17
Benedict of Poland OFM, 206
Berengar, abp of Narbonne, 7
Bergamo, confraternities of, 114, 119
Berlinghieri, of Florence, 112
Bernadone, Pietro, 29
Bernard, abbot of Fontecaude, 21
Bernard Gui OP, Inquisitor, 194
Bernard of Prim, 23
Bernardino, St, of Siena, OFM, 224
Bible: academic study of, 138-9, 142-3; vernacular translations, 20-1; text and correctoria, 139-40; scholastic commentaries, 140-1; concordances of, 120, 140; languages of, 140; the Paris Bible, 139
Bigod, Hugh, Justiciar, 175
Black Death, 119, 223
Blanche of Castile, qn of France, 45, 167
Bogomils, sect of, 4
Bologna: jurist universities of, 10, 12, 79; canon law studies at, 10, 13-14; Dominicans at, 72, 73; nunnery of St. Agnese, 78; church of St Nicholas (S. Domenico), 72, 109; general chapters at, 79; Carmelite studium at, 97; the Inquisition at, 193

Bonagrazia, gen of OFM, 60, 61, 199
Bonaiuto, Andrea di, 110
Bonaventure OFM, St (of Bagnoregio): regent at Paris, 57; Franciscan gen, 51, 53, 57-9, 122, 171, 199; cardinal bp of Albano, 57; his Life of St Francis, 26, 28, 47; commentary on the Sentences, 57; on Ecclesiastes, 41; his apologia, 56-7, 58; his Apologia Pauperum, 58-9, 60, 158; his part in the Council of Lyons, 200
Bonaventura di Mugello OFM, 199
Boniface VIII, pope, 160
Boniface of Savoy, abp of Canterbury, 172
Bonites, 99
Brandenburg, margraves of, 179
Brettini, hermits, 99
Brugliano, hermitage, 223
Buddhists, 211-12, 214
buildings of the friars, 46, 53, 62, 108-11, 166
Buonagiunta, gen of the Servites, 90
Byzantine Empire, 194-201 passim; emperors of, see John III Vatatzes, Michael Palaeologus VIII, Baldwin I, Baldwin II

Caesarius of Speyer OFM, prov of Germany, 44
Caleruega, 65
Calimala, guild of, 109-10
Camaldolese monks, 117
Cambridge, studia of Franciscans, Dominicans and Carmelites, 133
canonization, of lay saints, 18
canons regular, 16, 66
Canterbury: Franciscans at, 45; Dominicans at, 168; abps of, see Langton, Boniface, Kilwardby, Pecham
Cardinal Protectors, of OFM, 181-2; of OP, 182; of Cistercians, 182; and see Ugolino, Rainald of Segni, John of Toledo, Hugh of St Cher
Carmelites (Order of Our Lady of Mount Carmel): their eremitical origins, 94-5; become cenobites and mendicants, 96-7; internal conflicts, 97-8; schools of, 97, 134, 135 & n; royal confessors, 171
Carpini, John de Piano di, OFM, 206-8
Cathars, heresy of, 4-8, 67, 68-9
Cathay, Latin Church of, 214-17
Catherine, St, of Siena, 101, 224, 226
chapters general: of the Franciscans, 37, 43, 49, 51-2; of the Dominicans, 78,

79, 82–3, 87, 169; of the Carmelites, 96, 98; of the Austin Friars, 100
chapters, provincial, 82, 83–4, 168–9, 187
Charles of Anjou, kg of Italy, 195, 198–9, 201
Chaucer, Geoffrey, 164–5
Christina of Markyate, 9 n.5
Cîteaux, Order of: mission to the Cathars, 8, 67–8; use of *conversi*, 75; general chapter of, 77; relations with women, 77; recruitment to the friars, 73 & n; abbot of, *see* Arnaud-Amaury
Clare of Assisi, St, 41–2
Clarendon, royal palace, 170
Clement IV, pope, 57
Clement V, pope, 216
Clement VII, Avignon pope, 223
Clement of Sant'Elpidio OAE, gen of Augustinian Friars, 100
clergy, secular: unbeneficed, 164, 219; education of, 18–19, 21, 219, 220, 227; hostility towards the friars, 152; in conflict with the friars, 153–65; criticism of, by the friars, 164–5
Coiac, chamberlain to the Khan, 210
Cologne: Cathars at, 3–4; friars at, 48; clergy of, 107; Dominican school at, 133
commerce, ethics of, 123–5
communes, 12
confession, to friars, 125–6, 160–1, 162, 170–1
confraternities: of lay penitents, 17, 19, 89, 112–16, 122; their constitution and observances, 115; of the Romagna, 113; of Faenza, 114; of Bergamo, 114, 119; the Laudesi, 115; of the Blessed Virgin, 115; *Disciplinati*, 119; Society of the Faith, 193; Third Orders, 115
Conrad, bp of Hildesheim, 152
Conrad of Marburg, Inquisitor, 190
Conradin of Hohenstaufen, 198
consolamentum, rite of, 4–5
Constantinople: church of Hagia Sophia, 195; Franciscan convent at, 140, 199; Dominican convent at, 203; sack of by the 4th Crusade, 195; Charles of Anjou's plan to conquer, 198–9; negotiations with Rome, 194–200; Greek patriarchs, *see* Germanos, Joseph; Latin patriarch, *see* Morosini *conversi*, *see* lay brothers
Cordova, Caliphs of, 144
Crescentius of Iesi OFM, Franciscan gen, 27, 50

Crusade: First Crusade, 188; Fourth Crusade, 195; of Frederick II, 185; of Louis IX, 177, 208; the Baltic Crusade, 185; against Christian rulers, 185–7; Crusade of the Shepherds (Pastoureaux), 178; Albigensian Crusade, 8, 69, 189; preaching of by friars, 185–7; indulgences for, 186; Bacon's criticism of, 203
Crutched Friars, 91, 135
cum ex eo of Boniface VIII, 226
cum inter nonnullos of John XXII, 63
Curzon, cardinal Robert, 126, 144

Damascus, Sultan of, 204
David of Dinant, 144
Diana d'Andolo, 74, 78
Diego, bp of Osma, 67–8, 75
diffinitors, 51, 83
disciplinati, 119
Dominic, St: his family and personality, 65–7; his ideas of poverty, 68–9; his visit to Rome, 70–1; his ministry to the Cathars, 68–9; his ministry to women, 75–6; his meeting with St Francis, 68, 182, 221; receives Sta Sabina from Honorius III, 76; chooses Bologna as centre, 79
Dominicans (Order of Preachers): origins of, 68–72; constitution of, 82–4; provinces of, 80; general chapters of, 69, 72, 79, 82–3; visitations, 84; recruitment, 72–3, 74; studies in, 84–7; training of preachers, 87–8; buildings of, 108–9; service as Inquisitors, 190–2; papal penitentiaries, 182–4; Observants, 224–5; Second (female) Order, 76–9
dualists, *see* Cathars
Dunstable, canons of, 168
Duns Scotus OFM, 150
Durandus of Huesca, 23

Eccleston, Thomas of OFM: his chronicle, 45, 108–9, 132
Eckhart, Meister OP, 226
Edward I, kg of England, 111, 171, 175
Eleanor of Provence, qn of England, 172
Elias, Brother OFM, Franciscan gen, 27, 40, 47, 48–9
Engelbert, abp of Cologne, 107
Erfurt, Augustinian Friars of, 224
etsi animarum of Innocent IV, 155
Everlasting Gospel, the, 56
Evesham, battle of, 176
exiit qui seminat of Nicholas III, 60

Ezzelino of Cremona OP, 207
Ezzelino da Romano, 117, 193–4

Fasani, Ranieri, 117
Federico Visconti, abp of Pisa, 227
Felix de Valois, 91
Ferrier OP, Inquisitor, 190
Filioque controversy, 196, 199–200
Fioretti (Little Flowers of St Francis), 27
Fishacre, Richard OP, 133, 142–3
FitzRalph, Richard, abp of Armagh, 161, 162–3
Flagellants, 117–19
Florence: Franciscan convent of S. Croce, 61, 105, 109–10; Dominican convent of S. Maria Novella, 105, 109, 112, 153; Servite convent of the Annunziata, 90, 105; Austin Friars and Carmelites at, 105; cathedral of, 110; church of S. Paolo, 105; hospital of S. Gallo, 105; of S. Pancrazio, 105; of Fontemanzina, 112; lay confraternities at, 112, 114; Calimala guild, 109–10; bp of *see* Ardingo
Fonte Colombo, hermitage, 31, 38
Foulques de Neuilly, 120
Francis of Assisi, St: *Lives* of, 26–8; his family, 29–30; conversion and career, 30–1; the stigmata, 32; his companions, 34–5; his *Testament*, 26, 29, 36, 39; idea of poverty, 33–4, 39; the eremitical life, 31; the imitation of Christ, 32–3, 39; on learning, 46; his Rules, 29, 31, 32, 38, 203; his style of oratory, 36; mission to the Sultan, 37; his meeting with St Dominic, 43, 68, 182, 221
Franciscans (Order of Friars Minor): origins of, 31–40; constitution of, 51–3; their liturgy, 37; clericalisation, 49; observance of poverty, 53; organisation of studies, 52; service to the Inquisition, 191; the Spirituals, 27, 61, 62–3, 222; the Fraticelli, 63; the Observants, 223–4; schism in, 63–4, 223–4; Second (female) Order, 41–2; Third Order, 115
Frederick II of Hohenstaufen, emp, 118, 179–80, 184, 186, 189, 193
Friars of the Sack (Order of Penitence of Jesus Christ), 93–4, 105, 106, 167
Fulk, abbot of the Thoronet, bp of Toulouse, 69–70

Gaetani, cardinal Benedict, 160; and *see* Boniface VIII

Geoffrey de Beaulieu OP, confessor and biographer of Louis IX, 167
Geoffrey Hardeby OAE, 162
George Acropolites, grand logothete, 199
Gerard, cardinal of S. Sabina, 160
Gerard of Abbeville, 158
Gerard of Borgo San Donnino OFM, 56, 154–5
Gerard of Fracheto OP, 73
Gerard de Prato OFM, 117, 217
Germanos II, patriarch of Constantinople, 195, 197
Germanos III, patriarch of Constantinople, 199
Ghengis Khan, 205
Ghibellines, 118, 187, 193
Gilbert de Fresney OP, prov of England, 72
Giles of Assisi OFM, 47, 54, 130
Giles of Rome OAE, gen of Austin Friars, abp of Bourges, 99–100, 148
Giotto, 228
Giovanni della Valle OFM, 223
glossa ordinaria of the Bible, 138
Golden Horde, land of, 205
Gosset, 209
Gratian, 142, 182
Great Devotion, the, 116–17
Great Khan: *see* Ghengis, Ogodai, Kuyuk, Mongka, Kublai; capital of, 212–3, 215; palace of, 212
Great Schism, 223, 224
Greccio, hermitage, 32, 38
Greek Church, negotiations with, 194–201
Greek language, knowledge of, 140
Gregory VII, pope, 7
Gregory IX, pope, 40, 49, 99, 145, 152, 182, 183, 184, 190, 191, 195–6, 204, 206, and *see* Ugolino
Gregory X, pope, 57, 158, 199–200
Gregorian Reform programme, 7, 16
Grosseteste, Robert, bp of Lincoln, 21, 132, 142–3, 152, 172, 219
Guelfs, 118
Guido, bp of Assisi, 37
Guildford castle, friars at, 170

Haymo of Faversham, pro & gen OFM, 49, 50, 130, 196
Hebrew, knowledge of, 140
Henry III, kg of England, 111, 167, 169–70, 222
Henry IV, kg of England, 171
Henry VII, kg of Germany, 179
Henry, cardinal bp of Albano, 22

Henry, d of Silesia, 295
Henry of Burford OFM, penitentiary, 183
Henry of Milan OFM, 193
Hildesheim, Franciscans at, 152; bp of, *see* Conrad
Homobuonus of Cremona, St, 18
Honorius III, pope, 38, 44, 71, 73, 92, 152
Hospitallers, Knights, 203
Hubert de Burgh, Justiciar, 106
Hugh, St, abbot of Cluny, 14–15
Hugh, Brother OP, 196
Hugh Bigod, 175
Hugh de Digne (of Barjols) OFM, 55, 61, 130, 173, 221
Hugh of St Cher OP, cardinal priest of S. Sabina, 78, 96, 183, 222; his Biblical commentaries, 141; Bible concordance, 144
Humbert, cardinal bp of Silva Candida, 197
Humbert of Romans OP, Dominican gen, 78, 83, 84, 102 120, 122–3, 200, 202
Humiliati, of Milan, 22, 23–4
Hyères, Franciscan house at, 55, 173

Innocent III, pope, 1, 7, 8, 13, 18, 21, 36, 47, 72, 82, 183, 185, 189, 218, 227; and the Waldenses, 23; and the Humiliati, 23–4; his meeting with St Francis, 34, 36, 228; and the Order of Preachers, 70–1; and the 4th Lateran Council, 70, 82, 218; and Constantinople, 195
Innocent IV, pope, 40, 42, 96, 98, 143, 155, 169, 179, 184, 185–6, 191, 198, 203, 204, 206, 209
Inquisition, the papal, 188–94
Isidore of Seville, St, 211

Jacob, leader of the Shepherds Crusade, 178
Jacobites, of Syria, 205
Jacques de Vitry, bp of Acre, 23, 24, 41, 204
Jaime I, kg of Aragon, 179, 193
Jean Bellesmains, abp of Lyons, 22
Jean de Meung, 163
Jean de la Rochelle OFM, 49, 130–1
Jerome of Ascoli OFM, 199
Jerusalem: Latin Kingdom of, 2, 95, 185, 204; church of Holy Sepulchre, 213; patriarch of, *see* Albert of Vercelli
Joachim of Fiore, prophecies of, 54–5, 118, 154

John XXII, pope, 63, 187, 216, 222
John III Vatatzes, emp of Byzantium, 196–7
John, cardinal priest of S. Sabina, 47
John Bono, St, 99
John Capistrano OFM, 224
John of Darlington OP, 170, 171, 174, 176–7
John of Hildesheim OC, 94
John Mansel, 69
John de Matha, founder of Mathurin Friars, 91–2
John of Montecorvino OFM, abp of Peking, 214–16
John Oliva OFM, 191
John Parenti OFM, Franciscan gen, 130
John of Parma OFM, Franciscan gen, 50, 56–7, 198
John de Penna OFM, 44
John of St Albans, 128
John of St Giles OP, 128, 129, 174
John de Sancto Lugo OFM, 174
John of Toledo, cardinal of St Laurence-in-Lucina, 182
John Travers, sheriff of London, 45
John of Vicenza OP, 117
John of Wildeshausen OP, Dominian gen, 185
John, the weaver, 192
Joinville, Sire de, 167, 173, 209
Jordan of Giano OFM, 43, 44, 48, 180
Jordan of Saxony OP, Dominican gen, 67, 74, 78, 84, 127, 129, 131
Joseph I, patriarch of Constantinople, 200
judges delegate, 184

Karakorum, 211–12
Kilwardby, Robert OP, abp of Canterbury, cardinal bp of Porto, 62, 108, 110, 148, 149–50, 222
Knapwell, Richard OP, 150
Kublai, Gt. Khan, 213–15
Kuyuk Gt. Khan, 207, 208–9

Lambert le Bègue, 21
Lanfranc Septala OAE, gen of Austin Friars, 99
Langland, William, 164
Langton, Stephen, abp of Canterbury, 72, 131, 138–9
languages, study of, 140, 203
Laon, chronicler of, 19
Lateran basilica, Rome, 22; 3rd General Council of (1179), 11; 4th General Council of (1215), 70, 71–2, 82, 142, 189, 218–19

Laurence of Portugal OFM, 205
La Verna, 31
lay brothers, Franciscan, 47–8, 49; Dominican, 75
Lecceto, hermitage, 101
lectors, 80, 81, 85, 128, 134, 226
Legend of Perugia, 28–9
Legend of the Three Companions, 28–9
Leo X, pope, 224
Leo OFM, 28, 30, 54
lepers, 35–6
Lewes, battle of, 177
licet ecclesiae catholicae of Alexander IV, 99
Lincoln, sheriff of, 169
literacy, of the laity, 3, 8–10, 20
London: Dominican priory of (Holborn), 106, (Ludgate), 110; Franciscan house, 106; Carmelites at, 106; Austin Friars at, 107; Friars of the Sack at, 106; Crutched Friars at, 111; St Paul's cathedral, canons of, 108; mayor of, *see* William Joyner, Rokesley
Louis VIII, kg of France, 45
Louis IX, St, kg of France, 166–7, 169, 170–1, 172–4, 175, 176–7, 206, 208–9, 213, 222
Louis of Bavaria, emp, 64
Lucius III, pope, 22, 23
Luther, Martin OAE, 224
Lyons: Poor Men of, 22, 191; papal Curia at, 153, 184, 219; 1st General Council of (1245), 153, 179; 2nd General Council of (1274), 57, 59, 158, 199–200, and suppression of Mendicant Orders, 59, 93, 158–9; abp of, *see* Jean Bellesmains

Madrid, Dominican nunnery, 76
Mainz, Franciscans at, 44, 48
Maffeo Polo, 213
Manfred, kg of Italy, 118
Manselli, Raoul, 192
Marco Polo, 208, 213, 214
Margaret, qn of France, 209
Maria de Molina, qn of Castile, 179
Maronites, 205
Marseilles: Dominicans at, 105; Friars of the Sack at, 93; hospice of St Michael, 105; Fraticelli burned at, 63
Martin IV, pope, 159
Matthew of Aquasparta OFM, Franciscan gen, 61
Matthew of Bergevency OP, prov of England, 175
Matthew Paris, 166, 169, 172, 186, 205
Mathurin Friars, *see* Trinitarian Order

Maubuisson, Cistercian nunnery, 167
Maurice de Sully, bp of Paris, 91, 120
Metz, laity of, 19, 21
Michael Cesena OFM, Franciscan gen, 63, 222
Michael Palaeologus VIII, Greek emp, 195, 198–201
Milan, Inquisition at, 192
Mongka, Gt. Khan, 211–13
Mongols: invasions by, 197, 205–6; missions to, 206–17; Great Khan of, *see* Ghengis, Ogodai, Kuyuk, Mongka, Kublai
Montaperti, battle of, 118
Monte Senario, hermitage, 90, 105
Monte Subasio, Benedictines of, 37, 108
Montpellier: Franciscan convent at, 45; OFM general chapter at, 50; Carmelite schools at, 134
Morosini, Thomas, Latin patriarch of Constantinople, 195
Mount Carmel, hermits of, 95

Narbonne: province, 7; Inquisition of, 190; Franciscan general chapter of, 28; Franciscan statutes of, 51–3; cult of Olivi at, 61; abp of, *see* Berengar
Nestorians, 205, 208, 211, 212
Neville, Ralph, bp of Durham, 132
Nicaea, Greek empire of, 195, 197; ecumenical conference at, 196
Nicetas, Cathar bp, 5
Nicholas III, pope, 60, 183, 214
Nicholas IV, pope, 115, 214
Nicholas OFM, abp of Peking, 216
Nicholas Gallus OC, Carmelite gen, 97
Nicholas de Gorran OP, 223
Nicholas of Pistoia OP, 214–5
Nicholas of Troyes OFM, 174
Nicholas von Werle, 179
Nicolo Polo, 213
nimis iniqua of Gregory IX, 152
Norbert of Xanten, St, 17, 69
notaries public, 9
Nymphaeum, conference at, 197

Observants, *see* Franciscans, Dominicans, Augustinian Friars
Ocham, William OFM, 64
Odo Rigaud OFM, abp of Rouen, 175, 222
Ogodai, Gt. Khan, 206
Olivi, Pierre OFM, 60–1
Order of Preachers, *see* Dominicans
ordinem vestrum of Innocent IV, 40
Orsini, Romano OP, 137

Orte, 31
Orvieto, papal Curia at, 137
Osma: cathedral chapter, 65; canons regular of, 65–6; bp of, *see* Diego
Otto III, margrave of Brandenburg, 179
Oxford: university, 127, 134–5; chancellor of, 134; theology faculty, 128, 132, 135, 226; Dominican school at, 45, 131; Franciscan school at, 45, 131, 134; Carmelite school at, 97; Austin Friars at, 101; Friars of the Sack at, 93; parliament of, 176

Pacifico OFM, prov of France, 45
Padua, university, 74
Paolucci dei Trinci OFM, 223
Parastron OFM, 199
Paris; town of, 155; Treaty of (1229), 189, (1259), 175; abbey of Ste Geneviève, 13; church of St Mathurin, 92; hospice of the Dixhuit, 129; university of, 12–13, 129, 144, 153–5, great dispersal of, 131; chancellor of, 12, 203; arts faculty, 129, 133; theology faculty, 132, 153–4; secular masters of, 153–67; English-Picard Nation of, 129; Franciscan school at, 52, 130–1, 167; Dominican school at, 72, 128–9, 137, 155, 167; Carmelite school at, 97; Austin Friars' school at, 99, 167; Friars of the Sack at, 93, 167; Crutched Friars at, 167; Averroist controversy at, 146–8; bp of, *see* Maurice de Sully, Stephen Tempier
Parma, the Great Devotion at, 116–7
Pastoureaux, Crusade of, 178
patrons, of the friars 46, 93, 108–12, 166–9, 179; at the Curia, 181–2, 225
Pecham, John OFM, abp of Canterbury, 150, 222
Pedro d'Albalat, abp of Tarragona, 194
Peking: capital of Kublai Khan, 213–15; Latin church of, 215–17; abps of, *see* John of Montecorvino, William du Pré, Nicholas
penitentials, 126
penitential movement, *see* confraternities, Flagellants
penitentiaries, papal, 182–4
Peraldus, William OP, author of *Summa de Vitiis et Virtutibus*, 124–5
Peregrino of Castello, bp of Cathay, 216
Perigueux, Franciscans at, 45
Perugia, Flagellant movement at, 117–18
Peruzzi, of Florence, 109
Peter Catanii OFM, Franciscan gen, 38

Peter the Chanter, 138
Peter Chotard OP, 174
Peter Comestor, author of *The Histories of the Bible*, 85, 86, 138, 227
Peter of Corbeil, abp of Sens, 144
Peter of Corbie, 95
Peter Ferrandus OP, biographer of St Dominic, 67
Peter Lombard, author of the *Sentences*, 86, 141, 226
Peter of Lucalongo, 215
Peter des Rievaux, 171
Peter des Roches, bp of Winchester, 131, 171
Peter of Sézanne OP, 196
Peter of Verona OP (St Peter Martyr), Inquisitor, 109, 191, 192
Philip I, kg of France, 15
Philip IV, kg of France, 175, 222
Philip, chancellor of Paris, 145
Philip of Harvengt, abbot of Bonne-Espérance, 9
Pied Friars, 93
Piers Plowman, 164
Pisa, Franciscans at, 55; abp of, *see* Federico Visconti
Pistoia, 9
plurality, 220
podestà, office of, 10, 194
Poor Catholics, 23
Portiuncula, church of (St Mary of the Angels), 37, 46
Potter, Walter, 111
poverty: the Waldensian ideal, 19–20; in Franciscan observance, 33–4, 39, 60–3, 157–8, 223–4; in Dominican observance, 61–2, 68–9, 222–4; in the Austin Friars, 100; the poverty of Christ, 60, 63, 158; *see* also *usus pauper*
preaching: by lay people, 19, 24, 47; by the Cathars, 5; by the parish clergy, 119–20; by the friars, 120–4; sermon aids and the *ars predicandi*, 120; preaching at court, 171–2
Prémontré, customary of, 76
primitive Church, idea of, 15–16
Prouille, Dominican nunnery, 69, 70, 76
Pseudo-Dionysius, author of the *Ecclesiastical Hierarchy*, 156

quasi lignum vitae, of Alexander IV, 155
quo elongati, of Gregory IX, 40, 50, 112
quae honorem conditoris, of Innocent IV, 96

Rainaldo di Segni, Cardinal Protector of the OFM, 182, and *see* Alexander IV

Ralph of Reims OFM, 196
Raymond V, count of Toulouse, 6
Raymond VI, count of Toulouse, 8, 72, 189
Raymond Berengar OFM, 199
Raymond of Capua OP, Dominican gen, 223, 224
Raymond of Penaforte OP, Dominican gen, 78, 194; his *Summa de casibus*, 85, 125; and the *Liber Extra*, 182
Raynier Sacconi OP, author of *Summa de Catharis*, 194
recruitment to the friars, 34–5, 72–5, 103, 127
religiosam diversitatem, of Council of Lyons, 158
Richard of Ancona OFM, 39
Richard of Devon OFM, 45
Richard de Gray of Codnor, 95
Richard of Ingworth OFM, 45
Richard, Earl Marshal, 174
Richard of Middleton OFM, 150
Richard Rufus OFM, of Cornwall, 142
Richard of Stratford, 111
Rivo Torto, 33, 39, 41
Robert of Abrissel, 17
Robert le Bougre OP, Inquisitor, 190–1
Robert Holcot OP, 226
Rokesley, Gregory de, mayor of London, 110–11
Roland of Cremona OP, 73, 128, 142, 190
Roman de la Rose, 163
Rome: Lateran basilica and palace, 183, 228; St Peter's, 183; S. Maria del Popolo, 99; S. Sabina, 76; San Sisto, Dominican nunnery, 76, 77; papal Curia at, 79, 155, 181–3; *studium* of the Curia, 137, 184; bishops of, *see* individual popes
Rostock, prior of, 179
Rouen, Franciscans at, 45; abp of, *see* Odo Rigaud
Rudolf of Hapsburg, kg of the Romans, 180
Rufino OFM, 28
Rutebeuf, 163, 167

Sabatier, Paul, 26
Sacred Palace, lectors of, 184
Saint-Denis, Franciscans at, 45, 167
Saint-Julien, commune of, 104
Salamanca, university, 140
Salimbene de Adam OFM, 35, 48, 55, 116–17, 169
Sancho IV, kg of Castile-Leon, 179

Sartaq Khan, 209, 210–11
Sens, OFM chapter at, 169; abp of, *see* Peter of Corbeil
Sentences, lectures on at Paris and Oxford, 135, 142–3; and *see* Peter Lombard
Servite Friars, 89–91
Shrewsbury, Franciscans at, 46
Sicilian Vespers, war of, 187
Siegfried, bp of Augsburg, 44
Siena: commune of, 111; Servites of, 111
Siger de Brabant, 146–7
Simon de Montfort, the elder, 8, 66
Simon de Montfort, earl of Leicester, 172, 178
Simon 'Stock' OC, St, Carmelite gen, 96
Smaragdus, abbot of Verdun, 16
Society of the Faith, 193
Solomon OP, 62
Spirituals, *see* Franciscans
Stanford, OP chapter at, 169
Stephen of Saint-Thibéry OFM, Inquisitor, 192
Stephen Tempier, bp of Paris, 146, 149
Stephen of Tournai, 13
Strausberg, Dominicans at, 179
super cathedram, of Boniface VIII, 160, 161, 162
Sylvester OFM, 34

Tartars, 205, 206, 210
Tebaldo Visconti, *see* Gregory X
Templars, Knights, 203
Teutonic Knights, 185
Theobald de Columbariis OP, 174
Third Orders, *see* confraternities
Thomas OFM, lector, 198
Thomas of Cantimpré OP, 9 n.5
Thomas of Celano OFM, biographer of St Francis, 27, 28, 46, 47, 228
Thomas of Chobham, author of a *Summa Confessorum*, 124
Thomas of Spalato, 36
Thomas Waleys OP, author of the *ars predicandi*, 120
Thomas of York OFM, 134, 156
Toulouse: church of St Romain, 70; early Dominican house, 69, 72, 189; university of, 133, 184; Inquisition at, 192; bp of, *see* Fulk
Tours, Dominicans at, 178
Trent, commune of, 3
Trinitarian Order (Mathurin Friars), 91–2
Tuscany, hermits of, 98–9

Ubertino da Casale OFM, 63

INDEX

Ugolino, cardinal bp of Ostia, Protector of the OFM, 29, 38, 41, 47, 68, 181, 221, and *see* Gregory IX
Ulrich Engelberti OP, prov of Germany, 180
universities: rise of, 12; papacy and, 14; canon law studies at, 13–14; recruitment of friars from, 74, 127–9; and *see* Paris, Bologna, Oxford, Cambridge, Padua, Toulouse, Vercelli
Urban V, pope, 217
Urban VI, pope, 223
usus pauper controversy, 60–1

Ventura of Verona OP, 66
Vercelli: commune of, 193; university of, 74
Verona: Council of, 22, 189; preaching of the Great Devotion at, 117; notaries at, 9
Vézelay, Franciscans at, 169
Vienne, Council of (1312), 140
Violante, qn of Castile-Leon, 179
Visconti of Milan, 187
vita apostolica, see Apostolic Life

Wahlstatt, battle of, 295
Waldenses, 19–23
Waldes, 19–22
Walter de Brienne, Crusade of, 30
Walter Cantilupe, bp of Worcester, 175

Walter Winterborne OP, royal confessor, 171, 174
Whitefriars, *see* Carmelites
William of Holland, anti-kg of Germany, 180, 186–7
William, bp of Tartoûs, 96
William of Alton OP, 137
William Arnold OP, Inquisitor, 192
William of Auvergne, 145
William of Auxerre, 126
William of Colchester, 111
Willaim Flete OAE, 101
William Hothum OP, prov of England, 150
William Joyner, mayor of London, 110
William de la Mare OFM, 140
William of Moerbeke OP, 200
William of Nottingham, prov of England, 46
William Pelhisson OP, chronicle of, 189–90, 192
William du Pré OFM, abp of Peking, 217
William de Ruybrouck OFM, 209–13
William of Saint-Amour, 154–8, 163
William of Tripoli OP, 204
Williamite Friars, 93
Worms, canons of, 152; Franciscan house at, 152
Wyclif, John, 163

245